Arabic–English–Arabic Translation
Issues and strategies

Arabic–English–Arabic Translation: Issues and Strategies is an accessible coursebook for students and practitioners of Arabic–English–Arabic translation. Focusing on key issues and topics affecting the field, it offers informed guidance on the most effective methods to deal with them, enabling users to develop deeper insights and enhance their translation skills.

Key features include:

- a focus on Arabic–English translation in both directions, preparing students for the real-life experiences of practitioners in the field
- in-depth discussion of the core issues of phraseology, language variation and translation, legal translation and translation technology in Arabic and English translation
- authentic sample texts in each chapter, taken from a variety of sources from across the Arabic-speaking world to provide snapshots of real-life language use
- source texts followed by examples of possible translation strategies, with extensive commentaries, to highlight the best translation practices and methodologies
- a range of supporting exercises to enable students to practise their newly acquired knowledge and skills
- a wide range of themes covering both linguistic and genre issues, offering multidimensional perspectives and depth and breadth in learning
- a list of recommended readings and resources for each of the topics under discussion
- a comprehensive glossary and bibliography at the back of the book.

Lucid and practical in its approach, *Arabic–English–Arabic Translation: Issues and Strategies* will be an indispensable resource for intermediate to advanced students of Arabic. It will also be of great interest to professional translators working in Arabic–English–Arabic translation.

Ronak Husni is a Professor of Arabic and Department Head at the American University of Sharjah, UAE. Her research interests include Arabic language and literature, Translation Studies and Gender Studies.

Daniel Newman is a Professor of Arabic and Head of Department at the University of Durham, UK. His research interests include the history of translation, linguistics and Arabic literature.

Arabic–English–Arabic Translation

Issues and Strategies

Ronak Husni and Daniel L. Newman

LONDON AND NEW YORK

First published 2015
by Routledge
2 Park Square, Milton Park, Abingdon, Oxon OX14 4RN

and by Routledge
711 Third Avenue, New York, NY 10017

Routledge is an imprint of the Taylor & Francis Group, an informa business

British Library Cataloguing-in-Publication Data
A catalogue record for this book is available from the British Library

Library of Congress Cataloging-in-Publication Data
A catalog record for this book has been requested.

ISBN: 978-0-415-47884-7 (hbk)
ISBN: 978-0-415-47885-4 (pbk)
ISBN: 978-0-203-88329-7 (ebk)

Typeset in Sabon
by Bright Lantern Publishing

Contents

Acknowledgements

The seeds for this book were sown over a long period of time by successive cohorts of students, who, together with their present (and future) counterparts, constitute the primary target group for the present book.

It was their thought-provoking and often complex questions that prompted us to start thinking about designing a work of this kind. And so, our first thanks must go to all our students, some of whose questions will, it is hoped, be answered here.

In addition to students, we benefited from equally thought-provoking – and critical – exchanges with colleagues both at home and abroad.

However, the single biggest thanks is also an apology, to our long-suffering editor at Routledge, Andrea Hartill, whose patience we severely tested. We can only hope that the result was worth the wait and thank her for what at times seemed boundless endurance and forbearance.

Naturally, it goes without saying that any remaining flaws are entirely the responsibility of the present authors.

We should also like to thank the following copyright holders for permission to use the following material:

Chapter 1

Figure 1.4: example of search results in arabiCorpus (http://arabiCorpus.byu.edu; web host: Brigham Young University). Used with kind permission of the creator Prof. D. Parkinson, Brigham Young University.

Figure 1.5: example of search results in Leeds Arabic Corpora. Wilson, J., Hartley, A., Sharoff, S., & Stephenson, P. (2010). Advanced Corpus Solutions for Humanities Researchers. In PACLIC (pp. 769–778). http://anthology.aclweb.org//Y/Y10/Y10-1089.pdf. Used with kind permission from Dr Serge Sharoff, of Leeds University.

Figure 1.6 (results of a word search in the Online Corpus Concordancer) and table on page 26 (results for 'fire' collocations in the Online Corpus Concordancer). Used with kind permission of Mr Tom Cobb.

Chapter 2

Extract from Rajaa Alsanea's *Banāt al-Riyāḍ* (Girls of Riyadh) © Dar al Saqi, Beirut, Lebanon, 2007. This excerpt was published with permission from Dar al Saqi.

Extract: page 4 (213 words) from *Girls of Riyadh* by Rajaa Alsanea, translated by Rajaa Alsanea and Marilyn Booth, copyright © 2005 by Rajaa Alsanea. Translation copyright © 2005, 2007 by Rajaa Alsanea and Marilyn Booth. Used by permission of The Penguin Press, a division of Penguin Group (USA) LLC and also reproduced by permission of Penguin Books Ltd.

Extract from Fu'ād al-Takarlī's *Khazīn al-lāmar'iyyāt*. Used with kind permission of Saqi Books.

Extract from *Down and Out in Paris and London* by George Orwell, copyright © George Orwell, 1933. Used with kind permission of the Estate of the Late Sonia Brownell Orwell.

Extract from Yūsuf Idrīs' *Ḥikāya Miṣriyya jiddan*. Reproduced with kind permission of the author's estate.

Chapter 4

Figure 4.1: example of Arabic–English text alignment in Déjà Vu. Used with kind permission of Atril Solutions SARL, creator of Déjà Vu.

Figure 4.2: example of search results page of Almaany. Used with kind permission.

Figure 4.3: search page of arabiCorpus (http://arabiCorpus.byu.edu; web host: Brigham Young University) and Figure 4.8 (example of search results in arabiCorpus for كمبيوتر). Used with kind permission of the creator Prof. D. Parkinson, Brigham Young University.

Figure 4.4 (search page of the International Corpus of Arabic) and Figure 4.9 (example of search results in the International Corpus of Arabic for كمبيوتر). Used with kind permission.

Figure 4.5: example of search results in Leeds Arabic Corpora. Wilson, J., Hartley, A., Sharoff, S., & Stephenson, P. (2010). Advanced Corpus Solutions for Humanities Researchers. In PACLIC (pp. 769–778). http://anthology.aclweb.org//Y/Y10/Y10-1089.pdf. Used with kind permission from Dr Serge Sharoff, of Leeds University.

Figure 4.6 (search page of *Corpus Concordance*) and Figure 4.7 (results for 'resistance' in Corpus Concordance). Used with kind permission of Mr Tom Cobb.

Daniel Newman
Ronak Husni

Transliteration

ḍ	ض	'	ء
ṭ	ط	b	ب
ẓ	ظ	t	ت
ᶜ	ع	th	ث
gh	غ	j	ج
f	ف	ḥ	ح
q	ق	kh	خ
k	ك	d	د
l	ل	dh	ذ
m	م	r	ر
n	ن	z	ز
h	ه	s	س
w	و	sh	ش
y	ي	ṣ	ص

Abbreviations and symbols

adj.	adjective
adv.	adverb
Alg.	Algerian (Arabic)
CA	Classical Arabic
Chr.	Christian
DET	determiner
ECA	Egyptian Colloquial Arabic
Eg.	Egyptian (Arabic)
Eng.	English
Fr.	French
f.s.	feminine singular
imp.	imperfect
Isl.	Islamic
Jord.	Jordanian (Arabic)
Kuw.	Kuwaiti (Arabic)
Leb.	Lebanese (Arabic)
lit.	literally
Mor.	Moroccan (Arabic)
m.s.	masculine singular
MSA	Modern Standard Arabic
NE	Near East
part.	participle
perf.	perfect
pl.	plural
phon.	phonology
prepo.	preposition
RP	Received Pronunciation
sg.	singular
SL	source language
s.o.	someone
ST	source text
sth.	something
subj.	subjunctive
Syr.	Syrian (Arabic)
TL	target language
trans.	translation/translated

TS	Translation Studies
TT	target text
Tun.	Tunisian (Arabic)
/	precedes alternative translations
*	precedes erroneous linguistic forms

Figures

Introduction

Over the past two decades the field of Translation Studies (TS) has increased exponentially and research conducted at doctoral level on issues relating to Arabic/English translation has been holding its own. If we turn to the publishing world, however, we find that the crop is much more modest and many, if not all, of the resources tend to be little more than manuals containing bilingual texts with commentaries on the translations.

This, then, leads us to the next question of where the present book fits into the field. One way of answering this is by saying what the book is *not*. It is not, nor does it have any pretensions to be, a comprehensive textbook on Arabic/English translation, or a Translation Theory manual. Nor does it deal with the history – fascinating though it is – of translation between the two languages.

Rather, it focuses on a number of key issues and topics within Arabic/English translation that are of interest to those working between the two languages in a wide variety of fields and subjects.

Aims and structure of the book

This book fills a number of gaps in what is still a very small niche market in the field of Translation Studies (TS). It deals with translation between the two languages, in *both* directions; most, if not all, of the books available to the student concentrate on one translation direction, English into Arabic *or* Arabic into English.

Our decision to take the 'bidirectional' approach is predicated on a number of considerations. First, in our experience, students, irrespective of which language they are working into, often express the need to know how a certain expression or construction, usually one they have erroneously put forward as a possible rendering of a given Source Language (SL) string, translates into the foreign tongue. Second, it also recognizes that in the real world most practitioners working in the field of Arabic find themselves translating into both directions.

As stated above, rather than attempting to cover a wide canvas, the book focuses on a number of issues in Arabic–English–Arabic translation and some relevant strategies, grounded in contemporary theory, in order to deal with them.

We are aware that any selection is, by its very nature, flawed since it reflects the subjective choices of the authors. However, choices have to be made and we have been guided by both our experience as teachers and translators, as well as by practical concerns such as space constraints. We have tried to cover a range of themes, which cut across the micro- and macro-levels, straddling both linguistic and textual issues.

Chapter 1 discusses the way compounding, collocation and idioms work between the two languages, how this affects the translator and how it impacts on the various translation strategies to be employed.

Chapter 2 deals with language variation and differences in style, register and dialect in relation to translation. It also addresses the issue of diglossia, which is of particular relevance to Arabic.

Chapter 3 provides a detailed overview of Arabic/English legal translation and its constituent types.

Chapter 4 examines the translation technologies available to the Arabic/English translator, both on- and offline.

A glossary of some of the technical terms used in the book appears at the end.

Each chapter contains authentic sample texts, drawn from a variety of sources from across the Arabic-speaking world. The examples are generally unedited and unemendated, thus providing snapshots of real-life language use that the translator is actually faced with, rather than a sanitized version thereof. Naturally, any deviations from normative usage are discussed and contextualized.

The source texts are accompanied by numerous examples of possible translation strategies with extensive commentary, as well as exercises to enable the user to apply the newly acquired knowledge and skills. In addition, the reader is guided towards useful specialized resources and literature when appropriate.

The primary aim of the book is a practical one in that it aims to improve insight into various strategies as well as provide the necessary skills in order to employ them both judiciously and effectively. As a result, the book will:

- develop users' ability and skills in translating between Arabic and English;
- raise awareness of particular problem areas in Arabic>/<English translation;
- increase competency by providing the appropriate strategies for effective translation.

Who is the book for?

This book is aimed at a number of potential audiences. These include university-level students of translation and professional translators. And while it was originally designed for those whose mother tongue is either Arabic or English but who possess proficiency in the other language, it can be used by all those who have attained the required level in both these languages.

How to use the book

The advantage of a 'topical' approach is that it gives considerable freedom to the reader, who is untrammelled by a predetermined order of use. The book has been designed to allow users to focus on the various topics in the order of their choosing, depending on their individual needs and/or course syllabus.

Whilst it was originally intended for class use with a teacher, its structure and detailed explanations make it eminently suitable for home use as well.

1 Phraseology

Collocations, compounds and idioms

INTRODUCTION

Phraseology refers to fixed or idiomatic expressions, which may consist of a word, a noun phrase or even a sentence. Because of their highly idiomatic nature, their meaning can often not be deduced from the constituent components. For instance, how can an idiom like *to feel under the weather* (= 'to feel unwell') be 'deconstructed' or parsed without knowing the context? Often, the context is so culture- and language-specific as to make the item incomprehensible to the 'alien' observer.

The fact that these phrases are rarely signposted means that they are a potential pitfall to the translator who does not recognize them and, as a result, will translate them literally, thus stripping them of all connotative meaning they might be endowed with. For instance, a phrase such as لله دَرُّه may be rendered by the inexperienced and/or careless translator by a mock-exoticism like 'his milk is due to God/Allah', rather than as 'how wonderful so-and-so is!'.

Expressions such as these are often grouped together with other composite or multi-word items (MWIs) such as *collocations* and *phrasal verbs*, all of which will be discussed in this chapter.

COLLOCATION

The term 'collocation' denotes the way in which words tend to be used with others, or 'the company that words keep' (Firth 1968: 182). Within phraseology, collocations (مُتَلازِمات/مُتَصاحِبات لَفْظِية، مُتوارِدات) occupy the biggest field in terms of number and incidence, and are thus most often encountered by the translator and language-learner alike, to whom they pose a formidable obstacle. Correct use of collocations, these 'odd comings-together-of-words', to use the words of the first linguist to examine this phenomenon (Palmer 1933: 13), is one of the key features of idiomatic, i.e. natural native, language use.

As speech consists of strings of words, there is considerable danger of choosing the wrong constituent component, and the long odds can depress even the most arduous student of language. This is true not least because collocation seems to be a law unto itself, its rules often defying logic and, thus, *unpredictable*. For instance, why is it idiomatic to say *kind*, *best* or *warm(est) regards* (at the end of a letter or e-mail), but not *sweet, good* or *hot regards*? Why can one *ride* on a bus, but not a car? How come you *make a mistake*, but *do an exercise*? Why is the opposite of '*salt* water' not *sweet*, but '*fresh* water' and why is the opposite of '*dry* wine', '*sweet* wine'? Similarly, in Arabic an 'applause' is a 'storm' (عاصِفة <مِن> التَّصْفِيق), rather than 'thundering' in English, whereas a reception is 'tepid' in Arabic (اِسْتِقبال فاتِر), but 'indifferent' in English.

Does this mean that collocation is entirely random? Not quite. First of all, collocation presupposes a semantic relation of some sort between the elements. Unfortunately, this relationship is not always transparent as it may be figurative. In some cases the link is arbitrary to some extent, in others it is much less so.

Connotative meaning plays an important role as a factor restricting co-occurrence. For instance, it is unlikely to have positive collocates with a word that has negative connotation: e.g. *clean dirt*. This is an example of a figure of speech known as *oxymoron*, in which two seemingly contrastive lexical items are linked for stylistic effect (or by mistake). In our example, it is predictable that adjectives like 'clean', 'spotless', etc. are *atypical* collocates for 'dirt'. In some cases, this kind of *pragmatic failure* is purposefully introduced to achieve comic or sarcastic effect: e.g. *Once again Johnny has scaled the depths of human achievement* (i.e. his marks are very low), where *scale* is associated with 'rising' and the expected noun with *achievement* is *heights*, rather than *depths*.

This results in conceptual semantic domains and El-Gemei[1] showed that the Arabic word إرْهاب ('terrorism'), for instance, has a tendency of occurring with words in the semantic military field. Additionally, collocates are often 'a function of the propositional meaning of a word':[2] for instance, only a human or animal can be said to be *loving*, whereas *blooming* tends to collocate with plants, except if it is used metaphorically.

Second, collocation may also be determined by whether or not it is a specialized term. For instance, one would not ordinarily link *white* and *noise*, except in certain scientific fields such as acoustics or telecommunication.

Generally speaking, the number of words that an item can collocate with is directly correlated to the degree of specificity of a word; the more generic the term, the greater its collocational range.[3] For instance, a verb like *to go* collocates with many more lexical items than *to motion*. Similarly, *shoulder* has more meanings than the technical medical term *clavicula*; in addition to denoting the part of the body between the neck and the upper arm, the former may refer to part of a road (*hard shoulder*), the part of an item of clothing that covers the shoulder, or a cut of animal meat (the upper joint of the foreleg).

In its most general interpretation, *collocation* refers to all incidents in which words are put together. These range from completely free combinations to figurative phrases, whose meaning cannot be readily understood from its components (linguists would say that they are 'semantically non-compositional'). An example of the former would be *red* + *car*, neither of which has a tendency to co-occur with the other. At the opposite end of the spectrum, we have a phrase such as *stuffed* + *shirt*, whose meaning of 'an overly serious person' cannot be deduced from either individual elements or their combination. In between, there are combinations of elements that have a tendency to co-occur but are used in their literal meanings: e.g. '*to impose* + *a tax*', '*to follow* + *directions*' and '*to comply with* + *the law*'.

New collocations are being created every day; some of them will eventually find their way into a dictionary, but most won't as they are part of the linguistic creativity of the moment. They come in many guises in terms of the number of words they contain, the grammatical categories (verbs, adjectives, nouns, prepositions, etc.), degree of figurativeness, degree of cohesiveness, flexibility (variation) and syntactic productivity. What is certain is that guessing is never a good approach to collocations, and one could do worse than follow Palmer's advice that a collocation 'must be learnt as an integral whole and not pieced together from its component parts'[4] since their meaning often 'can hardly be deduced from a knowledge of their component words'.[5]

The above examples are all **lexical collocations** (LC), which may be contrasted with another large category, namely, that of **grammatical collocations** (GC), which includes combinations of verbs with prepositions and/or particles. These will be discussed below. In many cases, grammatical collocations are *embedded* in a collocational construct, as in:

[[*to comply with*][GC] + [*the law*]][LC]

Most of the taxonomies and divisions of collocations concentrate on either semantic[6] or syntactic[7] aspects, often within a lexicographical[8] or translation[9] context.

Lexical collocations may be divided into a number of subcategories, along semantic and syntagmatic criteria, i.e. whether both elements freely recombine with others, whether they are part of a specific set and/or whether they are used in their figurative or literal meanings. This is commonly referred to as the 'collocational range', that is, the number of words that they can co-occur with. At the maximal end of the range, the collocation may be said to be *free*[10] or *open*[11] when each element occurs freely with other components (this is known as full commutability), and is used in its literal sense.[12] It is important to add that the meaning of a lexical item may also vary, depending on the collocates with which it occurs: e.g.

to fire *a gun* (= 'to shoot')
an employee (= 'to dismiss')
ceramic (= 'to bake')
a wound (= 'cauterize')

Combinations where one or both of the elements are subject to some restrictions insofar as they operate within a narrow semantic field, related to its collocant (the word it is used with), are referred to as ***restricted***. In the example of *to perpetrate a crime* and its Arabic translation إرْتَكَبَ جَرِيمَة the verbs conjure up a limited set of nouns for most native speakers of the respective languages. The verb is said to be restrictive since it has a limited collocational range and only joins up with words that are related, in one way or another, to 'crime' (or another negative activity):

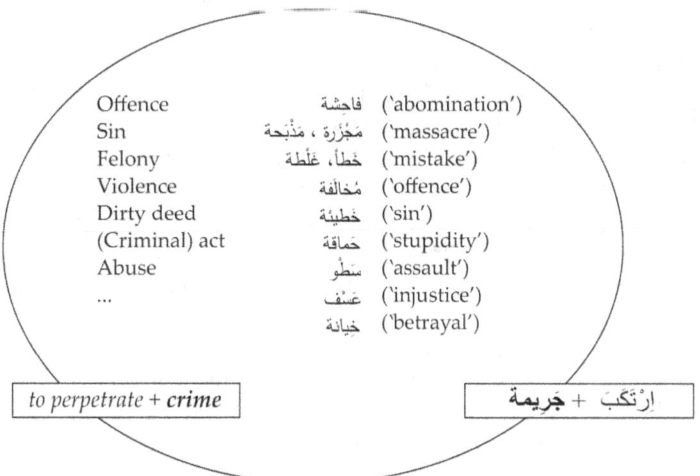

Figure 1.1 Collocational range of 'to perpetrate'

Other examples in this group include *grave + concern* (عناية فائقة), *well-informed + sources* (مَصادِر مُطَّلِعة) or *numerous + crowd* (جُمْهُور غَفِير), which have become set phrases, even if they allow for some variation: '*serious* concern' (عناية مُرَكَّزَة), '*authoritative* sources' (مَصادر مَسئولة/مُعْتَمَدة), '*large* gathering' (جَمْع [جُمُوع]/حَشَد [حُشُود] غفير). The number of collocates that the specialized item links up with may differ considerably. Consider the following examples, with the collocates listed in order of frequency in a large corpus of modern Arabic texts (arabiCorpus[13]):

Collocates	Item
(friend)(13) صَديق (reader)(4) قارِئ (critic)(3) ناقِد (opinion)(2) رَأْي	حَصيف (of sound judgement, discerning)
(price)(78) سِعْر (amount)(63) مَبْلَغ (fare)(41) أَجْر (expense)(20) كُلْفة (price)(12) ثَمَن (taxes)(8) رُسُوم (rent)(6) إيجار	زَهيد (small, trifling)
(winter)(10) شِتاء (cold)(11) بَرْد (air)(3) جَوّ	قارِص (biting, stinging)

There are 'significant correlations between restricted lexical co-occurrence and semantic features',[14] and thus the restrictions are not entirely unpredictable. For instance, it is not surprising that words like *love* or *like* will share many collocants. At the same time, one should never underestimate the idiosyncrasies in collocations, which resist rash generalizations![15]

A further distinction can be made within the class of *restricted collocations* inasmuch as one of the elements can be used in a figurative or metaphorical meaning.[16] For instance, in اِلْتَهَمَت النِّيران كُل شَيء, 'the fire consumed everything', the verbs اِلْتَهَمَ and *consume* are used metaphorically. In this case, the meaning of the construct is still transparent; conversely, if both elements are used metaphorically, the result is no longer a collocation, but an *idiom* (see below), such as *tough cookie* ('a strong-willed person').

Another type of restriction involves forms in which the collocational relationship can be extended. For instance, one *wears clothes*, *make-up* and *shoes*; these are rendered, respectively, by لَبِس (but when a garment is 'worn' in the sense of 'old, tattered', the verb is رَثَّ , with رَثّ and رَثِيث as the cognate adjectives), وَضَعَ and اِحْتَذَى !

The final semantic class is that of *bound collocations*, which denotes words that collocate uniquely with only *one* item. Syntagmatically, this category consists of noun phrases, genitive constructions (*iḍāfa*) and verb-object phrases. The restricted collocant has a figurative meaning, which is not transparent or deducible, as the following sample makes clear:

جرّار / لَجِب + جَيْش: 'huge army'
زُؤام + موت: 'sudden death'
رَؤوم + أمّ: 'loving mother to her children, doting mother'
وارف + ظِلّ: 'stretching, long shadow'
عَوان + حَرْب: 'endless war'
ضَرُوس + حَرْب: 'fierce, murderous war'
كَؤُود / كَأداء + عُقْبة: 'insurmountable obstacle'
خُلَّب + بَرْق: 'lightning without downpour'
أطْرَق + الرَأس: 'to bow the head'
طَأطَأ + الرَأس: 'to bend, incline the head'
اِشْرَأبَّ + العُنُق: 'to crane one's neck'
جَحَظ + العَيْن: 'to bulge (eye)'
اِستشاطَ + غَضَباً: 'to be fuming with rage'

It is worth noting that in some cases the fixed nature of the collocant in Arabic manifests itself in its non-agreement in gender with its noun: e.g. أم رَؤوم، حرب عوان.

Even if only the restricted collocant is figurative, this does not preclude the collocation as a whole from having an additional metaphorical meaning. For instance, برق خلب is usually semantically extended to mean 'an unkept promise', 'a let-down'.

This category is much bigger in Arabic than it is in English, and attracted attention from Arabic linguists very early on in history. A notable early example of this is the seminal thematic dictionary, entitled *Fiqh al-Lugha* ('On Philology') by Abū Manṣūr al-Thaʿālibī (d. 1038) which contains a multitude of bound collocations relating to a wide variety of subjects, such as body parts, defects, activities, etc.

Furthermore, collocations, just like *idioms*, are sometimes clearly culture specific: e.g. *Platonic love* / الحُبّ العَذْرِي (a reference to the ʿUdhra tribe). Other, less obvious examples are أم رَؤوم, which actually reveals a great deal about Arab social relations, while ظِلّ وارِف may conceivably tell us something about the climatic conditions of the cradle of Arab-Islamic civilization.

In English, on the other hand, examples of bound collocations are relatively rare: e.g. *to nod* + *head*, *to play* + *hooky* (= 'to play truant', to not go to school), *skewbald* + *horse*, *cete (of)* + *badgers*.[17]

These should not be viewed as idioms in the conventional sense since their meaning is not metaphorical; rather, it is the result of semantic specification or specialization. It is only when the collocation acquires metaphorical meaning that they should appropriately be considered *idioms*: e.g. *to drop a bomb* ('to make an unexpected announcement').

Similarly, there are *transitional combinations*,[18] which are phrases that are more fixed than other collocations, but can be set apart from idioms because their meaning is transparent: e.g. *to have/get one's foot in the door, for better or for worse.*

A final category of lexical collocations is made up of so-called **binomials** (**lexical couplets**), i.e. sets of coordinated near-synonyms (usually two) that tend to be fixed. English examples include:

- *might and main*
- *(last) will and testament*

- *hue and cry*
- *aid and abet*
- *each and every*
- *first and foremost*
- *ways and means*
- *trials and tribulations*
- *null and void*

For Arabic, the following may be cited:

- الصَّالِح والطَّالِح, 'the sound and the wicked'
- الشَّتْم والسَّبّ, 'insults and abuse'
- اِضطِّراب وحِيرة, 'confusion and puzzlement'
- لا يُعَدّ ولا يُحْصَى, 'uncountable and innumerable'
- لايَجُوزُ ولايُمْكِنُ, 'impossible and unfeasible'

These couplets share a number of basic features in both English and Arabic:

1 The elements are (near-)synonyms, as a result of which, there is semantic repetition.
2 Both elements belong to the same grammatical class.
3 The meaning of binomials is transparent, and can be easily deduced from its constituents.
4 Some binomials are culture-specific.
5 The entire set refers to a single referent.
6 Coordination typically occurs through *and* (more rarely, *or*).
7 The construct is usually fixed and formulaic, and does not allow any morphological or syntactic modification. For instance, one cannot separate the set by other words (e.g. adjectives) and the order of the elements cannot be reversed: e.g. **means and ways*, **every and each*.

In addition, Arabic couplets (known as مُزاوَجة) reveal some distinctive features, some of which are related to the derivational nature of the language:

- They often rely on *paronomasia* (تَجانُس),[19] i.e. word play, which usually involves a combination of words that are similar in form, i.e. root pattern (وَزْن), but not necessarily similar in meaning, often consisting of antonyms (opposites): e.g.

  هَرْج وَمَرْج, *confusion and turmoil*
  مِنْ كُلّ صَوْبٍ وحَدَبٍ, *from every direction and elevated place* ('from everywhere')
  الكَبِير والصَّغِير, *the big and the small* ('everyone')

- In contrast with English, many Arabic binomials are not lexicalized units, and many of them are nonce forms, i.e. coined for the occasion.[20]

Unlike in English, where most of these sets have been fixed a long time ago, the phenomenon remains very productive to this day in Arabic, where it is deemed a highly valued stylistic feature, as well as an emphasizing device.

A particular type of binomials in Arabic relies on reduplication as an intensifying device, with a *homoradical* (i.e. of the same root) modifier serving to intensify the meaning of the head noun. This is known in Classical Arabic grammar as إتّباع ('subordination'), and involves repetition of the word with the exception of one radical: e.g.

عَطْشان نَطْشان, *very thirsty*, لَيْل لائل, *a long night*

Repetition with a view to intensifying meaning is something we find elsewhere in Arabic, for instance in the so-called 'cognate accusative' (مَفْعُول مُطْلَق), where a verbal noun (مَصْدَر) of the main verb is added to emphasize the meaning of the latter. The verbal noun (which is usually indefinite accusative) can be further modified by an adjective: e.g.

غَضَبَ غَضْباً شَدِيداً, *he was extremely angry*
جَرَى جَرياً سَرِيعاً, *he ran very fast*
أقدِّرُ الأصْدِقاء تَقْدِيراً عَظِيماً, *I greatly value my friends*
سَيَنْجَح نَجاحاً عَظِيماً, *he will go far / he will be very successful*

It is also common in Arabic to simply repeat a word (usually an adjective) in order to add emphasis: e.g.

يُؤَكِّدُ لِي أَنَّ الغُرْفَة سَتَكون نَظِيفة نَظِيفة, *he assures me the room will be spotless*

The phenomenon of إتباع is unknown in standard English varieties, but a similar device is known in American English in the form of the so-called *shm-reduplication*.[21] Unlike its Arabic counterpart, it has a connotation of irony or derision, as in the following example:

– 'He is an accountant.'
– '*Accountant shmaccountant*! He was just the only one in the family who could count!'

In some cases, the elements within the binomial set may be antonyms and/or semantically unrelated, but 'yoked' together through joint use, which is why some authors refer to them as 'established collocations'[22] or a 'contrastive lexical couple'.[23] Both languages share a number of similar sets, whereas Arabic binomials often display euphonic root pattern repetition.

For our purposes, this category is subsumed into the 'couplets' because these phrases share the basic semantic features and raise similar issues in translation. Examples include:

fish and chips
chalk and cheese
knife and fork
life and death
black and white
bed and breakfast

السَّيْف والقَلَم, 'the sword and the pen' (*scholars and warriors*)
الحَياة والمَوْت, 'life and death'
الخَيْر والشَّرّ, 'good and evil'

The various levels/subdivisions of collocation may be represented as follows:

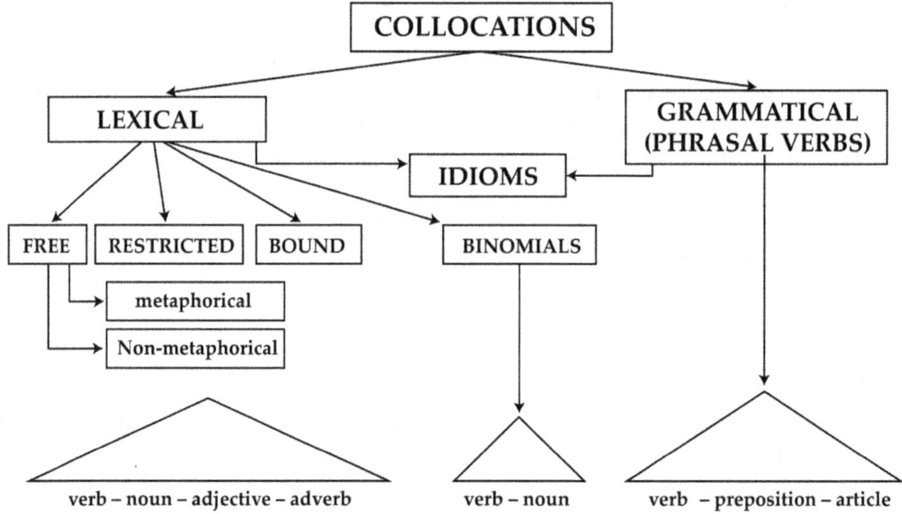

Figure 1.2 Collocational levels

Let us now take a closer look at the syntactic composition of collocational phrases. In English the following main types may be identified:

1 NOUN + NOUN: e.g. *brainstem*
2 VERB + NOUN (object): e.g. *to commit a crime, a dog yelps*
3 VERB + ADVERB: e.g. *to love dearly*
4 ADJECTIVE + NOUN: e.g. *vehement opposition*
5 ADVERB + ADJECTIVE: e.g. *sound asleep*
6 COLLECTIVE NOUN + OF + UNIT NOUN: e.g. *swarm of bees*

In Arabic, the principal categories are:

1 NOUN + NOUN (*iḍāfa*): e.g. بَيْت الشَّباب, *youth hostel*
2 VERB + NOUN: e.g. أَفَلَت الشَّمْس, *the sun went down*
3 NOUN + ADJECTIVE: e.g. رَجُل وَسِيم, *handsome man*
4 ADJECTIVE + NOUN (*iḍāfa*): e.g. طَوِيل الأناة, *long-suffering*
5 NOUN + [PREP.] + NOUN: this category is particularly productive in combinations of collective and unit nouns: e.g. جَماعة السَّمَك, *school of fish,* شَرِيحة مِن اللَّحْم, *slice of meat.*

GRAMMATICAL COLLOCATION

Grammatical collocation refers to 'a phrase consisting of a head word (noun, adjective, verb) and a preposition or grammatical structure such as an infinitive or clause.'[24] Both languages include many instances of this in a variety of combinations: e.g.

FOR + *the attention* + *OF* [PREP. + NOUN + PREP.], مُوَجِّه إلى
to be keen + *ON* + *-ing* [ADJECTIVE + PREP.], شَدِيد الرَّغْبة فِي
an attempt + *TO* + *INF.* [ADJECTIVE + PREP.], مُحاوَلَة
to say + *THAT* [VERB + THAT-clause], قال إن
a feeling + *THAT* [NOUN + THAT-clause], شُعُور بِأَنّ

بِمُناسبة, *on the occasion of* [PREP. + NOUN]
عَلَى رَغْمَ مِنه، رَغْماً عَن, *reluctantly* [PREP. + PREP.]
إِعْتِداء على, *attack on* [NOUN + PREP.]
أَعْلَنَ أن, *to announce* [VERB + THAT-clause]
مُعْفىً مِن , *free from* [ADJECTIVE + PREP.]

A particularly challenging category is that of the so-called *phrasal verbs* (الأفْعال العِبارِيَّة، الأفْعال المُرَكَّبة). Syntactically, these are simple verbs that occur with prepositions and/or particles, the result of which 'is called "phrasal" because it looks like a phrase rather than a single word. Although it looks like a phrase, it functions as a single word. It is a unit.'[25]

Semantically, their status is distinct since the meaning cannot generally be deduced from the constituent parts, which is why they are often classified as idioms. They are rightly considered one of the black spots in both English language learning and translation. Miscomprehension can even be lethal, as the unfortunate passenger on the train who mistook the meaning for *to look out* and 'took a look' outside the train, rather than 'take care', which is what his fellow traveller intended.[26]

When talking about phrasal verbs, a distinction must be made between, on the one hand, *prepositional* verbs and, on the other, *phrasal* verbs. The former category includes verb compounds consisting of a *verb* and a *preposition*, whereas the latter is made up of a *verb* and an *adverb particle*, which is why they are also known as *particle verbs*. Phrasal verbs can also contain both a particle and a preposition, in which case they are known as *phrasal-prepositional verbs*.

Not every preposition occurring with a verb results in a prepositional verb; the criterion is that the combination gives rise to a new semantic and syntactic *unit*. For instance, in the sentence *Johnny's father said that he should get* [VERB] *out* [PREP.] *from* [PREP.] *under* [PREP.] *the chair*, the only unit is *get* + *out*, whereas the prepositions *from* and *under* are not part of the construct.

The meaning of prepositional verbs is literal and transparent inasmuch as the meaning is *additive*; in other words, the meaning can be easily deduced from the meanings of the verb and the preposition. Conversely, phrasal(-prepositional) verbs often have figurative meaning, even if 'a large number of phrasal forms are simply the grammatical operation of verbs of movement plus a particle of direction.'[27]

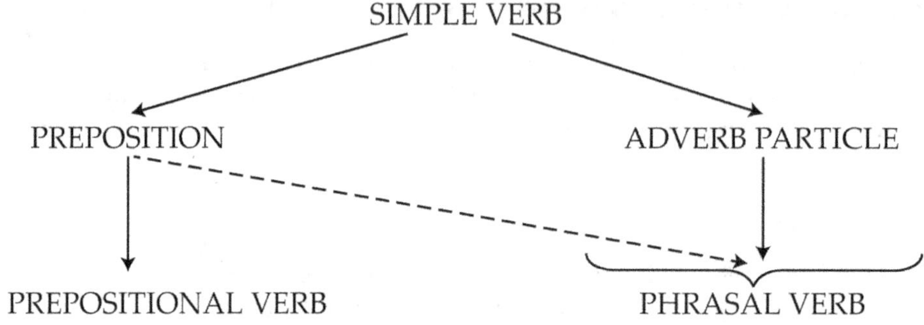

Figure 1.3 Structure of prepositional and phrasal verbs

Based on the semantics of the components, we may divide phrasal verbs into three groups:

1 Both elements retain their literal meaning (e.g. *to get up*, in the sense of 'to stand erect').
2 One of the elements – the particle – is used figuratively (e.g. *to meet up*).
3 The combination of both elements is entirely metaphorical (e.g. *to rub out* in the sense of 'to kill someone').

In the second group, the meaning is largely transparent, whereas in the third category, the meaning of the construct is entirely non-compositional, i.e. is not the sum of meanings of its parts.

In order to illustrate this, let us consider the prepositional verb *to look at*; its meaning is clear to anyone who is familiar with the meaning of *to look* and *at*. Conversely, the phrasal verb *to take off* can have any of the following meanings:

- 'to remove' (e.g. clothing), خَلَعَ
- 'to become airborne' (a plane), أقْلَعَ
- 'to imitate someone in an amusing manner', قَلَّدَ شَخْصاً
- 'to become successful', نَجَحَ
- 'to amputate', بَتَرَ
- 'to deduct', خَفَّضَ

What is particularly misleading is that the same word may, depending on the context, function as a preposition or as an adverb: e.g. *He took in the dog* (**prepositional verb**); *He was taken in* (= 'misled') *by her charm* (**phrasal verb**). From a syntactic point of view, the same phrasal verb can be either transitive or intransitive: e.g. *war broke out*, *they broke out the champagne* (= 'to open').

The following criteria distinguish phrasal verbs from prepositional ones:

- Phrasal verbs tend to be highly *polysemous*, i.e. they can have several meanings. In some cases, this is linked to the object: e.g.

 to put up + thing = 'to build'

to put up + person = 'to accommodate'

- Only a phrasal verb can be turned into the passive: e.g.

  the job ***was messed up*** (NOT **the man was stood up*)

- The preposition in prepositional verbs must be directly followed by its complement: e.g.

  he ***looked at*** *the girl* (NOT **he* ***looked*** *the girl* ***at***)

- Unlike prepositions in prepositional verbs, the particles in phrasal verbs are mobile, and can be moved to the end: e.g.

  they ***turned on*** *the light* OR *they* ***turned*** *the light* ***on***

- Some units *must* be separated: e.g.

  he ***pushed*** *me* ***around*** (NOT **he* ***pushed around*** *me*)

- The main stress in phrasal verbs falls on the particle, as opposed to the verb in prepositional verbs: e.g.

  to LOOK at, to take OFF

- When the verb is followed by two particles, one is a preposition and the other an adverb, whereas the adverb is always closer to the verb: e.g.

  to put down [ADV.] *to* [PREP.], أَرْجَعَ سَبَب إِلَى ('to ascribe to')
  to go through [ADV.] *with* [PREP.], أَنْجَزَ ، أَنْهَى
  to get fed up [ADV.] *with* [PREP.], سَئَمَ مِن

- When an adverb is added, it cannot appear between the verb and adverb particle: e.g.

  she ***carefully*** *looked up the word* (NOT **she looked carefully up the word*) [phrasal verb]
  she looked ***lovingly*** *at the boy* [prepositional verb]

- It is not generally possible to replace the verbs in phrasal verb constructs by synonyms or antonyms; for instance, while you can *see off* a friend at the airport, you can't *look/stare/...* her *off*.

- Only phrasal verbs can be turned into nouns: e.g.

  to break down → *breakdown*
  to kick off → *kick-off*

to knock out → *knockout*
to make up → *make-up*

NOTE: in some cases the nominalization process may be accompanied by inversion: e.g. *to cast down* → *downcast*; *to break out* → *outbreak*

- In addition to prepositions, some nouns and participles may act as adverbial particles to form a phrasal verb: e.g.

  to drive home ('to make clear, emphasize')
  to push shut (a door)

- Figurative phrasal verbs can generally be replaced by one word: e.g.

  to get over/to cross; *to pull up/to stop*; *to run into/to meet*

The coexistence of figurative and literal meanings in the same verb-preposition/particle combinations pose another problem, with only context being able to provide the answer: e.g.

to crack up: 'the house is cracking up (i.e. *cracks are appearing*)';
'we all cracked up (= *laughed violently*) when we heard his plan failed'.

Like so many areas of lexis, English phrasal verbs are not immune from differences between varieties of English. These can be both syntactic and semantic, or sometimes both: e.g. in British English you 'wait *for* someone', but in US English it is '*on* someone', which in the UK denotes 'to serve someone' (e.g. 'He expects me to *wait on* him just because I'm his wife')!

Sometimes, the differences can be much more dramatic, as in the classic example of *to knock up*, which in the USA means 'to get (a woman) pregnant', while in the UK it simply means (or, rather meant) 'to wake someone up by knocking on their door'! Other common examples include:

UK	**USA**
to do again	*to do over*
to fill in (a form)	*to fill out (a form)*
to trick into	*to rope into*
to fool about	*to fool around*
to clue up	*to clue in*

Turning to Arabic, one finds that the picture is slightly diffuse inasmuch as the very existence of 'phrasal verbs' has been doubted in Arabic, a view rooted in the non-applicability of the criteria used for English phrasal verbs: e.g. the lack of distinction between adverbial particles and prepositions, the need for an object with Arabic prepositions, and the relation between roots and their meaning.

These differences, however, are largely set off by the features of a subcategory of verb-preposition combinations in Arabic, which may be termed 'phrasal verbs' on semantic grounds even if, syntactically, they remain prepositional verbs.[28]

The following features may be listed for the subcategory under discussion:

- semantic non-transparency of combination, making it an *idiomatic phrase*;
- unpredictability of verb-preposition collocation;
- limited set of prepositions: بِ، في، على، لِ، إلى، مِن، عَن;
- preposition is essential for the meaning of the phrase;
- polysemy of prepositional verbs;
- combination may have both literal and figurative meanings;
- abstract meaning of preposition use;
- strong tie between the verb and its preposition.

The examples below reveal that in some cases the choice of preposition results not only in unrelated, but even in *opposite* (!) meanings:

to arrive at	إلى	أتَى
to bring	ب	
to mention sth.		
to destroy		
to finish, conclude	على	
to elaborate on sth.		
to devote oneself to sth.	إلى	اِنْقَطَعَ
to stop doing	عَن	
to look for	عن	بَحَثَ (a)
to study	في	
to consummate a marriage	على / ب	بَنَى (i)
to build on	على	
to revolt against	على	خَرَجَ (u)
to leave	عن/ مِن	
to go to	إلى	ذَهَبَ (i)
to bring	بِ	
to leave	عن	
to return to (e.g. صَوابِه, his senses, i.e. to regain consciousness)	إلى	رَجَعَ (i)
to withdraw from, refrain from	عن	

to ascribe sth. to s.o.	إلى	رَدَّ (u)
to dissuade s.o. from	عن	
to detest	عن	رَغِبَ (a)
to desire	في	
to love s.o. passionately	إلى	صَبَّ (u)
to make a raid on to befall s.o.	على	
to pour into	في	
to incline towards (a colour)	إِلَى	ضَرَبَ (i)
to turn away from something	عَنْ	
to roam about, travel in/through	فِي	
to play (music)	عَلَى	عَزَفَ (i)
to stop doing	عن	
to inflict upon s.o. to do away with s.o. to pass judgement against s.o.	على	قَضَى (i)
to judge	في	
to pass judgement in favour of s.o.	ل	
to be near to	إلى	قَعَدَ (u)
to sit on	على	
to have a liking for	إلى	مال (يَمِيلُ)
to be hostile to	على	
to deviate from	عن	
to move to	إلى	نَقَلَ (u)
to change gear (car) to	على	
to pass on from a source	عن	
to move from (a place) to copy from	من	
to become subject to	تحت	وَقَعَ (يَقِعُ)
to find	على	
to criticize s.o.	في	

Lexicogrammatical collocation

The subdivision we have applied up until now is too broad as it somehow seems to suggest that is a question of *either/or*; either it is a *lexical* collocation, or it is a *grammatical* one. It is not uncommon for both types to co-occur, with a particular lexical item collocating with a grammatical combination. For instance, *to pass up on* is a phrasal verb consisting of a preposition and a particle with a particular meaning ('to allow to go by'), but this knowledge alone will not lead to a correct idiomatic use of the phrase. Indeed, it is not possible to say 'to pass up on the bus', if you intend to say that you let it go by because it was too full, or 'to pass up on holidays', if you mean that you decided not to have any this year. In fact, the noun that typically collocates with *to pass up on* is *opportunity*: e.g. 'he passed up on the opportunity of seeing her off at the airport'.

The combination of lexical and grammatical collocants we shall call *lexicogrammatical collocation*, which is a common phenomenon in both languages: e.g.

> اِعْتَكَفَ فِي means 'to seclude, withdraw into a place', but usually collocates with words denoting 'mosque', i.e. جامِع، مَسْجِد;
> أَرْجَفَ بِـ usually appears with اِفْتِراءات, 'to spread calumnies'
>
> *to break up with* + lover
> *to fall out with* + friend, relative

Translating collocations

Over the past decade, the study of collocations in both English and Arabic has, to some extent, been driven by their implications in lexicography[29] and translation.[30]

The problems relating to the translation of collocation are situated at three levels: *recognition*, *comprehension* and *reproduction*. To put it differently, the translator has *three* obstacles to negotiate before arriving at the ultimate goal of successfully rendering a collocation. Some of these stages are easier to overcome than others. For instance, comprehension may be aided by means of a dictionary, provided, that is, the collocation is lexicalized and the dictionary is good! As we have seen, recognition can be particularly hampered by the fact that even the most basic words, when put together with others, obtain entirely different meanings.

While recognition is straightforward with *free collocations*, it is less so with those combinations that have a figurative meaning or with collocations used in specialized terminologies, as mentioned above.

As for comprehension, the Arabic>English translator was, until relatively recently, hampered by the dearth of dedicated lexicographical tools as general dictionaries are often not of great help. Collocations, much more so than idioms, reveal the limits of the dictionary because of their idiomaticity; more than anything else, it is about intuition, naturalness and instinct, which one associates with the native speaker. For instance, even the proficient language learner might find himself or herself in hot water when faced with examples like the following:

> *electrically charged*

imminent danger
unexpected danger
warm reception

Looking at the above purely from the point of view of *propositional meaning*, one would be tempted to translate these strings as follows:

مَشْحُون بالكَهْرَباء
خطر قَرِيب
خطر غَيْر مُتَوَقَّع
اِسْتِقْبال ساخِن

However, most native Arabic speakers would plump for:

مُشَبَّع بالكهرباء (lit. 'saturated with electricity')
خطر مُحْدِق (lit. 'encircling danger')
خطر داهِم (lit. 'suddenly descending danger')
اِسْتِقبال حارّ (lit. 'hot reception')

Even if there is no replacement for native speaker intuition, today's translators can resort to a number of dictionaries dedicated to collocations in both languages (see the list of resources at the end of this chapter).

Emery (1991) rightly claimed that the translation of Arabic collocation into English leads to a loss of 'attitudinal additional meaning', in view of the connotative features of many Arabic roots, i.e. the fact that a certain root has an inherently negative or positive meaning. However, connotative meaning affects all languages, and any loss – whether cultural and/or pragmatic (attitudinal) – is inevitable.

Translation may also be complicated by collocational variants within the same language. A case in point involves those between British and American English:[31] e.g. *to have a bath* (UK) / *to take a bath* (US). In some cases, the discrepancies can be greater with, for instance, some collocations being unknown in one variety: e.g. many British English speakers may have difficulty understanding the US *to take up a collection*, the UK equivalent being *to have a whip-round.*

By far the most intractable problem arises, of course, from the arbitrary nature of collocations, the most impressive example of which are the noun-adjective collocations with 'heavy' in English, where there are no fewer than thirty (!) possible Arabic equivalents, depending on the noun which it modifies:

heavy + sleep	سُبات **عَميق**†
+ seas	بِحار **هائجة**†
+ rain	مَطَر **غَزير**†
+ industry	صِناعة **ثَقيلة**†
+ fog	ضَباب **كَثيف** †
+ smoker	مُدَخِّن **مُفْرِط**†

+ dish (food)	وَجْبة دَسِمة†
+ traffic/emphasis/wind/accent/bleeding	مُرُور / تَرْكِيز / رِيح / نُطْق/ نَزْف **شَدِيد**
+ losses	خَسائر **هائلة**
+ armour	دِرْع **مُصَفَّح**
+ responsibility	مَسْؤُلِية **عَظِيمة**
+ sacrifices	تَضْحِيات **جَسِيمة**
+ blow	ضَرْبة **قاسِية**
+ investment(s)	إسْتِثمارات **مُكَثَّفة**
+ earthquake	زَلْزَلة **مُدَمَّرة**
+ investor	مُسْتَثْمِر **بارِز**
+ odour	رائِحة **قَوِيَّة**
+ legs	أَرْجُل **سَمِينة**
+ voice	صَوت **واطِى**
+ coat	مِعْطَف **غَلِيظ**
+ schedule	بَرْنامِج **مَشْغُول**
+ line	خَطّ **سَمِيك**
+ step	خَطَوات **صَعْبة**
+ risk	مُغامَرة **خَطِيرة**
+ breathing	نَفَس **ضَيِّق**
+ skies	سماء **مُغَيِّمة**
+ style (writing)	أُسْلُوب **مُبْهَرَج (مُتَحَذْلَق)**
+ turnout	جُمْهُور **كَبِير**
+ artillery	مِدْفَعة **ضَخْمة**
+ bombing	قَصْف **عَنِيف**

†(Helliel 1989)

Naturally, a similar situation occurs in the other direction, with one Arabic collocant having many equivalents, as shown by the list of some of the collocations involving the Arabic verbs أدّى and ضَرَبَ, each of which is rendered by a different verb – sometimes several – in English, in compliance with the latter language's collocation patterns:

to **do** one's duty	أدَّى واجِبَهُ
to **sit** for/take an examination	أدَّى اِمْتِحاناً

to **provide** a service	أدَّى خِدْمة
to **greet**	أدَّى السَّلام
to **perform** a ritual	أدَّى مَناسِك
to **render** a musical composition	أدَّى لَحْناً
to **accomplish** a task	أدَّى مَأْمُورية
to **swear** an oath	أدَّى يَمِيناً
to **bear** witness, testify	أدَّى شَهادة
to **fulfil** a function	أدَّى وَظِيفة
to **carry out** a mission	أدَّى رِسالة

to **draw** a line	ضَرَبَ خَطّاً
to **play** a musical instrument	ضَرَب آلة مُوسِيقِية
to **give** a military salute	ضَرَب السَّلام
to **knock** on the door	ضَرَب الباب
to **impose** a tax	ضَرَب ضَرِيبة
to **hull** rice	ضَرَب الأرُزّ
to **ring** the bell	ضَرَب الجَرَس
to **make** bricks	ضَرَب طُوباً
to **pitch** a tent	ضَرَب خَيْمةً
to **slap** s.o.'s face	ضَرَب كَفاً
to **imitate** (sth.)	ضَرَب قالِب
to **break** a record	ضَرَب رَقْماً قِياسِياً
to **administer** an injection	ضَرَب حَقْناً
to **cover** a she-camel	ضَرَب إبلاً
to **give** an example	ضَرَب مَثَلاً

The above applies to all types of collocation, and a restrictive or bound collocation in one language may re-emerge as a free one, or vice versa. For instance, while *swarm* (of bees) and *school* (of fish) are respectively translated by سِرْب من النَّحْل and جَماعة السَّمَك, Arabic uses the same word for *herd* (of elephants) and *pack* (of wolves): قَطِيع الفِيل/الذِّئاب.

Many collocations are *polysemous*, that is, they have different meanings, often a literal one and a figurative one. For instance, a child can 'wet his/her pants', but when it is used in relation to an adult, it usually means 'to be very afraid'. Similarly, in Arabic, you can be charmed by the melody of تَطْبِيل وتَزْمِير ('drum beating and flute playing') but more often than not it denotes *propaganda* (cf. *to beat someone's drum*). Although the context will generally help determine whether the literal or figurative meaning is intended, it may in some cases be quite ambiguous.

The above-mentioned cultural connotations conveyed by some collocations also affect translation decisions. Let us consider the following two common English combinations: *patient owl*, *cunning fox*. While the latter can easily be translated as ثَعْلَب ماكِر/مَكّار, the cultural specificity of the former poses a problem. In Western culture, an owl is a symbol of wisdom, whereas in Arab culture the owl has many negative connotations as it is considered a harbinger of bad luck, which is reflected in the fact that it is also known as غُراب اللَّيْل ('night crow'). As a result, the use of the word *owl* in Arabic in positive contexts often results in a cultural (pragmatic) mismatch that jars with the target readership. In this case, one is faced with the following possible solutions:

1 omission of the anthropomorphic element and paraphrase: e.g. شَخْص صَبُور;
2 equivalent animal metaphor: e.g. أصْبَر من الهُدْهُد / الجَمَل ('more patient than the hoopoe/camel').

The cultural specificity may flummox translators in seemingly straightforward cases. A particularly intractable example is the English collocation *common sense*, for which there is no single recognized equivalent in Arabic, which wavers between the following:

- الفِطْرة السَّلِيمة ('sound disposition')
- الحِسّ السَّلِيم ('sound feeling')
- الحِس الفِطْرِيّ ('natural feeling')
- بَداهة ('naturalness')
- الفَهْم الشّائع ('widespread understanding')
- المَفْهُوميّة ('understanding')
- المَنْطِق ('logic')
- الحِسّ المُشْتَرَك ('common feeling')

In addition to literal translations (فهم شائع, حس مشترك), the list, which has been drawn from written MSA sources only, comprises an Egyptian colloquialism (مفهومية) and functional equivalents. So much for collocational 'feeling'!

We have already mentioned the specificities of collocation within **specialized** – or terminological – **collocations.** Their collocational behaviour cannot be predicted or explained through the usual semantic or syntactic rules. Instead, they are subject to the conventions applied within the field of specialized language that they occur. More crucially, these restrictions tend to exist in the Target Language as well. For instance, in the field of computing the English word *processing* collocates with a limited set of conceptually similar collocants (e.g. *data, information*) determined by the specificities of the specialized language domain, or technical jargon, if you will. Similarly, in Arabic computing language, we find that its equivalent, مُعالَجة, behaves largely in the same way, and collocates with words like بَيانات and مَعْلُومات. The shared semantic features of specialized terms also results in shared collocational behaviour in many cases. For instance, terms within the semantic field of diseases will share many of their collocants:

> disease X ... *affects/hits/*... a *patient*
> disease X ... can be *chronic/treatable/ crippling/*...

In research examining specialized lexical combinations in French, it was found that collocants 'selected' terms that belonged to the same semantic class.[32]

The length and extent of contact between Arabic and European languages – English in particular – has resulted in a large number of *calques*, i.e. borrowings, to which collocations have not remained immune: e.g.

> وَقَعَ في الحُبّ, *to fall in love*
> زُواج المَصْلَحة, *marriage of convenience*
> السِتار الحَدِيدِيّ, *the Iron Curtain*
> كِذْبة بَيْضاء, *white lie*
> خَطّ ساخِن, *hot line*

While it is important to stress the need to choose the right collocant, this is perhaps a simplification since naturalness and idiomaticity may dictate the translation of a collocation by means of:

1 equivalent collocation: e.g.

> *to shed tears*, ذَرَفَ دُمُوعاً
> *to shed skin*, انْسَلَخَ جِلْداً
> *to shed hair*, نَسَلَ شَعْراً
> *to shed leaves*, أسْقَطَ وَرَقاً

2 a paraphrase: e.g. *to hose down*, نَظَّفَ بِالماء

3 functional equivalent: e.g.

> *to shed blood*, قَتَلَ ('to kill')
> *to wreak havoc*, دَمَّرَ ('to destroy')
> *firebrand*, قَبَس ('live coal')

4 borrowing; depending on whether or not the borrowing is semantically transparent, it may be glossed or paraphrased: e.g. الحَرْبُ البارِدة (*the Cold War*).

In many cases, there are several competing possibilities: e.g.

dead end: طَرِيق مَسْدُود [form- and meaning-equivalent collocation]
عَمَل لامُسْتَقْبَلَ لَهُ [paraphrase]
فِكْرة لاطائل من وراءها [paraphrase]
وَرْطة، لاطائلَ فيه [functional equivalent]

The above translations of the collocation assume that we are talking about its figurative of a 'situation in which no progress can be made', an 'impasse'. If the literal meaning of a 'blocked road', 'cul-de-sac' is intended, the first phrase is the only possible translation.

In addition, the translator's choice will be determined by:

- text type and genre (e.g. literary, non-literary);
- register (e.g. formal, informal);
- target audience (e.g. specialist, non-specialist).

From a syntactic point of view, there is some variability, which reflects the creativity of collocation:

English		*Arabic*
noun + noun	→	noun + noun (*iḍāfa*): e.g. *passenger train*, قِطار رُكّاب
	→	adjective phrase: e.g. *railroad*, سِكّة حَدِيدِيّة
adjective phrase	→	adjective phrase: e.g. *high treason*, خِيانة كُبْرَى/عُظْمَى
	→	noun + noun (*iḍāfa*): e.g. *high seas*, عُرْض البَحْر
prepositional phrase	→	prepositional phrase: e.g. *at least*, على الأقَلّ
verb + preposition/ particle	→	verb + preposition: e.g. *to look at*, نَظَرَ إلى
	→	simple verb: e.g. *to cover up*, غَطَّى
	→	verb phrase: e.g. *to eat out*, أكَلَ خارِجَ البَيْت

The translation of **binomials** is subject to a number of features that set it apart from other types of collocation discussed. Generally speaking, the following strategies may be applied:

1 **similar binomial in TT**: e.g.

> الجَنَّة والنار, *heaven and hell* (lit. 'heaven and fire')
> عاجِلاً وآجِلاً, *sooner or later* (lit. 'urgent and postponed')
> الطُول والعَرْض, *length and breadth*
> فِي السَّرّاء والضَرّاء, *for better or for worse, in good and bad times* (lit. 'in prosperity and adversity')

In many cases, segments occur in the same position in both languages: for instance, in sets consisting of a positive/negative, or nearness/farness, the former in each appears first. In other instances, however, often some changes are necessary: e.g.

sweet and sour, حامِض وحَلْو
near and far, القاصِي والدّانِي

2 **another binomial in the TT:** e.g.

فتَّشَ عَن مُوَظَّفٍ جَدِيدٍ عَلَى السَّهْل والوَعْرِ, 'He looked for a new member of staff *high and low* (lit. 'the plains and the rugged terrain', i.e. everywhere).'
بِكُلِّ قُوَّةٍ وحَماسٍ, *with might and main* (lit. 'with power and zeal')

3 **omission of (near-) synonym:** e.g.

بِلا قَيْد أو شَرْط, *unconditionally* (lit. 'without restraint or condition')
تَهْدِيد ووَعِيد, *threats* (lit. 'threats and menaces')

This is the rule, for instance, for binomials that occur in legal English (see Chapter 3): e.g.

بَيْنَ, *between and among*
كُلّ, *each and every*

4 **compensation:** as binomials may serve as a means of emphasis, the loss of one or other element in the construct is offset by, for instance, the addition of an adjective: e.g.

إِشْتَغَلَ عَلَى كِتابِهِ لَيْلَ نَهارَ, 'He worked on his book *every single day* (lit. 'day and night').'
رَأَيْتُ التَّخْرِيبَ وَالتَّدْمِيرَ بَعْدَ تَفَشِّي النَّارِ فِي المِنْطَقَةِ, 'I witnessed the *total destruction* (lit. 'destruction and demolition') after the fire spread throughout the area.'

5 **functional equivalent or paraphrase:** the binomial is rendered by a word or phrase conveying the referential meaning of the combination: e.g.

قَلْباً وقالِباً, *wholeheartedly, completely* (lit. 'heart and form')
أَتَى عَلَى الأخْضَرِ واليابِس, *to destroy everything, wreak havoc* (lit. 'to finish off the green and dry vegetation')
الخاصَّة والعامَّة, *the entire population, all classes* (lit. 'the elite and the general population')

The more a binomial is culture specific, the less likely it is that there will be an equivalent construct, and in those cases strategies 3–5 would normally be used, especially the paraphrase: e.g. الصَّغائِر والكَبائِر, *venial and mortal sins* (lit. 'the small and the great').

As for the translation of **phrasal verbs**, here, too, identification is key, and the most common mistakes are the result of the translator misjudging the semantic composition of the phrase. This is particularly true for English, which has a higher number of non-transparent phrasal verbs.

Comprehension, as we have seen, is further complicated by polysemy, especially of English phrasal units, as well as the lack of one-to-one correspondence between phrasal verbs in both languages.

The strategies for dealing with phrasal verbs to a large degree depend on the transparency of meaning. In the case of *semi-transparent* phrasal verbs (many of which have an intensive aspect), the translation will involve one of the following strategies:

1 **change in preposition:** e.g.

to look for: بَحَثَ عَن
to look at ('to inspect'): دَقَّقَ فِي

2 **omission of the particle altogether:** e.g.

'The car has been *fitted out* with a new engine.'
تَمَّ تَزْوِيدُ السَّيّارةِ بِمُحَرِّكٍ جَدِيدٍ

'I *checked over* the article yesterday.'
راجَعْتُ المَقالَةَ أَمْسِ

'He *met up* with his old friends.'
اِجْتَمَعَ بِأَصْدِقائِهِ القُدَماءَ

to go with, رافَقَ
to go under (ship), غَرِقَ

3 **compensation through addition of a prepositional, adverbial or noun phrase:** e.g.

to cover up ('to cover completely'), غَطَّى بِالكامِلِ
to piece together, جَمَّعَ قِطْعةً قِطْعةً
to hit out, هاجَمَ بِعُنْفٍ

4 **paraphrase:** as many English phrasal verbs are idioms, it is sometimes necessary to paraphrase their meaning: e.g.

to brick up, أَغْلَقَ بِقَوالِبَ الطُّوبِ
to get over, أَوْصَلَ المَعْنَى

5 **new verb incorporating the intensive aspect:** e.g.

to drink up (= 'drink until the end'), أَنْهَى ('to finish'), جَرَعَ ('to pour down')
to screw down (= 'fix down tightly'), ثَبَّتَ ('to secure')
to pile up, تَراكَمَ

to bottle up (in the sense of 'to seal in a bottle'), عَبَّأَ
to finish off, أَنْهَى

This strategy will often include specific verb forms that are associated with an intensive (e.g. II) or resultative meaning (e.g. VII): e.g.

to smash up, كَسَّرَ
to rip apart, مَزَّقَ
to die off, اِنْقَرَضَ

Other factors that determine the translation include whether or not the phrase has a transitive/intransitive meaning (bearing in mind that Arabic prepositions always need an object) and the object with which the phrasal unit collocates: e.g.

to take off (intransitive), اِنْصَرَفَ
to take off (transitive), خَلَعَ (مَلابِس)
to break off (work), اِنْقَطَعَ (العَمَل)
to break off (an engagement), فَسَخَ (خُطُوبة)

Non-transparent, i.e. wholly figurative, phrasal verbs and those that are culture-specific, of course, pose the biggest problem. As their meaning cannot be deduced from their constituent components, there is no option but to resort to the dictionary. Naturally, this presupposes recognition, which is the translator's main stumbling block.

As regards lexicographical tools, the coverage of phrasal verbs in English–Arabic dictionaries is, at best, sketchy, and often it is necessary to turn to specialized phrasal verb dictionaries, but even then the polysemous character of phrasal verbs means that context remains a crucial element.

When translating phrasal verbs, it is important to pay due attention to *register*, particularly in English as many phrasal verbs are linked to informal or even slang usage. As a result, the translator has to make sure to avoid register mismatches, with an informal unit being used in formal contexts, and vice versa. For instance, it would be inappropriate to use phrasal verbs like *to botch up* ('to mess up'), *to fork out* ('to pay') or *to fess up* ('to confess') in formal prose.

In addition to dictionaries, the translator may have recourse to a number of electronic tools in the field of collocation. The main ones are *concordancers* and *corpora* (see Chapter 4), which provide a truly unique service hitherto unavailable. For instance, Figure 1.4 shows that شَعْواء only collocates with the noun حَرْب, while Figure 1.5 reveals that the Arabic word حَرِيق ('fire') collocates with the verb شَبَّ (i, u) – 'to break out' – or التهم ('to consume'), and the adjective هائل ('terrible').

Some corpus concordancers even provide handy collocational commentary. For instance, Figure 1.6 contains (part of) the search results for the word 'fire'.

Figure 1.4 Results of a word search in arabiCorpus (http://arabicorpus.byu.edu/)

Back to the query window

See 97 examples of '[word="حريق"] cut 100' in I-AR-LEMMA

& gt; فحم & gt; طيور و دواجن حية & gt; طيور زينة حية & gt; **حريق** طفايات & gt; طائرات & gt; ضأن و ماعز حى & gt; و بقالات

يتعين أن يستغرق هدم مبنى مماثل لمركز & quot; وقال & quot; . **حريق** من مسؤولين أنّه لم يحدث في التاريخ أن انهار مبنى حديدي بسبب

أمسي فاطمئني إنْ جُنَّ قلبي الطفلُ وانتفضتْ على __UNDEF__ **حريق** على رمادٍ __UNDEF__ ناقِضا __UNDEF__ بالياسمين وبالقرُنفل

أو مساوٍ له ، تعين ترك الحج والإتيان بالواجب __UNDEF__ **حريق** كانقاذ غريق أو __UNDEF__ الإتيان بالحج ترك واجب أهم من الحج

، أو غريق ونحوهما ، يجوز له الفطر ، وعليه القضاء بعد ذلك ، **حريق** يجوز لمن يحتاج الفطر لإنقاذ إنسان من هلكة ، مثل إنقاذ من في

وكلها نظمتها وأنا في الثالثة عشرة من عمري. سيرى القارئ ، **حريق** أهلها لأنها أحبت ، وأخرى في رثاء طفل غريق ، وثالثة في وصف

يمكن استعادة المعلومات الموجودة في السجلات ، إلا أن هذا ، **حريق** أصابه الغرق ، أو كمية من بقايا أوراق سجل سوداء أبقى عليها

أتى على أشجار اللوز والتين والزيتون والصنوبر التي كانت **حريق** حجرية تُستعمل أيضاً أدراجاً لنزول الوادي. في سنة 1989 ، شبّ

الم بها. وكانت قد رممت قبل ذلك بعد غزوة تيمورلنك سنة 1401 **حريق** تجديدها في أيام السلطان قاتيباي سنة 893 ه / 1488 م في اثر

أما أصحاب الكهرباء فيأتون إلى هنا ويذهبون بدون عمل أي شيء **حريق** منزلنا وهروبنا ونحن لا نستطيع النوم بسبب الخوف من حدوث أي

أو تسرب غاز أو بوتاجاز من بيت أو شق س: من حق ظباط المطافي **حريق** من داخل البيت. س: زي إي الحالات دي ؟ ج: مثلا لو كان في

..أو مصيبة في البيت قد تموت بسبب أنه لا مفر لا مخرج لها **حريق** يغلق جميع الأبواب حتى تكون في سجن وحتى إذا حصل لا قدر الله

أوروبي __UNDEF__ استمر ما يقارب ثلاث ساعات تحالف سعودي **حريق** استئناف العمل بمصنع « حديد 2 » بالجبيل بعد & quot; فايز

تحصل على ،(1999 __UNDEF__ الأخيلة.. 13 - فتحي غانم (1924 **حريق** ، الروايات منها رامة والتنين ، الزمن الآخر ، أبنية متطايرة

الأيام المكسّرة يضيءُ حطب الأوهام في البال إلى .... ؟ ضيّع **حريق** من الأصدقاء إلى أين مضينا ؟ ما بيننا مسافة طلقة وحروب خضراء

الثانوية الثالثة بمحاسن أرامكو / الأحساء مهم - صوت للاحساء **حريق** ريف الاحساء. حريق يلتهم إحدى ثانويات البنات بالأحساء. نشوب

Figure 1.5 Results of a word search in the Leeds Arabic Corpus (http://smlc09.leeds.ac.uk/query-ar.html)

Figure 1.6 Results of a word search in the Online Corpus Concordancer, based on the British National Corpus (http://lextutor.ca/conc/eng/)

The list shows that the possible collocates with 'fire' (within the corpus) are:

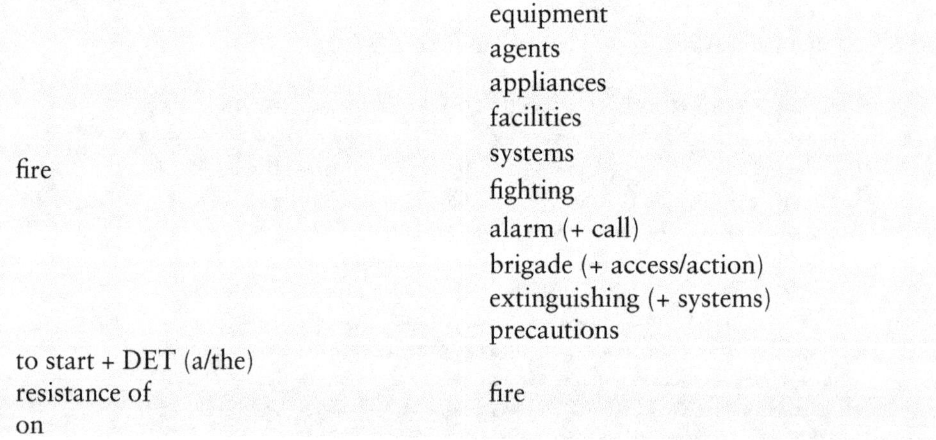

fire	equipment agents appliances facilities systems fighting alarm (+ call) brigade (+ access/action) extinguishing (+ systems) precautions
to start + DET (a/the) resistance of on	fire

IDIOMS (تعابير / عبارات اِصْطِلاحِيَّة)

We have mentioned the words 'idiom' and 'idiomatic' a number of times. While the latter simply refers to 'natural native-like usage of language', the former is a technical term. For our purposes, we consider an 'idiom' to be a *fixed expression with figurative or metaphorical meaning*, whereas 'the essential feature of an idiom is its non-literal, metaphorical meaning. The meaning of an idiom is not the sum of the meaning of its parts, its constituent words.'[33]

Although it is impossible to deduce the sense of idioms from their constituent parts, there are often degrees of transparency and Cowie (1994, 1998), for instance, distinguished between:

1 *pure idioms* (entirely opaque and invariable), e.g. *brass monkeys* ('to be chilly'), *to smell a rat* ('to suspect something is wrong');
2 *figurative idioms* (slightly variable, with a figurative and a rarely used literal interpretation), e.g. *change one's tune* ('to express a different and, often, contradictory opinion');
3 *restricted collocations* (one figurative and one literal element, with restrictions on use with elements outside the phrase); e.g. *early bird* ('someone who wakes up, or arrives early');
4 *open collocations* (both elements used literally and freely combinable), e.g. *take a ride* (e.g. in a car, a circus attraction, train).

Despite the fact that they are considered to be 'frozen expressions', idioms often allow variability, whether grammatical (e.g. verbs can be conjugated, or appear in another tense) or lexical (some words may be replaced by synonyms): e.g.

> *to put/set a foot wrong* ('to make a mistake')
> *to follow/walk into someone's footsteps*
> جامِد النَّفْس/القَلْب/العاطِفة, *hard-hearted*
> على النَّار / مِثْل النار / مِثل الجَمْرة, *anxiously*

However, there are limits to the variability and it is usually not possible to:

- replace one of the core lexical items: e.g.

> *dead letter,* but NOT **dead envelope*
> شَقّ طَرِيقَهُ, but NOT *شَقّ سِكّتَهُ/سَبِيلَهُ

- change the word order of an idiom: e.g.

> *topsy-turvy,* but NOT **turvy-topsy*
> بَيْنَ المِطْرَقة والسِّنْدان, but NOT *بَيْنَ السِّنْدان والمِطْرَقة

- omit or add a word (except for a modifier): e.g.

> *save one's breath,* but NOT **save breath*
> *head over heels, completely/totally head over heels,* but NOT **head over high heels*
> تَلَقَّى الضَّوء الأخْضَر ('to get the green light'), but NOT *تَلَقَّى الضَّوء
> الخَطّ الأحْمَر ('red line'), but NOT *الخَطّ الأحْمَر الفاقِع

The above rules may be broken for stylistic reasons, or for comic effect: e.g. 'I was head of swimming trunks when I came out of the pool!'

Idioms are highly language- and culture-specific, and the translator needs to know, for instance, that *red tape* (bureaucracy) is 'red wax' (شَمْع أحْمَر) in Arabic; that opposites are *apples and oranges* in English, but 'fat and fire' (شَحْم ونار) in Arabic; that something that is *heart-warming* in English, 'cools the breast' (أثْلَجَ الصَّدر) in Arabic, a language whose origins are rooted in the burning desert heat, which also explains how the *easy life* is عَيْش بارِد ('cold life')! When the English heart *trembles*, the Arabic one 'dances' (تَرَقَّصَ). In Arabic, childhood is conjured up by a reference to a 'smooth nail' (ناعِم الظفْر), while in English it is a *tender age*; in Arabic a 'prey' is 'cold' (غَنيمة بارِدة) or 'easy to swallow/pleasant to eat' (غَنيمة سائغة), rather than 'easy', etc.

Identical expressions may have widely varying meanings, one figurative (making it an idiom), another purely literal: e.g. *to be on a trip*, either to be travelling, or to be experiencing the effects of taking the hallucinogenic drug LSD.

Often, the metaphorical meaning derives from a one-time literal one, which has since been lost; e.g. *to be in the limelight* ('to be the centre of attention') goes back to a time when theatre stages were lit by limelight. Even the most cited of all idioms *to kick the bucket* ('to die') has quite literal origins; according to one etymology listed in the Oxford English Dictionary it refers to the bucket that was kicked away from under a person to be hanged, who would then die because 'the bucket had been kicked'!

So, in most cases idioms are rooted in history as well as culture, which makes them such a problem for the language learner. That is not to say that the difficulty is the same between all languages; those that are culturally closer will have more common areas of origins, and vice versa.

In English, idioms may be traced back to:

- folklore: e.g. *old wives' tale*, *the Grim Reaper*;
- the Bible: e.g. *pearls before swine*, *speaking in tongues*, *patience of Job, to turn ploughshares into swords*;
- literature: e.g. *neither a lender nor a borrower be* (W. Shakespeare, *Hamlet*, 1:3);
- historical events: e.g. *to cross the Rubicon* ('to go beyond the point of no-return', referring to Julius Caesar's army crossing of the river by that name);
- historical figures: e.g. *Platonic love*;
- calques: e.g. *let them eat cake* (< alleged quote from the French queen Marie-Antoinette);
- popular culture: e.g. *the full Monty* (film).

In Arabic, we find similar categories:

- Qur'an: e.g. مُسْلِم حَنيف ('true Muslim');[34]
- Hadith: e.g. فَريسة بارِدة ('easy prey' – in reference to fasting during winter time);
- historical figures: e.g. قَيْس ولَيْلَى;
- the Bible: e.g. سَفينة نوح (Noah's Ark), كَبْش الكَفارة ('scapegoat');
- literature: e.g. خَيْر جَليس في الزَّمان كِتاب ('the best companion is a book'), which is part of a verse by al-Mutanabbī (the first half of which is أعَزُّ مَكانٍ فِي الدُّنْيا سَرَجُ السّابِحِ, 'the best place in the world is on the back of a steed').
- calques, most of which have come from English in recent times: e.g.
  دُمُوعُ التِّمْساحِ, *crocodile tears*
  سَحَبَ البِساطَ مِنْ تَحْتَ قَدَمَ, *to pull the carpet from under someone's feet*

عَضَّ اليَدَ الَّذِي أَطْعَمَتْهُ, *to bite the hand that feeds one*
زُوْبَعةٌ فِي فِنْجانٍ, *a storm in a teacup*
وَضَعَ العَرَبَةَ أمامَ الحِصانِ, *to put the cart before the horse*
شِيك (صَكّ) عَلَى بَياض, *blank cheque*
سِتار حَدِيدِيّ, *Iron Curtain*

In some cases, however, the meaning may change in the process of borrowing, with the creation of so-called 'false friends' (expressions that look similar but differ in meaning), as a result of:[35]

a Reinterpretation: e.g. the Arabic equivalent of the English expression *to lose one's nerve* (= 'to lose one's courage') is فَقَدَ أعْصابَهُ ('to lose his nerves'). Though a near-literal translation, the Arabic phrase denotes 'to lose one's temper', i.e. become angry.
b Partial borrowing: the original expression has several meanings and only one is borrowed: e.g. the English idiom *cover story* can mean either 'an important news story that appears on the cover of a periodical', or 'a made-up story to hide the truth'. The Arabic calque مَوْضُوعُ الغِلافِ is only used in the latter sense. Naturally, this has significant implications and the translator has to be wary not to assume meaning is always transferred with form.

Similarity in form does not necessarily imply borrowing as different cultures have similar reactions to things. For instance, although فَتَحَ أُذْنَيْهِ is often cited as a calque of the English 'to open one's ears', it is, in fact, a wholly Arabic construct, whose origins can be traced to the Middle Ages, and one cannot even exclude that English (and other European languages) ultimately borrowed it from Arabic! Similarly, does 'he was fuming'/كان يَغْلِي, for instance, reveal any cultural specificity, or rather a similarity in metaphorical target and source domains, which are common to both English and Arabic communities?

Meanings may differ altogether, as in *for your eyes* and مِنْ أَجْلِ عَيْنَيْكَ; while the former has a connotation of secrecy or confidentiality (as in the case of documents marked 'for your eyes only'), the Arabic idiom means 'for your sake': e.g.

كانَت تعاديه مِن أَجْلِ عَيْنَيْ زَوْجِها
'She made an enemy of him for the sake of her husband.'

It is also not uncommon to find idioms with similar meaning, but of varied origin, competing with one another. For instance, 'to return empty-handed' can be folklore-based, as in عادَ/رَجَعَ بِخُفَّيْ حُنَيْنٍ ('to return with Hunayn's shoes'), have its roots in a proverb, like جاء بِقَرْنَيْ حِمار ('to return with the two horns of the donkey'), which is a compression of ذَهَبَ الحِمار يَطْلُبُ قَرْنَين فعادَ مَصْلُوم الأذْنَيْنِ ('the donkey went in search of horns and returned with his ears cut off'), or be rendered through a technical term, رَجَعَ/عادَ خالِي/خاوِي الوِفاض ('to return with empty saddle bags').

It is often argued that Arabic uses far more idioms than English; whether or not this is true is difficult to tell. What is undoubtedly clear to even the most casual observer is that religion-based idioms are more frequent in Arabic.

Syntactically, idioms may come in the following guises:

- NOUN (English/Arabic): e.g.

  brick ('reliable person')
  ثَعْلَب ('cunning person')

- NOUN + NOUN (English/Arabic): e.g.

  hobby-horse
  حَيْص بَيْص ('higgledy-piggledy')

- NOUN + ADJECTIVE (English/Arabic): e.g.

  dark horse ('a virtually unknown competitor that wins something unexpectedly')
  لِسان طَوِيل ('long-tongued', i.e. given to gossip)

- PREPOSITIONAL PHRASE (English/Arabic): e.g.

  in a pickle ('in difficulty')
  في غَمْضةِ عَيْن ('in the blink of an eye')

- VERB PHRASE (English/Arabic): e.g.

  to have a fit ('get very angry')
  شَدَّ الحِزام ('to tighten the belt')

- GENITIVE CONSTRUCTION (English/Arabic): e.g.

  man of substance ('wealthy person')
  days of yore ('bygone days')
  رِباطُ الجَأشِ ('self-control')

- SENTENCE (English/Arabic): e.g.

  to hit the ceiling ('to get angry')
  طَوَى صَفْحة الماضِي ('to turn the page')

Translating idioms

The translation of idioms is complicated by a number of factors:

- The absence of an equivalent idiom in the TL;

- Deceptive transparency of components; this applies particularly to idioms that have both a literal and a metaphorical meaning. In many cases, the literal and figurative meanings are rendered by different translations in the target language: e.g.

  to go down, (lit.) 'to descend, sink' (نَزَلَ), (fig.) 'to be accepted (e.g. idea, proposal)' (لَقِيَ قُبُولاً)
  to pay back, (lit.) 'to return money borrowed' (سَدَّ دَيْناً), (fig.) 'to take revenge' (اِنْتَقَمَ)

- Lack of transparency of components, often due to archaic meanings: e.g. in the Arabic idiom ضَرَبَ اللَّيْل بِأَوْراقِه, the meaning of أوراق as 'the front and side of a house' is a very classical one which many Arabic speakers would no longer be familiar with;

- Variability of one of the lexical items in idioms (see above);

- The cultural specificity of many idioms. For instance, the very common phrase مِسْمار جُحا ('Joha's nail') is a reference to a story involving the fictional figure of 'Joha', the Arab counterpart of Till Eulenspiegel, whose adventures are the object of innumerable tales all over the Near and Middle East (appearing in the guise of *Nasrettin Hoca* in Turkey and Naṣr al-Dīn in Persia), as well as in Central Asia. Conversely, an example for English would be *'all Christmases rolled into one'*, which may pose a problem for readers who do not celebrate Christmas. In this case one might draw a comparison with the Muslim cultural equivalent عيد (*Eid*). In English>Arabic translation, the idioms relating to, for instance, *alcohol* (e.g. *bottoms up*, *hair of the dog*) or certain sports such as *cricket* (e.g. *to throw a googly, a good innings*) are also particularly challenging;

- Misleading similarities between idioms in the source and target languages. Despite the existence of certain human universals, there are many examples of similar idioms having very different, often opposing meanings across languages. For instance, the English translator coming across the expression شَدَّ حِزامَهُ may be forgiven for opting for the obvious translation 'to tighten one's belt', i.e. 'to live frugally'. Whilst this may be the correct translation in some cases, in others it would be completely nonsensical since the same idiom is also used to mean 'to prepare oneself', and is then synonymous with شَدَّ إزارَهُ or شَدَّ مِئزَرَه. Similarly, the Arabic idiom سَحَبَ ذَيْلَهُ ('to withdraw one's tail'), though very similar to the idiom 'with one's tail between one's legs', could not be further in meaning from its English equivalent: the Arabic idiom means 'to strut', whereas the English phrase (which usually collocates with the verb *to leave*) means 'in shame and disgrace'! In Arabic you can 'bite your nails' (عَضَّ أنامِلَهُ) only 'in anger' but an English speaker does it out of anxiety, as in *a nail-biting wait*. In short, the translator has to guard against imposing SL meanings on TL idioms, irrespective of formal similarities;

- Connotational or contextual differences between established SL and TL idioms: e.g.

  a The expression *that ship has sailed* is best translated into Arabic as فاتَهُ القِطار but while the English expression appears in a variety of contexts, the Arabic idiom tends to collocate mostly with 'marriage', as in فاتَهُ (فات عَلَى) الزَّواج

('to lose one's chance of getting married').

b The established equivalent of سارَ فِي رِكابِهِ is 'to follow in someone's footsteps'; unlike the English idiom, the Arabic phrase implies to do so blindly.

- *Polysemy* of some idioms: e.g. صالَ وجالَ may mean either 'to discuss something in depth' or 'to do as one pleases, without any let or hindrance';

- *Language variation*: within a given language different communities coin different idioms, or attribute different meanings to identical ones. Whilst this is true for varieties of English, it is much more prominent in Arabic, where many idioms are *dialect*-specific but may filter through in the formal register of speakers of that particular dialect. Consider, for instance, the renditions of the English idiom *out of the frying pan into the fire*:

  اِسْتجارَ مِن الرَّمْضاء بالنّار (lit. 'to seek relief from the sun-baked earth in the fire') (MSA)

  هَرَب من الدُّبّ وَقَع في الجُبّ (lit. 'to escape from the bear only to fall into the pit') (Levantine Arabic)

  مِن تَحْت الدَّلْف لِتَحْت المِزْراب (lit. 'from under the drip to under the spout') (Levantine/Gulf Arabic)

  خَرَج مِن الحُفْرة ووَقَعَ في الدُّحْدِيرة (lit. 'to get out of the hole but fall down the slope') (Egypt)

  طالَع مِن الخَبّ طاحَ فِي الطَّوي (lit. 'to come out of the *khabb* but fall in the well') (Oman)

  طالَع مِن القَوم مَزْتُوه الغَزاية (lit. 'to escape from the troops only to be plundered by raiders') (Oman)

  طالَع مِن المَوت طاحَ فِي حَضْرَمَوت (lit. 'to be saved from death but fall in Hadramawt') (Oman)

In some cases, one finds that the dialects are more fertile grounds for idioms than the standard variety. From the point of view of recognition and comprehension this naturally complicates things greatly. In many cases, the differences in form are small but in others the same meaning is expressed completely differently, as the above examples reveal.

- *Register*; just like other lexical items, idioms are often linked to specific registers. This applies solely to English, where a number of them are associated with an informal style: e.g.

  to get on someone's case ('to monitor someone's behaviour')
  to be off his rocker ('to be crazy')
  on the q.t. ('on the quiet, secretively')

The most effective translation strategies are as follows (in order of preference):

1 a TL **idiom** that has similar meaning and form: e.g.

an iron fist in a velvet glove, قَبْضة حَدِيدِيّة في قُفّاز مُخْمَلِي
the naked eye, العَيْن المُجَرَّدة
face to face, وَجْهاً لوَجْه
lion's share, نَصِيب الأسَد
to fall in love, وَقَعَ في الحُبّ

In some cases, there are several possibilities: e.g.

topsy-turvy, رَأْساً عَلى عَقِب، العالَم بِالمَقْلُوب

2 a TL **idiom** with similar meaning but dissimilar form, i.e. with one or more different lexical items: e.g.

to fly off the handle, هاجَ هائِجُهُ
a drop in the ocean, غَيْض مِن فَيْض
to run with the hare and hunt with the hounds, لَعِبَ عَلى الحَبْلَيْن

3 to **paraphrase**, maintaining some SL cultural specificity, where necessary: e.g.

to back the wrong horse, راهَنَ عَلى الجَواد الخاسِر

4 a **functional equivalent**, i.e. 'descriptive' translation, which essentially entails 'neutralizing' the idiom by rendering it through a non-idiomatic phrase in the target language: e.g.

dark horse, شَخْص غامِض ('obscure person')

5 **omission**: this strategy is employed for the sake of specific text types and/or readership: e.g.

He was really angry when she came home late – it really got his hackles up.
اِسْتَشاط غَضَباً لَما دَخَلَت مُتَأَخِّراً

6 **addition**, particularly in cases where both figurative and literal meanings of an idiom coincide, as in the example *to shrug one's shoulders*, which should either be translated as هَزَّ كَتِفَيْه (literal) or هَزَّ كَتِفَيْه لامُبالاةً (figurative);

7 **borrowing**, i.e. literal translation. This is a useful strategy for highly culture-bound idioms. The borrowing may be of every lexical item in the original, or only some of them: e.g.

to have green fingers, يَدُهُ خَضْراء

With respect to the last strategy, it is important to point out that today's borrowing is often tomorrow's naturalized idiom, with its foreign origins being quickly forgotten. For instance, the English origins of *to cry crocodile tears*, ذَرَفَ دُمُوع التماسيح have been forgotten as the expression has become part of Arabic lexis. Similarly, most English speakers will be blissfully unaware that *a marriage of convenience* is, in fact, a calque from French, and the origins of the Arabic زَواج المَصْلَحة may thus go back to either language.

Naturally, a number of strategies are usually open to the translator, and in many cases, there are several possibilities within a given strategy: e.g.

to follow/take someone's lead:	حَذا حَذْوَهُ يَنْهَج مَنْهَجَهُ اِقْتَفى أثَرَهُ
an easy prey:	غَنِيمة بارِدة ('cold prey') فَرِيسة سائغة ('easy-to-swallow prey') صَيْد هَيِّن ('easy hunt') هَدَف سَهْل ('easy target')

In order to illustrate this further, let us consider some of the possible equivalents to the English idiom *it's raining cats and dogs*.

Literal translation (borrowing)	تُمْطِرُ (الدُّنيا) قِطَطاً وكِلاباً
Idiom similar in form and meaning	–
Idiom similar in meaning, dissimilar in form	إنَّ الدُّنْيا تُمْطِرُ كأفْواه القِرَبِ مَطَر جارٌ الضَبُّع سَحَّت السَّماء نَزَلَ عَلَيْنا الغَيْث اِنْهَمَرَ المَطَر تَهْطِلُ الأمْطارِ سَقَطَت هُطُول الأمْطار تَبِلُ الدُّنْيا أمْطَرَ وابِل مَطَر ذُو بُرايةٍ أغْدَقَ السَّماء اِنْبَعَقَ المُزْن بَغَت السَّماء أَلْقَت السَّماء بَرَك بَوانِيها اِنْباقَت المَطْرة أَثْرَت الأرْض

	جادَ المَطَر أصابَتْنا تَجاوِيد المَطَر حَفَلَت السَّماء دَرَّت السَّماء بِالمَطَر رَضَبَت السَّماء أرْهَجَت السَّماء
Functional equivalent/paraphrase	إنَّ الدُّنْيا تُمْطِرُ بِغزارةٍ تَسْقُط زَخّات من المَطَر

Despite the number of possibilities within each category, it is clear that one may distinguish between *degrees of figurativeness* of the expressions, depending on the presence of a literal component.

Viewed from this angle, we may say that إنَّ الدُّنْيا تُمْطِرُ كأفْواه القِرَبِ ('the rains pours as if flowing from the mouths of waterskins') is more figurative than أَغْدَقَ السَّماء (which contains the word 'sky'), which, in turn, is more figurative than اِنْبَعَقَ المُزْن (which contains the word 'clouds'), with the least figurative being the phrases that contain the word 'rain'.

As ever, register, text type and target audience are crucial considerations. With the exception of the first, the following translations are all idiomatically possible and grammatically correct, but belong to different registers, styles and degrees of formalcy, literariness, etc.; when selecting the appropriate translation of a given idiom, all of these have to be matched. For instance, the use of a borrowing may be too exotic for a general newspaper article, but the best option in a literary text aimed at a semi-specialist readership.

As mentioned above, the differences in idioms between language varieties, both between the standard (MSA) and the dialects, and between the individual dialects impact on translation. When translating into Arabic, a translator may arguably decide that it is more important to have an idiom in both SL and TL and, in the absence of an MSA equivalent, resort to one used in a particular colloquial variety. It is important to remember, however, that no matter how judicious a choice this may be for stylistic reasons, it should not be at the expense of comprehension. The decision should, therefore, be based on whether or not the idiom is specific to only one variety or whether it is used in several, on the one hand, and, on the other, on the extent to which it may reasonably be expected to be understood by the target readership.

A particular type of idiom that also merits to be treated here are **similes** (تَشْبِيه), a figure of speech comparing two things through *like*, *as*, or *than*: e.g. *as happy as a sandboy*, *to sweat like a pig*, *more cunning than a fox*. These may be problematic for a number of reasons. First, as they tend to be highly culture-specific, literal translation often results in unnaturalness. The translation of *as strong as a horse* into قَوِي مِثْل فَرَس would provoke ridicule from most Arabic speakers, as would سَكْران كلورد for *as drunk as a Lord*!

Second, seemingly similar comparisons may result in dramatically different uses. For instance, at first glance the English simile *as white as snow* or *as white as a sheet* both have *whiteness* as the aim of the comparison, and one would reasonably expect them to be used interchangeably as long as a high degree of whiteness is intended. In practice, however, there are contextual connotations; *as white as snow* is used, for instance, when talking about someone's reputation, whereas *as white as a sheet* is used exclusively to refer to the pallor of someone's face, usually after sustaining an emotional shock of some sort. Similarly, *to drink like a fish* only applies to alcohol, not thirst after eating a salty dish!

Further, one should not assume that there is an equivalent TL simile for all SL ones, as the cultural differences between languages often result in semantic gaps. This is particularly true for English–Arabic translation since similes are used more often in English than they are in Arabic, which seems to have a penchant for other idiomatic expressions.

Here, too, foreign influences are making themselves felt. For instance, the established equivalents in Classical Arabic of *as white as snow* are أبيض كالشَّمْع ('as white as wax'), أبْيَض مِثْل القَمَر ('as white as the moon') or أبْيَض مِثْل البَدْر ('as white as a full moon'). As a result of language contact, however, these have increasingly been crowded out by أبيض كـ/مِثل الثَّلج, which, in more ways than one, may be considered both a cultural and pragmatic mismatch. Another example is *as black as ink*, traditionally rendered as أسود كالفَحْم/كالقِير ('as black as tar/coal'), though كالحِبْر ('as ink') is frequently found in modern Arabic texts.

Similes may be rendered in one of the following ways:

- a TL **simile** with similar form and meaning to the original: e.g.

  as strong as a lion, قَوِي كـ/مِثْل الأسَد

- a TL **simile** with similar meaning, but dissimilar in form: e.g.

  as patient as Job, صَبْر أيُّوب

- **omission**; this strategy may be used either when there is no equivalent in the target language, or for stylistic reasons. As similes often have superlative meaning, it is necessary to compensate for the omission: e.g.

  as thin as a matchstick, في غايةِ الرِّقَّةِ

- **literal translation** (*calquing*); in some cases, one may opt for a literal rendering for stylistic purposes, either signposted or not: e.g.

  as fast as a bullet, سَرِيع كرَصاصة (كما يُقال بالإنكليزي)

PROVERBS (أمْثال)

Since both idioms and proverbs can have metaphorical uses or content, the distinction between them is perhaps not always clear. Generally speaking, the distinctive feature of proverbs is the fact that they (purport to) convey a (folk) wisdom or (supposed) general truth, and often have an exhortatory or advisory intent; in other words, there is a moral to them.

Linguistically, they differ from idioms in that they are even more invariable in form;

proverbs resist any change, even pluralization or conjugation. They also tend to be complete sentences, rather than phrases, as is the case for idioms. Let us consider, for instance, the idioms كان زَفِيرُهُ لَهِيباً / بَلَغ السَّيْلُ الزُّبَى and their English translations 'to blow a gasket', 'to have kittens' or 'to spit fire', on the one hand, and an idiom such as لِكُل جَوّاد كَبْوَة ('every steed can stumble'), which is most appropriately rendered as 'nobody's perfect'. All are metaphorical expressions, but the proverb has a moral and pragmatic purpose, which in the latter example may be paraphrased as 'don't be too harsh on X, nobody's perfect!'

Proverbs occupy a high status in Arabic language usage to this day, and they are conspicuous in most conversations across all social levels in Arab countries. For this reason, it is a significant issue in Arabic–English translation.

Proverbs are probably the most culture-specific of all idiomatic expressions. The generic Classical Arabic proverbs have often been subject to modification in the dialects, each of which has continued to create them and as a result there are often many intra-cultural, regional differences and/or nuances: e.g.

> الدَّهْرُ يَوْم لَكَ ويَوْم عَلَيْك ('fate is with you one day, and against you the next') (MSA)
> العَبْد في التَّفْكِير والرَّبّ في التَّدْبِير ('the believer may think about it, but God is the One who arranges it') (MSA)
> الدُّنْيا يوم عَسَل ويوم بَصَل ('one day, the world is filled with honey, the next with onions') (Egypt)
> ما كُلّ ما يَتَمَنَّى المَرْء يُدْرِكُهُ تَجْرِي الرِّياح بما لا تَشْتَهِي السُّفُن ('not everything that a man wants will be carried to him by the winds from jetsam and flotsam') (Gulf Arabic)
>
> → *man proposes, God disposes*
> → *life has its ups and downs*
>
> باب النَّجَّار مِخَلَّع ('the carpenter's door hangs awry') (Egypt)
> بِنْت الصائغ تَشْتَهِي الصُوغ وَبِنْت النَّسّاج عَرْيانة ('the jeweller's daughter craves gold and the weaver's daughter goes naked') (Oman)
> دار النَّجَّار بلاشِي مِغْرَفه ('the carpenter's house doesn't have a ladle') (Tunis)
> دار الحَدَّاد بِلا سِكِّينة ('the ironsmith's house doesn't have a knife') (Tunis)
>
> → *the cobbler's children are always ill-shod*
>
> ذَنَب الكَلْب أعْوَج وَلَو حَطَّيْت في خَمْسِين قالِب ('the dog's tail remains crooked, even if it is put in fifty moulds') Gulf)
> عُمْرُه ذيل الكَلْب ما يِنْعِدِل وَلَوْ عَلَّقوا عليه قالِب ('the tail of a dog will never be straight even if they hang a brick on it') (Egypt)
> الحَنْظَلَة لا تَتَقَلَّب جَحّة ('a colocynth gourd can never be transformed into a watermelon') (Oman)
>
> → *a leopard doesn't change its spots*

In addition to a 'top-down' movement, i.e. from the Standard to the dialects, there has also been a great deal of upward and lateral spreading, with many originally dialectal sayings spreading to other varieties – both dialects and the Standard – either with their original meaning or dressed up in a new one.

Unlike with the other types of idioms discussed, it is impossible for the translator to avoid contact with colloquial proverbs in most non-technical text genres. This throws up a significant linguistic problem in that the proverbs often contain vernacular vocabulary, which may constitute an obstacle for all except the native speakers of the variety in question. For instance, the Omani proverb كَعَوْر بِياق يبكّر رِشِبْتُه ويَلَوَّح عِشُقْتُه contains references to local geography (the town of Biyaq) as well as dialectal lexical items. Yet, even if one were given the literal translation – 'like the blind man of Biyaq who is always replenishing his hookah and waving the date-stalk about it' (!) – the meaning would still remain elusive. (In fact, the closest English equivalent would be *a great deal of sowing for very little reaping*.)

Though both English and Arabic draw a great number of their proverbs from religious sources, religious language appears much more often in Arabic than it does in English. As a result, many English non-religious proverbs re-emerge with a clear religious connotation in Arabic translation: e.g. *patience is a virtue*, العَجَلَة مِن الشَّيْطان والتَّأنّي مِن الرَّحْمان ('speed is of the devil and patience of the Merciful'), which is often to be preferred to the 'secular' الصَّبْر مُرّ وثَمَرُهُ حِلْو ('patience is bitter but its fruit is sweet').

Just like with other idioms, there have been numerous borrowings from European languages: e.g.

> الأَعْوَرُ فِي بِلادِ العُمْيانِ أَمِيرٌ, *in the land of the blind the one-eyed man is king* (originally coined by the sixteenth-century philosopher Erasmus)
>
> لا دُخانُ بِلا / بِدُون نارٍ, *no smoke without fire*

The following strategies may usefully be employed in the translation of proverbs, in order of preference:

1 an **equivalent proverb** similar in form and meaning; this is the usual method with many of the 'newer' proverbs: e.g.

> إذا كانَ الكَلامُ مِن فِضَّةٍ فالسُّكُوتُ مِن ذَهَبٍ, *if speech is silver, silence is golden*
>
> رُبَّ سُكُوتٍ أَبْلَغ مِن الكَلامِ, *silence speaks louder than words*
>
> عُصْفُورٌ فِي اليَدِ خَيْرٌ مِن عَشَرةٍ عَلَى الشَّجَرةِ, *a bird in the hand is worth two in the bush*
>
> الأعْوَر في بِلاد العُمْيان طَرْفة, *in the land of the blind, the one-eyed man is king*

2 an **equivalent proverb** similar in meaning, dissimilar in form: e.g.

> اليَدّ الفارِغة تُسارِع إلى الشَّرّ, *the devil finds work for idle hands* (also *idle hands are the devil's playthings*; *an idle brain is the devil's workshop*)

إذا كَثُرَ الرَّبابِنةُ غَرِقَت السَّفِينةُ ('if there are too many captains, the ship will sink'), *too many cooks spoil the broth*

بيضةٌ اليَوْم خَيْرٌ مِن دَجاجةٍ الغَد ('an egg today is better than a chicken tomorrow'), *a bird in the hand is worth two in the bush*

غابَتْ السِّباعُ ولَعَبَتْ الضِّباعُ ('when the lions were absent, the hyenas played'), *when the cat's away, the mice will play*

3 an **equivalent idiom**, which typically conveys the result of the proverb. In Arabic, this will often involve a so-called *wisdom* (حِكْمة) or a literary quote: e.g.

مَنْ حَفَرَ حَفْرةً لأَخِيهِ وَقَعَ فيها ('he who digs a hole for his brother will fall into it'), *to be hoisted with his own petard*

education is not received; it is achieved, لا تَقُلْ أَصْلِي وفَصْلِي أبَداً إنَّما أصْل الفَتَى ما قد فَعَلَ (verse by the Abbasid poet al-Mutanabbī)

4 **paraphrase**; in this case no phraseological item is used, and the meaning of the proverb is given: e.g.

أَهْلُ مَكَّة أَدْرَى بِشِعابِها, *to know a place you have to be from the place*

5 translation by **addition**; it is not uncommon for proverbs to be abbreviated, as it is presumed that the listener/reader is sufficiently familiar with it to complete it. Whilst the same process may be transferred into the TL, it is advisable to complete the proverb in the TT: e.g.

when in Rome ... (do as the Romans do), إذا كُنْتَ فِي رُوما فَأَفْعَلْ ما يَفْعَلُهُ الرُّمانُ

القَناعةُ مالٌ لا يَنْفَد ... (وَكَنْزٌ لا يَفْنَى), *contentment is a wealth that does not run out and a treasure that does not perish*

6 **borrowing** (literal translation), with or without explanation or nearest equivalent. This may be used when there is no equivalent proverb and the meaning is transparent, or if it is in line with target readership expectations or text type conventions. Due to the culture-bound content of proverbs and the above-mentioned issue of vernacular vocabulary, inappropriate use of this strategy will result in unnecessary exoticness of the text, which may even hamper comprehension. For instance, the Omani proverb أنا شايف دَم في الخِتانة والقيظ في شَرْجَبانة ('I have seen the blood of the circumcision and the summer in the *sharjaban* [a fruit resembling the colocynth]'), which is said in self-praise, loses all meaning to the average Western reader, and as a result, a clear gloss is vital in those cases: e.g.

الكِلاب تَنْبَح والقافِلة تَسِير, *the dogs bark, but the caravan moves on*

إِعْقِلْ وَتَوَكَّل, *rely [on God] but tether [your camel]*, i.e. *God helps those who help themselves*
القِرْدُ فِي عَيْنِ أُمِّهِ غَزالٌ, *in the eyes of its mother, the monkey is a gazelle*

COMPOUNDS (مُرَكَّبات)

The issue of compounding plays a considerable role in Arabic–English–Arabic translation. As is so often the case this is primarily, if not exclusively, due to the fundamental differences in lexical structure and formation between the two languages, with compounding being extremely active in English and far less so in Arabic. First of all, let us take a closer look at what makes compounds what they are and behave the way they do.

Essentially, words can be divided into *simple* and *complex* words, i.e. those that consist of one lexical unit and those that consist of either an affix, or another lexical unit attached to it, respectively. In this context, linguists refer to *free* and *derivational morphemes*. A simple definition of morpheme would be 'the smallest meaningful unit of a language'. Let us take the word 'drink' as an example. As this is a unit that can exist on its own and cannot be divided into underlying components, it is called a *free morpheme*. At the same time, it has a lexical meaning by itself, so it is a *lexical* morpheme.

We can, of course, add a number of 'stick-on-parts' to the word and make a new one. We could, for instance, add '-ER' or '-ABLE' to 'DRINK', which gives us 'DRINKER' ('someone who drinks') and 'DRINKABLE' ('something which can be drunk'). In adding '-ER' or '-ABLE', which are known as *suffixes* (i.e. something that is added at the end of a word), we have created two new words. Naturally, in so doing, we also change the grammatical category of the words in many cases, as becomes clear from the following representation: e.g.

[DRINK]VERB
[[DRINK]VERB +[ER]affix]NOUN
[[DRINK]VERB +[ABLE] affix]ADVERB

As an affix can never exist by itself – it always needs a word to hang on to – linguists use the term *bound morpheme*. Since the process involves *derivation*, i.e. new words are created (as opposed to *inflection*, say of a verb), these types of morphemes are also known as *derivational morphemes*.

A word comprising only one morpheme is called *simple*, whereas a *complex* word has more than one. English words often contain a large number of morphemes, as in the word *antidisestablishmentarianism*, which may be analysed as [anti][dis][establish][ment][arian][ism], and contains two prefixes and two suffixes.

A *compound* is a combination of two or more independent words – i.e. *free lexical morphemes* – that functions both grammatically and semantically as a single word: e.g. *sun + rise*. It is important at this stage to contrast this with the concept of *noun phrase*, which is also a group of words, but which consists of a noun and a *modifier*, typically a determiner (e.g. article) and/or an adjective, as in the 'beautiful girl'. An easy test to apply is the following: if the relationship between the elements is 'X is something that is Y', then it is a noun phrase; if 'X is a type of Y', then it is a compound. So, a *handbag* is a type of bag (not a bag that is a hand!), while *a nice car* is 'a car that is nice' (not a type of car).

Compounding (or composition) also differs from derivation in a number of ways. First, there are no phonological changes in the elements of the compounds, as opposed to those in derivation: e.g. *music* > *musician* (derivation), *music-hall* (compounding). Second, derivation always includes *bound morphemes*, whereas compounding involves a combination of roots or stems. Finally, there is a limit to the number of morphemes that can be added through derivation, while in theory no such restriction exists for compounds, which are said to be *recursive*: e.g.

first-class ticket
first-class ticket office
first-class ticket office customer service
first-class ticket office customer service assistance
first-class ticket office customer service assistance clerk
...

As far as spelling is concerned, we can distinguish between three types of compounds:

1 a compound consisting of two separate words: e.g. *firing squad*
2 single-word (or *juxtapositional*) compounds: e.g. *gamekeeper*
3 hyphenated compounds: e.g. *ice-cream*

Unfortunately, the spelling of compounds is highly inconsistent and, at times, positively haphazard, especially in the case of hyphenation, with variants co-existing quite happily.

Another way of subdividing compounds is based on the semantic relation between its components. The key element of a compound is the *head*, which determines both the meaning and the grammatical category of the compound. In English, the head is the right-most element, as a result of which English compounds are called *right-headed*. By far the bigger category is comprised of compounds in which the left element modifies the head, i.e. says something about the head in one way or another, often that X is a specific type (i.e. a subclass) of Y (head): e.g. *football stadium* (a specific type of stadium). This class is known as *endocentric* compounds.

Another group may be illustrated by units such as *bigwig* or *pickpocket*, which do not have a head and often have a metaphorical meaning; a *bigwig* is not a wig that is big, but 'an important person', while *pickpocket* is not a type of pocket, but someone who 'picks your pocket'. These are known as *exocentric* compounds.

A group that falls outside the former two consists of sets such as 'the *London–Durham* express train' and '*Southampton–Newcastle* match', in which each element functions as head. Syntactically, this category implies ellipsis (omission) of a preposition: 'London *to* Durham (express train)', 'Southampton *versus* Newcastle (match)'.

The following are some additional guidelines to distinguish (or, as linguists say, *disambiguate*) compounds, especially in relation to noun phrases (which sometimes look the same):

1 **stress** pattern: compounds have the main stress on the first element, noun phrases on the second: e.g.

*dark **room*** (a room that is dark) vs ***dark**room* (a special room in which a photographer develops films)
black**board* (board found in a classroom) vs *black **board (a board that is black)
green**house* (a building where plants are grown) vs *green **house (a house that is green)
white**fish* (a type of fish) vs *white **fish (any fish that is white)
flat**foot* (slang term for policeman) vs *flat **foot (a physical disorder)
White** House* (the US president's residence) vs *white **house (a house that is white)

In the above examples, the spelling (provided it is correct!) already provides the main clue since noun phrases can never be written in one word. However, below are some sets where spelling alone does not provide any clues:

French** teacher* (someone who teaches French) vs *French **teacher (a French national who is a teacher)
toy** factory* (a place where toys are produced) vs *toy **factory (a model of a factory, used as a children's toy)

2 **lexicalization**: only compounds can be lexicalized, i.e. acquire 'word status', as a result of which they appear in a dictionary: e.g. *ice-cream*. That is not to say that every compound is lexicalized, particularly as compounding is a highly productive process and new adhoc ones are coined every day: e.g.

crystal light bed treatment

3 **affixation** and **modification**: the first element of a compound does not take a suffix, and cannot be qualified (e.g. by *very*, *too*, *quite*): e.g. *a darker room* can only be a room that is darker, and you can't have a 'quite greenhouse'.

4 In the case of verb compounds, the **tense** is marked on the head: e.g.

I stir-fried the vegetables. (NOT **I stirred-fry*)

5 **transparency**: the meaning of compounds is often not transparent: e.g. a *blackberry* is often red and a *greenhouse* can be painted in any colour.

6 **pluralization**:

a In some cases, compounds have exceptional plurals. This is particularly noticeable in certain exocentric compounds; for instance, even though the plural of *leaf* is *leaves*, the Canadian ice-hockey team are the *Maple Leafs* (not *leaves*!). Similarly, the plural of *sabertooth* (a type of tiger) is *sabertooths*.
b There is generally no plural marking of the first element; only

the head takes the plural, even if the original word does not have a singular form, as in:

trousers vs *trouser-pocket*
pyjamas vs *pyjama bottoms*

Exceptions include *arms factory/race*, *systems analyst*, *sports doctor*, *goods train*, where there would be ambiguity if the plural were not used. For instance, in the case of *arms factory*, the use of the singular 'arm' could in theory refer to a place where they produce synthetic arms (i.e. limbs), as opposed to one where they make weapons, whereas a *good train* would quite naturally be analysed as 'a train that is good' (rather than a bad one). Another set of exceptions is a very small set of noun compounds which, for historic reasons, have an adjective as their second element, but only the nouns can take plural markers: e.g. *secretaries general*. These generally involve borrowings from French, where the adjective follows the noun.

7 **clipping**: (verb) compounds can be clipped, i.e. the second element dropped: e.g. 'This house is *guided* at £100,000', in which *guided* is shortened from 'guide-priced', i.e. 'has a guide price (at auction)' of £100,000.

Syntactically, compounds also come in many guises, some examples of which are shown in Table 1.1.

Table 1.1 Composition of compounds

+	*Noun*	*Adjective*	*Verb*	*Preposition*
Noun	handbook, ice-cream, shop window	ice-cold	to babysit, to shoplift	sit-in
Adjective	black market	bitter-sweet	to highlight	forthwith
Verb	swearword	diehard	to stir-fry	take-off
Preposition	underdog	overambitious	to backdate	hitherto

In addition to the above examples, compounds may also be comprised of a phrase – e.g. *good-for-nothing*, *off-the-peg* (clothes), *sweet-and-sour* (e.g. chicken) – or an idiom (e.g. *this cast-pearls-before-swine attitude of his*). The 'verb + preposition' (or adverb particle) category is also very productive, but these are phrasal verbs, which have been discussed above.

The grammatical category of the compound is determined by its head, so the columns refer to, respectively, *noun* (or *nominal*) *compounds*, *adjective compounds* and *verb compounds*. The exception here is the 'preposition' column, where the first element determines the part of speech of the compound.

Conversion plays a big role in English lexicology, i.e. a word can change grammatical categories, which also applies to compounds and many noun compounds are turned into verbs: e.g. *to blindfold*.

Compounds in Arabic

Arabic compounds differ significantly from those in English. Indeed, it is highly debatable whether Arabic has compounding (تَرْكِيب) in the sense it is applied to European languages.

Although Classical Arabic had a way of combining several words into one, a process known as نَحْت, one should resist comparing this to the type of units we have described above.[36] Examples of نَحْت are words including بَسْمَلَ ('to say بسم الله الرحمن الرحيم') and حَوْقَلَ ('to say لاحَوْلَ ولا قُوَّةَ إلا بالله'), or modern combinations (mainly restricted to science and technology) like (تَحْتَ + بَحْرِي <) تَحْبَحْرِي, ('underwater') and سَمْعبَصَرِي ('audiovisual'), most of which are adjectives. These are, in fact, 'blends', since the constituents are not free morphemes and, with the exception of the last one, are abbreviated (clipped).

The controversy arising from the discussions on compounds is inextricably linked with the fundamental differences in the morphology of Arabic and English. For a start, Arabic is said to be *non-concatenative*, meaning that it does not normally allow for lexemes to be juxtaposed to form a new unit, with a new specific meaning. But things are, unfortunately, not as cut and dried as all that, as the following examples make clear:

1 combinations with لا (to render the English *non-*, *un-*, *in-*): e.g. لاوُجُودِية (*non-existence*), لامَرْكَزِي (*decentralized*);
2 مابَيْن ('what' + 'between' – *antechamber*);
3 يانَصِيب ('oh' + 'fate' – *lottery*);
4 لَيْلَ نَهارَ ('day and night'), صَباحَ مساءَ ('morning and night');
5 طائرة هِلِيكُوبْتِر, ('aeroplane' + 'helicopter' – *helicopter*);
6 عرض حال / عَرْضُحال ('presentation' + 'state' – *petition*), رأس مال / رَأْسمال ('head' + 'money' – *capital*).

In 1–3, the first element is, once again, a bound morpheme and there is a strong case for reanalysing it as a prefix; hence, it involves *derivation* rather than compounding. The combinations under 4 have been called *blended compounds*;[37] in fact, *syntactically*, they are compounds but *semantically* they are idioms. The fifth example should be considered a calque, with the borrowing هليكوبتر being added in apposition. Only the last group comprises 'true' compounds insofar as here we have the juxtaposition of two nouns to form a new unit that functions as such both syntactically, and semantically, as is shown by the plural formation, for instance: رَساميل, عَرْض حالات (or رُؤُوس أمْوال).

Moreover, case is marked only on the second element: e.g.

> اِسْتَثْمَرَتْ الشَّرِكةُ رَأْسمالاً إضافياً في باريس ونيويورك, 'The company invested additional capital in Paris and New York.'
>
> قَدَّمَ عَرْضَ حالاً كانَ يُوَقِّعُهُ اِثْنانِ مِن المُوَظَّفِينَ, 'He submitted a petition signed by two of the employees.'

While the first group is very productive in Modern Standard Arabic, the others are made up only of the examples listed.

Does this mean that Arabic has no other compounds? Not quite. It does have lexical units that are involved in a semantic relation in which the second specifies the first, have one referent and 'function as one phrase or syntactic unit.'[38] However, *syntactically*, they are genitive constructions involving nominal annexation, known in Arabic as *iḍāfa*, and, as such, they are only *semantically* equivalent to English compounds. In itself, this is not that different from some English compounds, many of which are also in a genitive relationship with their co-element: e.g. *university spokesman* is a 'spokesman of the university'.

The claim that the Arabic *iḍāfa* is a compound must be further qualified since, clearly, not every genitive construction can be considered a compound! The answer lies in adding the criteria of:

- a semantic unit in a relation of specificity;
- the existence of 'one referent';
- idiomatic non-compositional meaning;
- the relationship that exists between the elements is adjectival or one of subject and object: e.g. تَأْمِيم البَنُوك ('nationalization of banks').

In these cases, the head (مُضاف) and its modifier, or governed noun (مُضاف إلَيْهِ), may be likened to constituents of English compounds.

In order to distinguish these from purely genitive constructions, the term *iḍāfa compound* is suggested here; it is a compound in the sense that it meets the above tests, while at the same time remaining fundamentally (syntactically) an *iḍāfa*.

At times, discussion of the *iḍāfa* within the context of Arabic compounds is based on how the Arabic construct is translated into English, or by the mere fact that the *iḍāfa* is a distinct syntactic unit. For instance, it is difficult to argue for the 'compound status' of مُدِير المَدْرَسة (*school principal*), for instance, as Ryding (2005) seems to do, or of رَأس السَّهْم (*arrowhead*), as Emery (1988) does, since these are purely genitive constructions. Indeed, if one applied the same principle to English compounds, 'seats of the bus' would have to be considered a compound. While there is a case for numeral constructions that occur with numerals to be considered compounds, syntactically, they do not fit the other criteria. The same is true for other compound constructs – e.g. آنذاك (*at that time*: adverbial compound), مُتَعَدِّد الأطْراف (*multilateral*: adjective compound) – none of which should be considered compounds in the sense discussed here.

In addition to *iḍāfa compounds*, there is another category of *syntactically compound units*, i.e. prepositional phrases: e.g. فَوْقَ البَنَفْسَجِي, 'ultraviolet', فَوْقَ الطَّبِيعة, 'supernatural'.

A summary of the typology of Arabic compounds is shown in Table 1.2. The table shows clearly that many of the compound combinations that exist in English are lacking in Arabic, with the empty slots in the 'verb' category being the most salient feature, even if verbs are represented by the deverbal nouns (مَصْدَر): e.g. غَسْل الدِّماغ ('washing' + 'brain' – *brainwashing*).

Table 1.2 Compositions of Arabic compounds

+	*Noun*	*Adjective*	*Verb*	*Preposition*
Noun	قَمِيصُ نَوْمٍ ('shirt' + 'sleep' – *nightgown*), طَبِيبُ أسْنانٍ ('doctor' + 'teeth' – *dentist*), شَنْطَةُ اليَد ('bag' + 'hand' – *handbag*)	يَد بَيْضاء ('hand' + 'white' – *benefit, favour*), ساعة إضافِية ('hour' + 'additional' – *overtime*)	–	–
Adjective	سَلِس القِياد ('docile' + 'guidance' – *compliant*), طَوِيل القامة ('long' + 'stature' – *tall*), قَصِير الباع ('short' + 'ability' – *powerless*), دائم الخَضْرة ('always' + 'greenness' – *evergreen*)	–	–	–
Verb	–	–	–	–
Preposition	فَوْقَ العادة ('above' + 'habit' – *extraordinary*), تَحْتَ الشُعُور ('below' + 'feelings' – *subconscious*), ضِدَّ الماءِ ('against' + 'water' – *waterproof*)	–	–	–

A particularly productive set in the noun + noun and adjective + noun categories are compounds with a fixed set of items such as غَيْر or عَدَم (to render the English *non-*, *un-*, *in-*), فَرْط ('excess' – cf. English *hyper-*), قابِل لِ ('subject to' – cf. English *-able*, *-ible*, *-ive*), قابِلِية ل ('ability for' – cf. English *-ability*, *-ibility*), شِبْه ('similar' – cf. English *semi-*, *demi-*, *quasi-*), مُتَساوٍ (*equi-*, *iso-*), مُتَعَدِّد (*poly-*, *multi-*), to name but a few: e.g.

عَدَم الإسْتِحْياء, *shamelessness*
عَدِيم النَّظِير, *unequalled*
مُتَساوِي الإضْلاع, *equilateral*
فَرْط الحَرَكة, *hyper-activity*
شِبْه كَرِيم, *semi-precious*
قابِل لِلكَسْر, *breakable*
مُتَعَدِّد الخَلايا, *multicellular*

These combinations are particularly productive in MSA in neologization in science and technology.

Just like in English, it is possible to distinguish between *endocentric* and *exocentric* compounds in Arabic (Emery 1988): e.g. قميص نوم (endocentric) and نَجْمة البَحْر ('star' + 'sea' – *starfish*, exocentric). The latter category is especially productive in proper nouns denoting flora and fauna, nearly all of which have terms of kinship as the head, and often contain a *bound modifier*, i.e. a مضاف إليه that occurs only with a particular مُضاف: e.g.

أمُّ الحِبْرِ, 'mother' + 'ink' – *cuttlefish*
أبُو سُعْن, *marabou*
اِبْن آوَى, *jackal*
بِنْت الأَرْض, *insects and worms*

Another common category of Arabic compounds have head words that denote ownership or agency, such as ذو and رَبّ، صانع، صاحِب: e.g.

رَبَّةُ البَيْتِ, *landlady, mistress of the house*
ذو القُرْبَى, *relative*
صانِع القَرار, *decision-maker*
أصْحاب الشُّبُهات, *people of ill repute*

Unlike English compounds, those in Arabic are *left-headed*, i.e. the first element determines the grammatical category and meaning of the whole.

Though, at first sight, the prepositional compounds appear to be an exception since they are right-headed, this may be explained by the fact that the prepositional part is to be reanalysed as a prefix; hence, there is a strong case for not considering them compounds at all.

Compounds in Arabic do not have a specific stress pattern, in contrast to their English counterparts. As a result, there is no way of distinguishing between *iḍāfa* compounds and noun phrases on the basis of stress alone.

Unlike in English, compounds in Arabic cannot consist of more than two elements, and cannot be *nested*, i.e. form part of a larger compound unit: e.g. 'town hall clock'. In Arabic, the compound would have to become part of another annexed structure: e.g. وَرَقةُ دَفتَرِ الحِساباتِ (*account book sheet*).

Grammatically, the adjective compounds are the odd ones out since, despite being an *iḍāfa*, the first element can also take the definite article, which is why these are commonly known as 'impure' or 'false' *iḍāfa*s. In addition, the adjective agrees with the noun in gender: e.g.

الرَّجُلُ الطَّوِيلُ القامةِ, 'the tall man', vs الرجلُ طَوِيلُ القامةِ, 'the man is tall'
البِنْتُ الطَّوِيلةُ القامةِ, 'the tall girl', vs البِنْتُ طَوِيلةُ القامةِ, 'the girl is tall'

Other criteria for distinguishing between the genitive construct phrase and syntactically identical *iḍāfa* compounds include pluralization and modification.

In *iḍāfa*s, the number (singular vs plural) of the non-head substantially changes the meaning of the set, as opposed to compounds, where the meaning is independent of the number of the non-head: e.g.

قَلَمُ الطَّالِبِ, 'the student's pen'
أَقْلامُ الطَّالِبِ, 'the pens of the student'
قَلَمُ الطُّلابِ, 'the students' pen'
أَقلامُ الطُّلابِ, 'the pens of the students'
vs

نَجْمُ البَحْرِ, ‘starfish’ (sg.)
نُجُومُ البحرِ, ‘starfish’ (pl.)
نجم / نجوم البِحار *

It is not possible to split up a compound in any way, but it is allowed for *iḍāfa*s: e.g.

قَلَمُ الطُّلابِ الثَّلاثةِ وَالمُدَرِّسِ, ‘the pen of the three students and of the teacher’
شَنْطةُ هذِهِ اليَد *, ‘the bag of this hand’
مَكْتَبٌ جَميلٌ لِلمُدِيرِ, ‘the director’s beautiful office’

The non-head of compounds cannot be modified, but that of an *iḍāfa* can: e.g.

حَقِيبةُ الزَّبُونِ الطَّوِيلِ, ‘the tall customer’s suitcase’

Translating compounds

The difficulties involved in translating compounds between English and Arabic may be summarized as follows:

- The identification of compounds is not always self-evident: e.g. *French teacher*.
- The meaning of compounds is often not transparent: e.g. *pickpocket*.
- In the case of nested compounds, grammatical (i.e. *morphosyntactic*) analysis can be ambiguous: e.g. *processor system modelling language*.
- The number (singular/plural) of the constituent elements is often not the same in both languages: e.g. *travel agency*, وِكالةُ أسْفارٍ.
- Often, a compound in one language is not translated by its grammatically equivalent construction: *application program*, بَرْنامِجُ تَطْبِيقِيٍّ.
- A compound in one language may be rendered by a simple word in another: e.g. *daybreak*, شُرُوق, *bathtub*, مَغْطِس.

Generally speaking, English compounds are rendered into Arabic in one of the following ways:

1 ***iḍāfa***, which can take the form of:

a noun + indefinite noun: e.g. غُرْفةُ نَوْمٍ, *bedroom*
b noun + definite noun: e.g. آلةُ التَّصْوِيرِ, *camera*, مَصْرُوفُ الجَيْبِ, *pocket money*
c noun + لِ + noun: e.g. لابِسُ لِلنَّوْمِ, *sleeping clothes*

2 **noun phrase** (noun + adjective): e.g. وِكالة عَقارِيَّة, *real-estate agency*; طَيَّارة مائية, *seaplane*

3 **prepositional phrase** (preposition + noun): e.g. تَدْرِيبٌ عَلَى إطْفاءِ الحَرِيقِ, *fire drill*; طاقةٌ عَلَى الإنْتاجِ, *output capacity*

4 **finite clause:** e.g.

نِظامُ اِسْتِرْجاعِ المَعْلُوماتِ أَلتِي تُعالَجُ كَمِياتٍ نَصِّيَّةٍ كَبِيرَةٍ, *batch-data retrieval system*

A rule of thumb is that the majority of endocentric English compounds are rendered by an *iḍāfa* in Arabic, with the exceptions being either due to idiomatic or figurative usage: e.g. *chainsmoker,* مُفْرِط في التَّدْخِين. Since exocentric compounds always have figurative meaning, the translation is entirely unpredictable and based purely on meaning: e.g. *flatfoot,* شُرْطِي. As a result, recourse to the dictionary is the only option.

Of particular note are compounds involving noun-preposition collocations such as تَدْرِيبٌ عَلَى / بـ / في إطْفاءِ الحَرِيقِ (NOT * تدريب إطفاء الحريق), *fire drill*. Unlike in English, where the preposition of a verb usually 'disappears', in Arabic it must be included, as it may result in mistranslation.

As stated above, Arabic compounds tend to consist of only two elements, whereas English compounds are, in theory, infinitely expandable. The fact that it is very easy in English to juxtapose a string of nouns has resulted in a large number of multi-word compounds, particularly in scientific and technical terminology, but also in everyday vocabulary. Multi-word compounds pose a particular problem in view of their grammatical and semantic complexity and compression; their structural ambiguity naturally grows when they are extended. Any successful translation depends on the successful identification of the semantic relations between the constituent components of the compound.

In some cases, spelling may come to the rescue as nested combinations are hyphenated, as in *colour-picture tube*, where *colour* and *picture* together modify *tube*; in other words, it is not a *picture tube* that is *coloured*. Things can easily get very complicated, however: e.g. in *linear frequency-modulated signal detection* the presence of the hyphen tells us that the signal is *frequency modulated*, rather than 'being *of a linear frequency* that is modulated'. Unfortunately, this doesn't remove the ambiguity at other levels, which is not resolved by identifying the head of the compound; depending on what it is modified by, the whole can be deconstructed as 'detection of a linear signal that is frequency modulated', 'the linear detection of a frequency-modulated signal' or 'linear frequency-modulated detection of a signal'. The various possible relations are represented below:

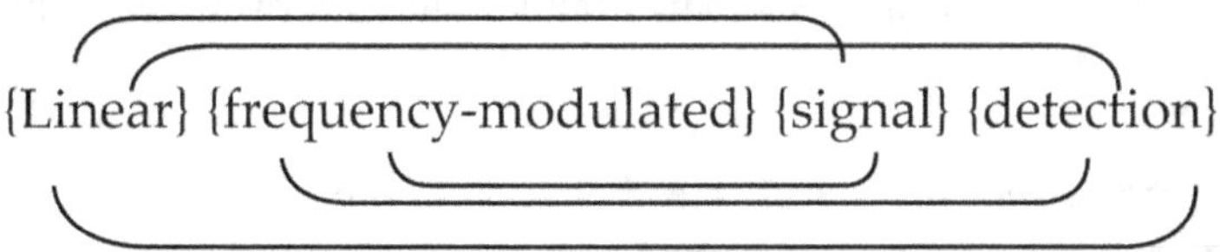

The choice of one or the other dramatically changes the translation, and grammar alone cannot provide a conclusive answer in these cases. As a result, the translator has to carry out some research into the subject in order to ascertain which of the possible interpretations is actually used in the field (in this case, it is the first).

It stands to reason that the complexity of English multi-word compounds defies easy solutions and one finds that in Arabic they often require several *iḍāfa*s and/or prepositional phrases, possibly embedded in finite clauses: e.g.

broadband integrated services digital network, شَبَكة رَقْمِيّة لِلخَدَمات المُتَكامِلة العَرِيضة الحزمة
patent cooperation treaty, مُعاهَدةُ التَّعاوُنِ بِشَأْنِ البَراءاتِ
remote administrator control server, بَرْنامِجُ للتَّحَكُّمِ بِالأَجْهِزةِ عَن بُعْدٍ
multichannel multipoint distribution service, نِظامُ التَّوْزِيعِ مُتَعَدِّدُ القَنَواتِ وَالنُّقاطِ
dial-up postpaid internet service, خِدْمةُ الإِيجارِ فِي الإِنْتَرْنَت عِبْرَ الهاتِفِ لاحِقةِ الدَّفْعِ

The strategies for multi-word compounds may be summarized as follows:[39]

- to recover the underlying structure, i.e. the syntactic relations between the components ('syntactic recovery');
- to break down the compound into its constituent sub-units. Whilst in many cases this is a straightforward linear operation, in others things can be somewhat more complicated;
- to translate both the semantic and syntactic relations accurately and idiomatically.

Up until now, we have concentrated on translating English compounds into Arabic as this is arguably the more complicated process, not least because of the already-mentioned complexity. That is not to say that translating Arabic 'compounds' is devoid of difficulties.

The first problem that arises is related to the figurative meaning of certain *iḍāfa* compounds, both endocentric and exocentric: e.g. اِبْن السَّبِيل does not mean that someone is born to the road but, rather, a *wanderer*; أَهْلُ البَيْت, lit. *people of the house*, refers to those related to the Prophet Muhammad, and may be contrasted with أهل الدَّار, which simply means 'the people living in the house'.

The main stumbling block, in fact, lies in the incorrect – or rather unidiomatic – rendering of *iḍāfa*s and certain noun phrases into English, where the latter requires a compound. What complicates matters is the fact that in many cases, several constructions are possible, but only one will be idiomatic. The single biggest mistake that is perpetrated in the translation of *iḍāfa*s is to render them consistently as an English *of*-genitive construction (the so-called Norman genitive), instead of a compound or *'s*-genitive: e.g.

> مَطار القاهِرة, **the airport of Cairo* instead of *Cairo airport*
> أُمّ سَلْوَى, **the mother of Salwa* instead of *Salwa's mother*

In theory, all translations are correct but most native speakers of English would probably opt for the latter of each set as being the more idiomatic. In many cases, however, the genitive is both possible and idiomatic: e.g.

> مُنَظِّمُو المُؤْتَمَر, *the organizers of the conference*, *the conference organizers*

Note that both **the organizers' conference* and **the conference's organizers* are impossible here; the former because this implies a possessive relationship, rather than one of subject-object, and the latter since the *'s*-genitive construction is not ordinarily used with inanimates.

Bearing in mind the above provisos, one may put forward the following general principles for the rendering of *iḍāfa*s as compounds in English:

- when the second element of the *iḍāfa* limits the meaning of the first in some way, i.e. denotes a 'type of' relation: e.g.

  شَنْطَةُ اليَد, *handbag*

- when the second element is the object of an action and the first – the subject – an active participle: e.g.

  صانِعُ القَرارِ, *decision-maker*

- when the second element denotes the purpose of the first: e.g.

  صُنْدُوق التَّوْفِيرِ, *savings bank*
  BUT: سَيَّارَةُ الإِسْعافِ, *ambulance*, قُنْبُلَة اليَد, *grenade*

This does not mean that the translation of any of the above can only be a compound or that this is the most idiomatic solution, and semantics can often throw a spanner in the works: e.g.

فِنْجانُ قَهْوَةٍ, *coffee-cup* (= the receptacle)
a cup of coffee (= the receptacle but filled with coffee)

LEXICOGRAPHICAL RESOURCES

The following is a list of relevant specialized lexicographical resources on various areas of phraseology.

Collocations

Benson, M., E. Benson and R. Ilson (1997): *The BBI Combinatory Dictionary of English: A Guide to Word Combinations*, rev. ed., Amsterdam/Philadelphia, PA: John Benjamins.

Ghazāla, Ḥasan (2007): *Dar El-Ilm's Dictionary of Collocations. English–Arabic/ Qamus Dār al-ᶜIlm li 'l-mutalāzimat al-lafẓiyya, ᶜArabī-Inklīzī*, Beirut: Dār al-ᶜIlm li 'l-Malāyīn.

Ḥāfiẓ, al-Ṭāhir Ibn ᶜAbd al-Salām (2004): *Muᶜjam al-Ḥāfiẓ li 'l-mutaṣāhibāt al-ᶜArabiyya, ᶜArabī-Inklīzī*, Beirut: Librairie du Liban.

Kjellemer, G. (1994): *A Dictionary of English Collocations*, Oxford: Clarendon Press.

Oxford Collocations Dictionary for Students of English, Oxford: Oxford University Press, 2002.

Idioms

ᶜAbd al-Nāṣir, Kāẓim (2001): *al-Qāmūs al-shāmil li-mufradāt wa 'l-taᶜābīr al-ᶜāmmiyya al-Amrīkiyya. A Comprehensive English to Arabic Dictionary of American Slang*, Beirut: Librairie du Liban.

Abū Saᶜd, Aḥmad (1987): *Muᶜjam al-tarākīb wa 'l-ᶜibārāt al-iṣṭilāḥiyya al-ᶜArabiyya*, Beirut: Dār al-ᶜIlm li 'l-Malāyīn.

Abu-Ssaydeh, Abdul-Fattah (2005): *Dictionary of Semantic Extensions, Similes and Conceptual Metaphors, English–Arabic*, Beirut: Dār al-Rawsha/Dār al-ᶜIlm li 'l-Malāyīn.

Abū-Zalal, ᶜIṣām al-Dīn (2007): *al-Taᶜābīr al-iṣṭilāḥiyya bayna al-naẓariyya wa 'l-taṭbīq*, Beirut: Ajyāl li 'l-Khadamāt al-Taswīq wa 'l-Nashr.

Cowie, A. P., R. Mackin & I. R. McCaig (1983): *Oxford Dictionary of Current Idiomatic English. Vol. 2: Phrase, Clause and Sentence Idioms*, Oxford: Oxford University Press.

Dāwūd, Muḥammad Muḥammad (2003): *Muᶜjam al-taᶜābīr al-iṣṭilāḥiyya fi 'l-ᶜArabiyya al-muᶜāṣira*, Beirut: Dār Gharīb li 'l-Tibāᶜa wa 'l-Nashr.

Dictionary of English Idioms English–Arabic/Muᶜjam al-taᶜābīr al-iṣṭilāḥiyya, Inklīzī–ᶜArabī, Beirut: Librairie du Liban, 1989.

El-Batal, Mohammed (2005): *A Dictionary of Idioms. Egyptian Arabic–English. With an English–Egyptian Arabic Glossary. Muᶜjam al-taᶜābīr al-iṣṭilāḥiyya ᶜArabī Miṣrī–Inglīzī, maᶜa masrad Inglīzī–ᶜArabī Miṣrī*, Cairo: Egyptian International Publishing Company/Longman.

Ghalib, Ḥannā (2003): *Kanz al-lugha al-ᶜArabiyya al-mawsūᶜa fi 'l-mutarādifat wa 'l-aḍād wa 'l-taᶜābīr*, Beirut: Librairie du Liban.

Ḥusām al-Dīn, Karīm Zakī (1985): *al-Taᶜbīr al-iṣṭilāḥī*, Cairo: Maktabat al-Anjil al-Miṣriyya.

Kāmil Fāyid, Wafā' (2007): *Muᶜjam al-taᶜābīr al-iṣṭilāḥiyya fi 'l-ᶜArabiyya al-muᶜāṣira*, Cairo, n.p.

Kharma, N. A. (1985): *Dictionary of English Idioms, English–Arabic*, Beirut: Librairie du Liban.

Muᶜjam al-taᶜābīr al-iṣṭilāḥiyya Inklīzī–ᶜArabī. A Dictionary of English Idioms, English–Arabic, Beirut: Librairie du Liban, 1985.

Kikano, Antoine Bishara (2002): *Muᶜjam al-taᶜābīr. Dictionary of Expressions*, Beirut: Librairie du Liban.

Selver, P. (1957): *English Phraseology: A Dictionary Containing more than 5,000 Idiomatic and Colloquial Words and Expressions*, London: J. Brodie.

Sieny, Mahmoud, M. Hussein & S. Al-Doush (1996): *al-Muᶜjam al-siyāqī li 'l-taᶜbīrāt al-iṣṭilāḥiyya, ᶜArabī–ᶜArabī. A Contextual Dictionary of Idioms. Arabic–Arabic*, Beirut: Librairie du Liban.

Sunbulī, Husayn Taqī (2002): *Muᶜjam al-irshād li-muṣṭalaḥāt wa 'l-taᶜābīr al-iṣṭilāḥiyya al-Inklīziyya. Al Irshad Dictionary for English Idioms and Phrases*, Beirut: Dār al-Irshād li 'l-Nashr.

Wajdī, Rizq Ghālī (2003): *al-Sarrāj al-Wajīz. Muᶜjam al-mutarādifat wa 'l-ᶜibārāt al-iṣṭilāḥiyya wa 'l-aḍād al-ᶜArabiyya*, Beirut: Librairie du Liban.

Phrasal verbs

El-Nagar, H. Y. (1998): *Phrasal Verbs*, Cairo: Dar El-Talae.

Helliel, Hilmi M., Tom McArthur & Beryl Atkins (2000): *York Dictionary of Phrasal Verbs and their Idioms, English–Arabic*, Beirut: Librairie du Liban.

Khalaili, K. (1979): *English Phrasal Verbs in Arabic*, London: Hodder and Stoughton.

Sunbulī, Ḥusayn Taqī (2002): *Muʿjam al-irshād li-muṣṭalaḥāt wa 'l-taʿābīr al-iṣṭilāḥiyya al-Inklīziyya. Al Irshad Dictionary for English Idioms and Phrases*, Beirut: Dār al-Irshād li 'l-Nashr.

Taha, A. (1996): *York Dictionary of Two-word Verbs in English*, Beirut: York Press-Librairie du Liban.

EXERCISES

Exercise A

Use both dictionaries and authentic texts to identify the meaning and usage of the following multi-word items, as well as any variants. Then, provide as many translations as possible, together with the contexts, text types and readerships for which they can be used.

1 جاءُوا بِلَفِّهِم وَلَفِيفِهِم
2 تَسْتَكّ مِنْه الأسْماع
3 تَمَخَّضَ الجَبَلُ فَوَلَدَ فَأْراً
4 ألقَى بَصِيصاً مِن النّور عَلَى
5 خَفَضَ جِناح الذُّلّ
6 رُفِعَت الأقْلام وجَفَّت الصُّحُف
7 رِيشة في مَهَبّ الرِّيح
8 سَبَقَ السَّيْف العَذَل
9 صِفْر عَلَى الشِّمال
10 فَصْل الخِطاب
11 كُلُّ إناء بالذِي فيه يَنْضَحُ
12 كَناطِح صَخْرَة
13 كَما تُسَلُّ الشَّعْرة مِن العَجِين
14 مَزَّقَهُم كُلَّ مُمَزَّق
15 لَقَّنَ دَرْساً
16 جَمَال الرَّجُل فَصاحَة لِسانِهِ
17 إنَّ الكَذُوب قَد يَصْدُقُ
18 أعَزُّ مِن الكِبْرِيت الأحْمَرِ
19 يَأكُل وَسَطاً وَيَرْبُضُ حَجْرَةً
20 كَلْب عَسَّ خَيْر مِن أسَدٍ رَبَضَ
21 لا تُعَلِّم اليَتِيم البُكاء
22 المِكْثار كحاطِب اللَيْل

23 إسأل المُجَرِّبَ وَلا تَسْأَلْ الحَكِيمَ
24 إبْعد عَن الشَّر وغَنِّي لَهُ
25 العاقِل تَكْفِيه الإشارة
26 دَع الخَلَق للخالِق
27 إنَّ الحَديد بالحَدِيد يَفْلُحُ
28 دُهاقِين السِّياسة
29 جُبِلَ عَلَى
30 شاعِر بِلاط

31 a red herring
32 to bring to heel
33 to count one's chickens before they are hatched
34 seek and ye shall find
35 to make a mountain out of a molehill
36 blood is thicker than water
37 talk of the devil ...
38 it's no skin off my nose
39 every cloud has a silver lining
40 people in glass houses shouldn't throw stones
41 to pass out
42 to do up
43 to get through with
44 to pick up
45 in sackcloth and ashes
46 on a sticky wicket
47 one-track mind
48 off the rails
49 at loggerheads
50 to wring one's hands

Exercise B

Identify the possible collocants of the following words and translate them.

1 ظاهِرة
2 كِذْب
3 خَطا
4 سِجْن
5 شُغْل
6 مَرَض
7 إجْراء
8 سِياسة

9 رأي
10 أخْبار

11 conclusion
12 control
13 crisis
14 damage
15 decision
16 difficulty
17 doubt
18 education
19 hope
20 power

2 Language variation and translation

IDENTIFYING VARIETY

Variety in language comes in many guises and levels. One way of talking about variety at what may be considered the generic level is through differences in terms of 'dialect' or 'accent'.

The sounds of a language – any language – can be pronounced in a variety of ways, typically linked to geographical locations; these manners of pronunciations are commonly referred to as **accents**. If there are also differences involving grammar and lexis (vocabulary), then we use the term **dialect**. In most language communities, one variety (or dialect, if you like) has at some point in history been elevated in that it is considered the **norm**, or the **standard** with which people are expected to comply. Usually, this normative language has grown out of a speech variety that gained prestige through its use in the most powerful or influential region of the community. This is the case, for instance, for both English and French, whose standard varieties go back to the language of the areas around their capital cities. Indeed, what today is called **Standard English** (also 'BBC English' or 'the Queen's English') in Britain is simply a dialect 'which has acquired greater importance than the other dialects for reasons which are in the main non-linguistic.'[40] It is also the normative language that is the one that tends to be written and used in formal contexts, whereas there is often a social connotation in that this variety is associated with the higher social classes.

Standard varieties are called **prestige dialects** (or **acrolects**) by linguists for the very simple reason that they enjoy the highest esteem within the language community. This fits in with the distinction that is usually made between geographical (or regional) dialects/accents and social dialects/accents. The former denote differences between various places, while the latter refer to differences related to social background or class. Sometimes, differences may be restricted to specific social, cultural and/or age groups. This is the case for **slang**, which is considered a 'sub-standard' variety involving differences in grammar and, especially, vocabulary but not usually pronunciation. Examples include the specific vocabulary used by prison inmates. Often, slang originated as a secret language by which people conveyed belonging to a group, while enabling its members to talk about certain issues in a way that would not be understood by outsiders. In some cases, this led to very creative language use, indeed. For instance, in 'rhyming slang' (associated with the London 'Cockney' dialect), speakers will use a word or phrase that rhymes with the one that they wish to use, as in 'jam jar' for 'car'.

It is not always the 'supradialectal' variety that has the highest prestige and we often find that the dialect of a particular region enjoys greater esteem than others, without, however, being considered 'normative' in the way that we have outlined above. For instance, the London dialect enjoys more prestige than, say, the dialect of Birmingham and has sometimes been adopted by people who originally hailed from other regions (and thus dialects).

The situation in Arabic is somewhat more complex, as we shall see. Although Classical Arabic (CA), *fuṣḥā*, or its modern offshoot, Modern Standard Arabic (MSA), is considered the prestige 'dialect', not least because it is associated with the Qur'an, it is always a *learned* variety since no Arabic-speaker is a mother-tongue speaker of CA.

When language variation affects only vocabulary, as in the terminology linked to a given profession, we use the term **jargon**. Examples include the use of language within the legal profession (which is known as 'legalspeak') or the computing industry.

Naturally, the above varieties do not exist within a vacuum and are subject to differences resulting from context, interlocutor, individual style, intended pragmatic effect, etc. Of particular relevance to translation are the shifts that occur as a result of 'register', which generally refers to a stylistic level that is to be situated along an informal–formal continuum.

Register is a crucial component in natural idiomatic speech and getting it wrong can lead to pragmatic mismatches, shifts in meaning, as well as unwanted comical effect if it doesn't fit the text type, character and context. For instance, it would be considered inappropriate in English academic discourse to refer to something as 'codswallop' (nonsense) as this is a highly colloquial word. Similarly, it is unlikely to hear someone involved in a fight address his opponent by saying 'I say, old fellow, will you kindly desist from hitting me?', as the degree of formalcy it conveys is at odds with the context.

In some cases, getting the register 'wrong' is, itself, used to achieve a certain stylistic – often humorous – effect, as in the following exchange:

– 'What happened to the watch?'
– 'It was stolen.'
– 'What?'
– 'Nicked, pinched, *purloined*.'

Native speakers would be quick to pick up on the fact that the last word sticks out because it is incongruously formal, even archaic, next to the highly colloquial British English words 'nicked' and 'pinched'. In this case, the incongruity of the word is signposted in writing by the italicization, which is usually reserved for foreign words or expressions.

Register is an extremely difficult thing to get right in translation as it is very difficult to determine it accurately. In addition, there is often no one-to-one correspondence of the various levels/nuances and their connotations across languages.

At the same time, register and variety are influenced by the individual speaker and his/her 'creative' or personalized use of language, which is referred to as an **idiolect**. This may come through in speech as well as in writing. It may include certain turns of phrases that a particular individual will use often, or a more general 'style' of expression. In literature, idiolectal use of language is often used to mark characters off from one another, whereas the author's idiolect is also clearly visible in many instances. Arguably, this is particularly true for good authors, whose individual use of language means that it is almost immediately recognizable.

The issue of register is particularly relevant in Arabic>/<English translation in view of the issue of diglossia, which will be discussed briefly in the next section.

Diglossia

The linguistic situation of Arabic is a highly complex one in that there is a standard variety (*fuṣḥā*) coexisting with a huge number of colloquials (*al-ᶜāmmiyya*, *al-dārija*), many of which are mutually unintelligible, even if the advent of global satellite television and the internet have exposed Arabic speakers to a great deal of dialectal variation that they have learned to cope with.

It is the colloquial that is the Arabic speaker's native tongue, whereas the normative variety is acquired at school and contact with this level of the language is restricted to formal writing and speech (e.g. news broadcasts). This dichotomy, which, in effect, is tantamount to bilingualism in a monolingual community, is known as 'diglossia'.

The phenomenon goes back to the very beginnings of Classical Arabic, i.e. the literary dialect of the Qur'an and pre-Islamic poetry, the so-called 'poetic *koiné*',[41] which has traditionally been associated with the dialect of the Quraysh, the Prophet Muhammad's tribe. Whatever the case may be, there is little doubt that this *koiné* was distinct from spoken varieties of the Arabic spoken in the Arabian Peninsula.

Already during the Prophet's lifetime, the new faith was propagated beyond its cradle. Naturally, the Arabian armies that swept across the region were composed of warriors from various tribes and thus spoke different dialects. It has been argued that it is the *lingua franca* or *koiné* used among the soldiers in foreign settlements that would ultimately give rise to the modern dialects.[42]

The issue of diglossia in Arabic has been the subject of an increasingly expanding body of research and a great deal of controversy, especially in regard to its implications in the classroom, with students having to acquire several varieties in order to be able to communicate within the Arabic-speaking community.

The term 'diglossia'[43] was introduced by the Greek philologist Ioannis Psicharis (Jean Psichari, 1854–1929) towards the end of the nineteenth century in his *Essais de grammaire historique néo-grecque*, published in Paris in 1886–9. Literally meaning 'bilingual' in Greek, the word denoted the Greek bilectal situation, split between the vernacular *demotiki* and the formal *katharevousa*.[44]

The famous French Arabist William Marçais was arguably the first scholar to use the term 'diglossia' in relation to Arabic, in his article entitled 'La Diglossie arabe' ('Arabic Diglossia'), which was extracted from a report the author had drawn up regarding Arabic teaching in North Africa. He distinguished between two 'distinctly different aspects' of Arabic, one, which is

> a literary language, referred to as written, standard, literal or classical Arabic, which has always been a written variety and today is the only one used for literary or scientific works, newspaper articles, legal documents, private correspondence – in short, everything that is written. In the form in which it appears, this written language has probably never been spoken and is most definitely not spoken anywhere today.[45]

and another consisting of

> spoken varieties [...], none of which has ever been written [...] and which constitute the only conversation medium in all communities, both uneducated and educated.[46]

Even though the above contains elements that are factually incorrect – the main one being the claim that vernaculars are never written – it was the first time the question of diglossia was presented in relation to education, which until then had been focused on the literary variety of the language.

In modern scholarship, it was an article written by Charles Ferguson in 1959 which triggered not only the long-standing debate, but also marked the beginning of modern Arabic sociolinguistics. Ferguson defined diglossia as a situation 'where two varieties of a language exist side by side throughout the community, with each having a definite role to play',[47] distinguishing between a 'high' ('H') variety – the normative *fuṣḥā* – and a 'low' ('L') one, the latter referring to the vernaculars. Ferguson's definition, therefore, is remarkably close to Marçais':

> Diglossia is a relatively stable language situation in which, in addition to the primary dialects of the language (which may include a standard or regional standards), there is a very divergent, highly codified (often grammatically more complex) superposed variety, the vehicle of a large and respected body of written literature, either of an earlier period or in another speech community, which is learned largely by formal education and is used for most written and formal spoken purposes but is not used by any sector of the community for ordinary conversation.[48]

In order to illustrate his theory, Ferguson identified a number of contexts and the corresponding level:[49]

	H	*L*
Sermon in a church or mosque	x	
Instructions to servants, waiters, workmen, clerks		x
Personal letter	x	
Speech in Parliament, political speech	x	
University lecture	x	
Conversation with family, friends or colleagues		x
News broadcast	x	
Radio, soap opera		x
Newspaper editorial, news story, caption on picture	x	
Political cartoon caption		x
Poetry	x	
Folk literature		x

Aside from its static nature, the model has been accused of being too impressionistic and of oversimplifying the linguistic situation within the Arabic speech community, reducing it to extremes and ignoring other factors influencing individual speakers, as well as rhetorical and pragmatic aspects. Some of the contexts are also highly debatable. Two merit particular attention: poetry and political speeches. The former disregards Arabic dialectal literature, which exists all over the Arab world, the most famous being, for instance, the Egyptian poet Fouad Negm, who used his craft to great effect in composing inspiring nationalist verse.[50] As for political speeches, they are often examples of mixed speech with emotive content being conveyed by the use of the people's speech, i.e. the dialect.

Ferguson did not overlook the fact that there are areas in which the levels can intersect or overlap, resulting in 'communicative tensions [that] may be resolved by the use of relatively uncodified, unstable, intermediate forms of the language'. He suggested that in Arabic this involves a spoken form 'used in certain semiformal or cross-dialectal situations [which] has a highly classical vocabulary with few or no inflectional endings, with certain features of classical syntax, but with a fundamentally colloquial base in morphology and syntax, and a generous admixture of colloquial vocabulary.'[51] It is this variety that is also known as *al-lugha al-wusṭā* ('the Middle Language'), to which we shall return later.

One year later, H. Blanc (1960) conducted an experiment with a number of native Arabic speakers of different dialects, which resulted in his identifying additional levels: 'Standard Classical', 'Modified Classical', 'Semi-literary/elevated colloquial', 'Koineized colloquial' and 'Plain colloquial'. Once again, one is faced with a model that is at once too rigid and simplified as it presupposes speakers acting within one level. Furthermore, it implies the existence of a 'grammar' for each of the levels. Finally, there were procedural questions in terms of the representativeness of the participants in the experiment.

The first Arab scholar to conduct a detailed examinination of diglossia was El-Said Badawi (1973), who used a number of phonological variables (e.g. the realization of ث, ذ, ق) and grammatical variables (e.g. negation, use of verbal/nominal sentences) to identify a number of levels/categories in contemporary Egyptian speech:

- 'heritage' *fuṣḥā* (فُصْحَى التُّراث), this corresponds largely to Classical Arabic, or at least grammar 'heavily influenced by the Qur'anic variety', and its usage is restricted to religious scholars (*ʿulamā'*) from al-Azhar, in religious discourse;
- 'contemporary' (MSA) *fuṣḥā* (فُصْحَى العَصْر): this variety is closely linked with the previous one and is employed, for instance, in formal news broadcasts;
- educated speakers' colloquial (عامِيَّة المُثَقَّفين): the register that is used by educated speakers when conversing about 'civilizational' issues, such as politics, social matters, etc., in a formal context;
- 'enlightened' colloquial (عامِيَّة المُتَنَوِّرين): the variety usually employed by literate people in their daily lives, and may also resemble that heard in 'light' media content;
- 'illiterate' colloquial (عامِيَّة الأُمِيِّين).[52]

Badawi's is a dynamic sociolinguistic model inasmuch as it reflects the existence of mutually influencing levels, as shown in Figure 2.1.[53]

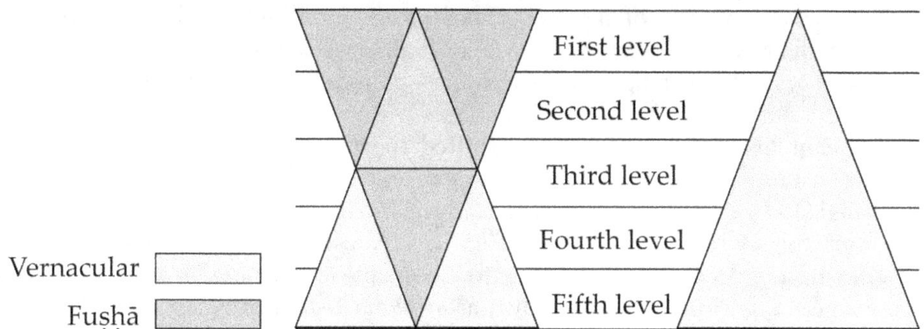

Figure 2.1 Intersecting levels of Arabic speech in Egypt (adapted from Badawi 1970)

This was later expanded as follows:

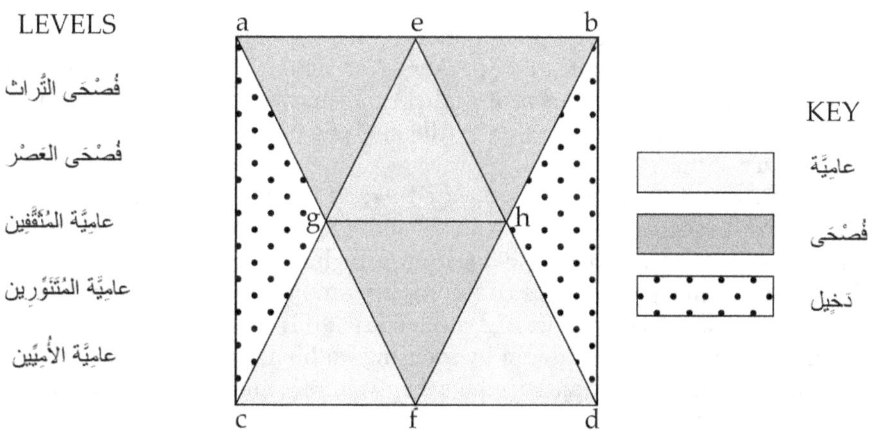

Figure 2.2 Mixed levels of Arabic speech in Egypt (adapted from Badawi 1970)

In Figure 2.2, the a–b axis represents the theoretically highest level of the literary *fuṣḥā*, with c–d denoting the theoretically lowest level of the colloquial. The diagonals a–f, b–f, c–e, e–d and f–b refer to the 'erosion' of features associated with the levels intersected. The area e–g–f–h, accordingly, represents the overlap of the literary and colloquial languages, while the areas a–g–e and e–h–b represent 'pure' *fuṣḥā* features and the areas c–g–f and f–h–d 'pure' colloquial features. The areas encompassed by a–g–c and b–h–d represent the proportional distribution of foreign (*dakhīl*) influence within the five levels.[54]

At the same time, this model is subject to a number of inconsistencies in that it, too, posits the existence of 'pure' registers, alongside the intermixedness. Secondly, it concentrates on the spoken language and completely disregards what goes on in the written language in terms of register changes, perpetuating the myth that all printed language is formal and written in one (the highest) register. Finally, the analysis is restricted to the situation of Arabic in Egypt without any attempt at comparison with the language situation in other Arabic-speaking countries.

The dynamic nature of the model, however, does allow for the inclusion of, for instance, the use (albeit extremely rare) of high-classicisms in the colloquial (e.g. the 'internal' passive in the Egyptian – Cairene – colloquial *hum bi-yuḍṭahadū*, 'they are being persecuted').[55]

In a similar vein, other scholars shifted the emphasis towards identifying and defining an intermediate form of the language, referred to as 'Modern inter-Arabic' by Bishai (1966), 'the Colloquial Arabic of the Intellectuals [...], used in various inter-Arab meetings which include representatives from different countries of the Arabic Middle East.'[56] In addition to the already-mentioned *al-lugha al-wusṭā* ('Middle Language'), this variety is also known as *al-lugha al-thālitha* ('the Third Language') *al-fuṣḥā al-mukhaffafa* ('*fuṣḥā* light') or *al-ᶜāmmiyya al-mushriqa* ('enlightened colloquial')[57] and essentially corresponds to Badawi's second and third levels. Salib, for his part, focused on what he called 'Spoken Literary Arabic' (SLA), comparing it against Richard Harrell's 'Egyptian Radio Arabic',[58] which he defined as 'standard oral Literary Arabic [...] which [...] is used normally through competent formal reading.'[59] It is difficult to see how one can still call it 'Literary Arabic' when the oral variety deviates in a number of key aspects (e.g. declension vowels). Salib, whose corpus, once again, consisted predominantly of Egyptian Arabic speakers, equated his SLA with Badawi's 'Educated Speakers' Vernacular',[60] stating, however, that it is 'merely a convenient and arbitrary label [...] [that] is not meant to argue for the existence of such a linguistic reality';[61] the analysis is based on the assumption that it is a distinct variety.

This interlanguage spoken by educated Arabs from different dialect areas soon became known as 'Educated (later also 'Formal') Spoken Arabic' (ESA),[62] though the term has, confusingly, also been defined as 'a higher, more formal register than the colloquial of primary discourses of familiarity among family and acquaintances'.[63] The main criticism levelled at the ESA model is that it is too restrictive and descriptive. It belies the reality of a continuum by focusing on binary constructs such as formal/informal, stigmatized/unstigmatized usage, and the mutual interference between colloquial and standard levels.

The studies essentially provided empirical evidence of interference between levels, across dialects, etc. but none that could contribute to what might be called a 'unified' grammar of this variety, for the simple reason that the notion that this type of cross-dialectal speech constitutes a distinct, clearly defined, codified and applied level within the Arabic speech community is a purely abstract construct that has no basis in reality. Equally, if not more, tenuous is the claim that 'the emergence of [this] new, intermediate form of Arabic [...] is [...] evidence that the diglossic situation is undergoing a dramatic change.'[64]

The 'quest' for levels continued by subsequent researchers, such as Meiseles (1980), whose division into 'Literary Arabic' (further subdivided into 'Ancient Literary Arabic' and 'Modern Literary Arabic'), 'sub-standard Arabic', 'Educated Spoken Arabic' and 'Vernacular Arabic' was redolent of Blanc's in some respects.

At a later stage, the study of diglossia shifted towards code mixing and code switching. Strictly speaking, these terms, which were first used in studies on bilingualism, refer to the shifting between two (or more) languages, for instance, Arabic and French/English within speech.[65] In Arabic sociolinguistics, 'code switching' has also been applied to shifts between MSA and the vernacular.[66]

Moving away from attempts at defining 'middle varieties', a number of scholars have focused on a highly fertile avenue of research involving speakers' intentions in the mixing of levels within discourse, often as part of a wider pragmatic framework.[67]

It is impossible to produce a grammar of the language used in interdialectal communication, except if one works within the idealized context of MSA and its contrastive use with the vernacular, which ignores the range of variation that exists in real-life speech, as well as the underlying processes that come into play when variation occurs. The shifts towards MSA are very variable and depend on the individual, topic and context.

Furthermore, 'dialectal' does not always equate with non-normative (or substandard) language use since a great deal of vocabulary considered 'colloquialisms' are in fact SA.[68] Dialects vary in terms of their use of 'standard' vocabulary and grammar in the extent to which the latter is added with dialectal features, ranging from phonological to morphological as well as semantic changes: e.g. the Egyptian *fihim* ('he understood', for standard *fahima*), *gawz* ('husband', for the standard *zawj*).

It is worth remembering that the *fuṣḥā–ʿāmmiyya* debate is a very old one indeed, and already in the seventeenth century Egyptian scholar Yūsuf al-Maghribī wrote a book, entitled *Dafʿ al-ʿiṣr ʿan kalām ahl Miṣr* ('Removal of the Burden from the Speech of the People of Egypt'), defending the *fuṣḥā* origins of the vernacular speech of the day.[69]

Hitherto, little attention has been paid to the implications of diglossia to translation – whether it be from or into Arabic – and, more importantly, its importance in the education and training of translators.

Variety in standards: English and MSA

Discussions of the nature of standard language are often blurred by emotional judgements as it is inextricably linked with questions of identity, nationhood, and so on. This is particularly relevant for Arabic, with *fuṣḥā* being widely considered 'the sole unifying force [...] and [...] allegiance to "perfect *fuṣḥā*" (*fuṣḥā salīma*) continues to be constructed as allegiance to the unity of the Arab world, its glorious Golden Age and magnificent heritage.'[70]

As a result, the standard language is sometimes irrationally viewed as an immutable entity that, unlike colloquial language, has not been subject to change in the course of its history. Of course, the opposite is true and standards do vary over time and any British English speaker listening to standard language usage of thirty years ago cannot fail to be struck by the extent to which it has changed, particularly as regards pronunciation and vocabulary.

While most scholars and users would probably agree that Modern Standard Arabic is the language variety that uses normative grammar, it would be difficult to find a consensus about much more than that, especially as far as vocabulary is concerned. Is it the vocabulary of the classical, mediaeval language? Of the Qur'an? Of the media? Or is it that which is used in modern literature and formal texts? Or is it, perhaps, a mixture of all of them? Once again, the split is in many ways a fictional one between the prescriptive and the descriptive, with proponents of the former school insisting on viewing language as something preserved in aspic.

So, what is Modern Standard Arabic? Any attempt at answering this question should start by stating what it is not; it is not Classical Arabic, i.e. the language of the

Qur'an or classical Arabic literature. Even if it is based on CA, there are significant differences in terms of syntax and, especially, lexis.[71] It is for this reason that A. Kaye referred to MSA as 'ill-defined'.[72]

In one of the first discussions of this register, El-Hassan described Modern Standard Arabic as 'the written language of contemporary literature, journalism and "spoken" prose'.[73] In reality, as Ibrahim pointed out, 'it seems clear that across the Arab world, there is a continuum for Modern Standard Arabic. Differences along this continuum are influenced by domains (such as literary, journalistic, political) and regions (i.e. geographical differences).'[74]

The above is bound up with the already-mentioned point that there is not, nor has there ever been, an Arabic speaker for whom *fuṣḥā* – classical or modern – is the mother tongue. To put it differently, Standard Arabic is a variety learned at school, whereas the true mother tongue, i.e. the only one that is 'acquired', to use the Chomskyan term, is the vernacular. This is not true for English, for instance, in that there are British English speakers who have RP as their native tongue.

A far more controversial question is that of a perfectly unified standard, normative variety of Arabic (whether it is called Classical Arabic or Modern Standard Arabic), which is another fiction, just like the notion that all Arabic colloquials are mutually unintelligible.

According to Z. Ibrahim,[75] Ibrāhīm al-Sāmarrā'ī was the first to remark upon the differences between the normative varieties across the Arab world in his *al-Taṭawwur al-lughawī al-tārīkhī*[76] ('Historical Linguistic Development'). In fact, this goes back much further as none other than the nineteenth-century reformist shaykh Muḥammad ᶜAbduh commented on the 'strange' language employed by Levantine, as well as – perhaps more surprisingly – Coptic authors.[77]

Lexical differences

The issue of cross-MSA variation has been studied by a relatively small number of researchers, with the primary focus on lexis[78] as it is here that the differences between the MSAs are most salient, especially in the media[79] and technical terminology. A good example is 'mobile phone', which, depending on the region or country, is rendered in six different ways: *jawwāl*, *naqqāl*, *mutanaqqil*, (*jihāz/hātif*) *khalawī*, *maḥmūl*, *sayyār*, *hātif mutaḥarrik*. The first three tend to be used more in North Africa, the fourth in Egypt, the fifth in the Levant (Lebanon, Syria), and the sixth in some areas of the Gulf. Naturally, the Arabic speaker *understands* all coinings, but in the standard variety of his/her native area, one of them will probably be used to the exclusion of the others. What is more, it is very likely that in informal contexts the same speaker will use none of the above, choosing instead the borrowing *mūbayl* ('mobile'), in the Near East, or جي أس أم ('GSM') in North Africa!

The extent of the differences means that in many cases most formal writing has features peculiar to one, or several, MSA varieties. Let us consider, for example, the following newspaper passages taken from various countries in which the variety-specific vocabulary has been underlined.

<table>
<tr>
<td>‘There were a number of strikes in the district of Mohamedia (Ben Arous Governorate), against the day-to-day administrative running of local affairs after the dissolution of the municipal council and the resignation of the mayor of the commune of Fouchana, whereas the district capital has remained in the state it has been after the looting and burning that occurred during the revolution of 14 January…
The vacuum left by the local authorities has in many cases led to chaos and breaches of the law. The number of illegal building activities and exploitation of land belonging to the municipality or the state has spread across an area of approximately 42 hectares, according to an official source.’</td>
<td>شهدت معتمدية المحمدية التابعة لولاية بن عروس العديد من اضطربات على مستوى السير العادي للشؤون الإدارية للمواطن بعد حل المجلس البلدي واستقالة رئيس بلدية المحمدية فوشانة كما ظل مقر معتمدية المكان على حاله بعد أن تعرض للتخريب والحرق إبان قيام ثورة ١٤ جانفي ...
وقد خلف الفراغ الذي تركته السلطة المحلية تفشي العديد من مظاهر الفوضى وخرقات كثيرة للقانون فانتشرت ظاهرة البناء الفوضوي والاستيلاء على أراض تعود ملكيتها للبلدية أو للدولة بلغت حسب مصدر مسؤول نحو ٤٢ هكتارا.

(Tunisia, *al-Ṣabāḥ*)</td>
</tr>
<tr>
<td>‘As Palestinians will soon commemorate the *Nakba*, the occupying forces have outlawed all events in Jerusalem and the Aqsa Mosque. Yesterday, they clashed with Palestinians, dozens of whom suffered various life-threatening injuries. A number of others were arrested during commemorative events in Jerusalem, while the Israeli military imposed a state of emergency.’</td>
<td>مع اقتراب إحياء فلسطين لذكرى نكبتها غدا، أحكمت قوات الاحتلال قبضتها على أحياء القدس المحتلة والمسجد الأقصى، ودخلت في مواجهات مع الفلسطينيين الذين أصيب منهم العشرات أمس، بجراح متفاوتة الخطورة، واعتقل من بينهم العشرات، في عدد من أحياء القدس المحتلة، فيما وضعت قوات أمن الاحتلال في حالة استنفار.

(Lebanon, *al-Safīr*)</td>
</tr>
<tr>
<td>‘A number of sectarian demonstations took place yesterday both in Cairo and a number of Governorates. Dozens of owners of companies that employ Egyptian workers abroad staged a demonstration outside the Council for Ministers to protest against the proposal, resubmitted by Dr Ahmed al-Baraei, the Minister for Labour, that is aimed at giving the Ministry the power to administer the Egyptian workers who are temporarily in Saudi Arabia during the hajj season.’</td>
<td>شهدت القاهرة وبعض المحافظات، أمس، عددا من مظاهرات الفئوية، وتظاهر العشرات من أصحاب شركات إلحاق العمالة المصرية بالخارج، أمام مجلس الوزراء للتنديد بمشروع قرار يعد له الدكتور أحمد البرعي، وزير القوى العاملة، يهدف إلى تولى الوزارة عملية إلحاق العمالة المصرية المؤقتة بالسعودية أثناء موسم الحج.

(Egypt, *al-Miṣrī al-Yawm*)</td>
</tr>
</table>

The above examples are part of what may be called a typology of variants. The following categories may be drawn up:

1 *Terms specific to one particular MSA variety*

In addition to *ḥālat al-istinfār* ('state of emergency') (Lebanon), which appears in the above passage, one may cite the following examples:

- للا, '*lalla*', term of address for high-born and royal women (Mor.)
- رَئِيس البَلَدِية, 'mayor' (Tun.) (vs Leb. مُخْتار; Eg. عُمْدة)
- خَصْخَصة, 'privatization' (Eg.) (vs Leb./Tun. تَخْصِيص)
- فَدان, 'feddan' (unit of area) (Eg.)
- قَيْدُوم, 'dean' (university) (Mor.) (in other MSAs عَمِيد)
- اِزْدِياد, 'birth' (Mor.) (in other MSAs وِلادة)
- تَحْسِيسِي, 'exploratory' (Mor./Alg.) (in other MSAs اِسْتِكْشافِي) [80]

This category may be further subdivided according to origin:

a calques (i.e. literal translations) from a (former or current) prestige language, which in many cases means French in North Africa/Lebanon and English in the Near East/Gulf: e.g. *takwīn*, for 'education' (< Fr. *formation*), as opposed to the Eastern *taᶜlīm*; *aydz* (< Eng. 'AIDS')/*sīdā* (< Fr. *Sida*);

b though in most cases the variations are unmistakably part of the standard normative language, there are a number of instances where borrowings from the *vernacular* have been incorporated into MSA usage: e.g.

إلى غاية, 'until' (Eg.)
سكربينة, 'high-heeled ladies' shoes' (Leb.)
دَوام, 'working time' (Syr.)
تاي, 'tea' (Mor.)
مِسَرّ, 'turban' (Oman)

2 *Words restricted to a number of MSA varieties*

These include names of the months, which vary between regions:[81]

	Near East/ Levant	*Tunisia/Algeria*	*Egypt*	*Morocco*
January	كانُون الثانِي	جانْفِي	يَنايِر	يَنايِر
February	شُباط	فِيفْرِي	فِبرايِر	فِبرايِر
March	آذار	مارْس	مارِس	مارْس

April	نِيسان	أَفْرِيل	أَبْرِيل/إِبْرِيل	إِبْرِيل
May	أيار	مايُو	مايُو	مايُو
June	حَزِيران	جُوان	يُونِيُو	يُونِيُو
July	تَمُوز	جُوِيلِيَه	يُولِيو	يُولِيو
August	آب	أوت	أغُسْطُس	غُشْت
September	أَيْلُول	سِبْتِمْبر	سِبْتِمْبر	شُتَمْبِر
October	تِشْرِين الأول	أُكتوبَر	أكتوبَر	أكتوبَر
November	تشرين الثانِي	نوفَمْبر	نوفَمْبر	نوَنْبِر
December	كانُون الأول	دِيسِمْبر	دِيسِمْبر	دِجِمْبِر

In the above Egyptian newspaper passage, *muḥāfaẓa* denotes a large administrative division in Egypt, Syria, Oman and Iraq, and is translated variously as 'province' or 'governorate' (when referring to Egypt and Oman), the latter of which is also the translation of Tunisian term *wilāya*. Another example from the field of politics is the use of *al-wazīr al-awwal* ('Prime Minister') in North Africa, as opposed to the more common *ra'īs al-wuzarā'* elsewhere.

Most words in this category are the result of lexical preference, for whatever reason, in certain countries/regions. For instance, *muẓāhara* is more commonly used as 'demonstration' in Egypt than it is in the Levant (or North Africa), whereas *baladiyya* ('municipality') and *ᶜamāla* ('administrative district') are less frequently found in the Near East than they are in North Africa. Other examples include:

- تَوْقِيف, 'arrest' (Leb., Mor.) (other MSAs قَبْض عَلَى)
- تَكْلِفَة, 'expenses' (Eg.) (Leb. كُلْفة)
- مُداهَمَة, '(police) raid' (Eg.) (Leb. دَهْم)
- مُخابَرات, 'intelligence services' (e.g. Eg./Jord.) (Leb. اسْتِخْبارات)
- إجْرامِي, 'criminal' [adj.] (Eg.) (Leb. جُرْمِي)

It is interesting to note that in a large number of cases, the differences are not so much different lexical items as variant *forms* of the same morphological root.

3 *Words that are common to a number (or all) of MSA varieties, but with different meanings*

A particularly sizeable subcategory in this group is composed of foodstuffs. For instance, while *laban* is the usual word for 'milk' in Egypt, it refers to buttermilk in North Africa and strained yoghurt in the Near East, where *halīb* is used for 'milk'. A rather more confusing case is that of *barqūq* and *khawkh*: the former denotes a plum in most places, except in the Levant, where *khawkh* is used, which refers to 'peach' in Egypt and Oman, but not in the Levant where it is *durrāq*!

Other examples include:[82]

muᶜtamadiyya	'legation' (NE) 'delegation'[83] (administrative district) (Tun.)
khallāᶜa	'summer vacation (usually in the countryside)' (Tun.) 'moral depravity' (other MSAs)
ijāza	'(university) degree' (Leb.) 'holiday' (Eg.)

In other cases, meanings may be added that are peculiar to particular MSAs, thus giving rise to polysemy. For instance, the word *sayyid* is the general term of address for men (Eng. 'Mr') in MSA, as well as being an honorific for descendants of the Prophet Muhammad. However, in Oman, the word is also used as an honorific for members of the royal family.

A rather insular – and often overlooked – category is that of religion-based linguistic differences, which may, however, also cut across regions. Although a number of terms and expressions are shared among Muslims and Christians, many are not. For instance, the word *sūra* denotes a chapter in the Qur'an but cannot be used to refer to a Book or Chapter in the Bible, for which only *sifr* and *aṣḥāḥ*, respectively, can be used. And although both the Qur'an and the Bible are holy books for their respective followers, only the latter is referred to as *al-Kitāb al-Muqaddas* ('The Holy Book'), just as *muṣḥaf sharīf* ('noble volume') can only be applied to the Qur'an. Conversely, both Qur'anic and Bible verses are known as *āyāt*. When it comes to the believer and his relationship to God, only Christians are referred to as *khādim rabbinā*, 'servant of our Lord'.

In some cases, there are even linguistic differences within Christian denominations, linked with specific practices, beliefs or dogma: e.g. *taqdīs* can mean 'sanctification, reverence, worship' but also 'Consecration' as part of a Roman Catholic service (but not, for instance, in the Coptic church). Other examples include *niyāfa* (a title for bishops and cardinals), which is only used in the Coptic church, whereas *shaykh* in the sense of 'religious scholar' can only be used for Muslims. The Arabic *al-marḥūm* (lit. 'he on whom [God] has mercy'), which may be translated into English as 'the late', is commonly added by Muslims and most Christian churches when mentioning a deceased person's name, but in the Coptic church, the word *al-mutanayyaḥ* is used, instead.

Syntactic differences

Although less prominent than lexical variation, syntactic differences are not infrequent between MSAs. Among the items investigated, we find prepositions, subject-verb argeement, the future particle and object pronouns. In the case of prepositions, more specifically in prepositional verbs, it has been found that, depending on the variety, they may be omitted, added, or change. For instance, a number of verbs which require a preposition in Egyptian formal written Arabic (as well as many other MSAs), appear without one in Lebanese: *iltaqā* and *taᶜahhada* collocate with *bi* (or *maᶜa*) in most MSAs, but not in Lebanese, as shown in the following examples drawn from the Egyptian *al-Ahrām* and Lebanese *al-Ḥayāt* newspapers:[84] e.g.

اِلْتَقَى الرئَّيس بِ/مَعَ نُخْبةٍ مِن كِبار المُثَقَّفِينَ
'The president met with the members of the cultural elite.'

تَعَهَّدَتْ الحُكُومةُ دَفْعَ مَبْلَغ ٨ بِلْيُون دولار
'The government is committed to paying $8bn.'

تَعَهَّدَ البَنْك الدُّوَلِيُّ بِحَفْزِ المُنَظَّماتِ لِتَوْفِيرِ المَبْلَغ المُتَبَقِّي
'The World Bank has pledged to compel the organizations to provide the remaining amount.'

The reverse is true for *baḥatha* in the sense of 'discuss', which tends to have *fī* in Lebanese MSA but occurs without a preposition in formal Egyptian Arabic:[85] e.g.

بَحَثُوا <في> عَمَلِيَّة السَّلامِ
'They discussed the peace process.'

When looking into expressions of the future, Parkinson[86] found that in the Egyptian newspaper *al-Ahrām*, the particle *sawfa* was used ten times more frequently (20% vs 2%) than in the Lebanese newspaper *al-Ḥayāt*, where the proclitic *sa-* was the preferred option.

Later on, the same researcher conducted another study, adding a Moroccan and Kuwaiti sample to his corpus, to investigate feminine agreement with sentence-initial 'modal' verbs such as *yumkinu* ('it is possible'), *yajibu* ('it is necessary') and *yanbaghī* ('it is desirable').[87] The results revealed dramatic differences, with not a single feminine agreement being found with *yumkin* in the Egyptian corpus, whereas in the case of *yanbaghī* and *yajib*, the Lebanese usage was 33 per cent, over three times higher than the average in the other corpora. As a similar, if not greater, discrepancy could be found with other modals, Parkinson concluded that 'even with [...] verbs that seem to prefer masculine agreement, the Lebanese are more likely than the others to use feminine agreement.'

Differences were also found between Egyptian, Syrian and Lebanese media MSA by Wilmsen, who examined the use of the free object pronoun *iyyā* and found that the Levantine writers tend to use it twice as often as Egyptians.

Finally, Ibrahim[88] remarked on variation in plurals, with one plural sometimes being more favoured in one variety than another: e.g. *manshūrāt*, 'leaflets' (Eg.), vs *manāshīr* (Leb.).

It is tempting to infer an influence from the colloquial or even of a foreign language. Whilst this cannot be excluded in some cases,[89] it does not hold true in the examples discussed. In the case of prepositions, there is no evidence that the recorded preference of Levantine colloquials for *bi* in cases where ECA speakers opt for *fī*[90] is carried through into the MSA. As regards the other items, the argument is even more tenuous since their use is almost entirely limited to the formal language. As a result, differences would seem to be attributable to separate historical developments within regional MSAs, the reasons for which are often not identifiable.

Syntactic variation also affects English normative varieties, albeit to a lesser extent than in Arabic. Examples include the use of the singular with collective nouns in US English, as opposed to the plural in British English; varying use of some irregular verb forms and tenses: e.g. 'the Government is [UK]/are [US]'; 'sawn' [UK] vs 'sawed' [US] (past participle of 'to saw'); 'I've already done it' [UK] vs 'I already did it' [US].

Orthographic differences

Differences in spelling, too, can be observed:[91] e.g.

- (non-)use of the *hamza*: e.g. تأريخ / تاريخ ; مؤقت / موقت
- *tā' marbūṭa*, with or without diacritical dots: e.g. مدرسة / مدرسه
- use/omission of diacritical dots in final *yā'*: e.g. صحفي / صحفى
- use of diacritical dots with *alif maqṣūra*: e.g. علي / على

In other cases, there are discrepancies between individual items that may be attributable to an influence from regional pronunciation or borrowing origins: e.g.

- إنكلترا (e.g. Tun.) / إنجلترا (e.g. Eg.), 'England'
- أميركا (e.g. Leb.) / أمريكا (e.g. Eg.), 'America'
- طكسي (e.g. Alg.) / تكسي (e.g. NE), 'taxi'
- صك (e.g. Leb.) / شيك (e.g. Tun.), 'cheque'[92]

One should be wary, however, of jumping to conclusions from the above. A great deal more research needs to be undertaken involving many more MSA variants, which will require an increase in relevant corpora. Recent research has tended to focus on only two varieties – Egyptian and Lebanese – due to the current availability of corpora from those countries. Also, the studies concentrated on only one register and genre of contemporary formal Arabic, i.e. media Arabic since the object of the research involved newspapers, in some cases only two (*al-Ahrām* and *al-Ḥayāt*).[93] Analyses of other types and genres of formal writing are conspicuous by their absence. Similarly, while there is undoubtedly some common ground within the broad North African and Eastern Arabic dialect families,[94] it would be overly simplistic to extrapolate judgements based on data from one country to other MSAs within the region as a whole, let alone beyond. This is particularly pertinent since at present only a partial picture of usage of 'Standard Arabic' is available.

The issue is a crucial one in the study of Modern Standard Arabic, or rather *Arabics*, and further to the above statement regarding the putative influence from the local vernaculars, one may cite the example of technical terminology, the wide variety of which is due not to colloquial influences but to the lack of coherence and resultant ineffectiveness of the Arabic Language Academies in this field.[95]

Most of the items discussed are part and parcel of the standard normative language. Nevertheless, in many, if not all, cases, they would sound 'foreign' to Arabic speakers of the other variants to varying degrees. Whilst syntactic variants would not generally affect intelligibility, the same cannot be said about lexical differences, as demonstrated in Ibrahim's study, where both Egyptian and Lebanese respondents experienced difficulty understanding some of the passages submitted to them.[96]

Naturally, the variation in standard also impacts on translation, both from and into Arabic, with problems occurring at various levels. When translating from Arabic into English, the translator must be aware of potential differences between the variants in order to produce an adequate translation. This also implies that the translator has knowledge of the geographic origin of the text (which is not always the case).

Semantic differences sometimes constitute major blackspots as in, for instance, the verb *taddaʿī ʿalā*, which is used in the sense of 'to sue' in Lebanese MSA, but means 'to falsely accuse' in Egyptian MSA.[97]

When translating *into* Arabic, an awareness of the differences is necessary not just to avoid confusion and potential misunderstanding, but also to avoid 'regionalizing' the text, which may antagonize readers from other areas. So, unless the readership of the text consists solely of a particular region, which in most cases is unlikely or, at least, unpredictable, a sensible strategy would be to opt for what may be called a 'neutral' or 'unmarked' term. Let us consider the example of *ṣalāḥiyya* ('appropriateness, fitness'), which is the common Near Eastern form; the Maghribi variant is *ṣulūḥiyya*, used in expressions such as *ṣulūḥiyya li 'l-akl* (edible). Although both terms have normative usage in the respective regions, it may be advisable for the translator to select the more neutral *qābiliyyat al-akl*, which is not regionally 'marked'.

In English, too, various standards (North American, Irish, Australian, British) co-exist and often have their own terminology, whereas shared lexical items may differ in meaning: *paddock* in Australia means field, whereas in the UK it means a small enclosure for livestock; *outback* (remote area, with sparse population) is peculiar to Australian English. The Irish 'jaded' means 'physically tired', rather than the usual British and North American 'unenthusiastic about something'.

British and US English often vary in everyday vocabulary, as the examples in Table 2.1 demonstrate.[98]

Table 2.1 Some examples of differences between British and US English

British English	*US English*
aubergine	eggplant
boot	trunk
cheque	check
chips	french fries
coriander	cilantro
courgette	zucchini
crisps	potato chips
flat	apartment
knickers	panties
nappy	diaper
pavement	sidewalk
petrol	gas / gasoline
public school	private school
rubber	eraser
spring onions	scallion
state school	public school
sweets	candy
tap	faucet
torch	flashlight
trousers	pants
zebra crossing	cross walk

Spelling, too, sometimes varies; for instance, many words that include 'our' in UK English have 'or' in US English (e.g. 'colour/color'), whereas UK English prefers '-ise' to US '-ize' ('surprise/surprize'). In addition, there are more isolated cases such as 'cheque' (UK) / 'check' (US).

Reasons for dialectal variety in writing

Before moving on to diglossia in translation, we should first examine the reasons why dialect, register shifts – language variation, in general – are used in source texts. In written texts, the issue mostly affects literature, whereas in speech it is of particular significance in what may be called persuasive discourse, such as political speeches, where politicians modulate language and idiom to achieve particular effect, such as promoting a sense of solidarity and communal spirit.[99]

Most of us in our everyday conversations use register and variety shifts at some point or another, for a variety of reasons, such as humour or context. Differences in language use, level and style convey differences in moods, socio-economic background, educational attainment and, even, racial differences. As such, it is as much about what one projects – or wishes to project – and how it is perceived (and received) by the listener or reader.

The rationale for switching may be driven by the following factors:

accommodation	adaptation to the interlocutor's language
group membership	to demonstrate belonging to a particular group
topic	e.g. an academic discussion vs an informal chat with friends about holiday plans
addressee	his/her social, hierarchical position or status
context	the circumstances in which the conversation takes place: e.g. a wedding, business dinner, family gathering
setting	the place where the discussion is held: e.g. office vs restaurant on holiday

Group membership is a particularly powerful driver as the use of a certain social dialect, or 'sociolect', identifies members of the same social group.[100] Conversely, deviation from the prevailing group sociolect may give rise to antagonism on the part of the members and constitute a barrier for inclusion. For instance, someone with a marked English accent might feel less than welcome at a Scottish nationalist rally! This factor plays a role more generally and is bound up with perceptions and attitudes towards the speaker's linguistic variant that are often rooted in preconceptions about the individual's background, class, etc.[101]

One context in which rendering the correct sociolect and idiolect is extremely important is dialogue in literature. In one of the classics of American literature *Huckleberry Finn*, its author, Mark Twain, was acutely aware of this and explained his strategy as follows in the introduction to the book:

> In this book a number of dialects are used, to wit: the Missouri negro dialect; the extremest form of the backwoods Southwestern dialect; the ordinary 'Pike County' dialect; and four modified varieties of this last. The shadings have not been done in a haphazard fashion, or by guesswork; but painstakingly, and with the trustworthy guidance and support of personal familiarity with these several forms of speech. I make this explanation for the reason that without it many readers would suppose that all these characters were trying to talk alike and not succeeding.[102]

Because of the issue of diglossia, things are more complex in Arabic literature, where the often significant differences between the vernaculars and the desire not to have regionalisms have led some authors, such as the Egyptian Naguib Mahfouz or the Moroccan Mohammed Choukry, to name but a few, to eschew dialect from speech. One of the staunchest proponents of this view was the great literateur Taha Hussein, who saw it as proof of the 'laziness' of authors.[103]

The result, however, is a glaring lack of authenticity and sometimes unintended comic effect when an illiterate farmer uses the same standard Arabic employed during a formal speech or academic presentation.[104]

Translation into English from Arabic has in the past also grappled with register, as B. Lewis pointed out:

> The cause of cultural communication has suffered some damage from a sort of Anglo-Arabese favored by many, particularly Victorian, translators—a pseudo-biblical, neo-gothic, mock-Elizabethan, bogus Oriental style which finds its ultimate form in Burton's translation of the *Thousand and One Nights* and still seems to contaminate some other translators, recent and even contemporary.[105]

This was naturally due to the time in which the translations were produced, as well as the source text genres. However, it is difficult to see how this argument can mitigate the following brief example of 'Burtonian' hyperbole, which scarcely reflected the language use of his own time, or indeed any other time:

> 'Allah upon thee!' cried he in wrath exceeding that lacked no feeding, 'O scanty of wit, expose not thy life to such peril! How durst thou address me in words so wide from wisdom and un-far from foolishness?'[106]

Interestingly enough, the author of these lines took the great E. Lane to task for the unidiomaticness of his translation of the *Thousand and One Nights* (1839),

> Worst of all, the three handsome volumes are rendered unreadable as Sale's Koran by their anglicised Latin, their sesquipedalian un-English words, and the

stiff and stilted style of half a century ago when our prose was, perhaps the worst in Europe.[107]

Whilst some may argue that Lewis' statement no longer applies to the current state of translation from Arabic, this is true no doubt for the renditions of modern literary works but less so for the translation of religious works, for instance, where one may sometimes still adumbrate more than a whiff of the mock-Biblical.

Navigating the pitfalls of diglossia is an important part of the translator's task and it is to this aspect that we shall turn next.

DIALECT AND DIGLOSSIA IN TRANSLATION

The issue of how diglossia impacts on translation in Arabic and, more importantly, how to deal with it has received relatively little attention.[108]

In his study of the translation (into German) of the vernacular in the above-mentioned book by Mark Twain, Berthele[109] states that one of the biggest challenges for the literary translator is finding equivalents of dialectal and sociolectal speech as it relies on understanding the relationship between the language levels in the source language and finding equivalents in the target language, which relies on *the often erroneous assumption that these exist.*

Any strategy necessarily 'reflect[s] the translator's assessment of the value the author places on the use of colloquial speech.'[110] It implies that the translator has to ascertain the author's idea about the relationship between standard and non-standard use of language; the author's purpose and intention of non-standard varieties and to marry this with his/her own idea about this and attempt to render it into the TL, based on his/her understanding.[111]

This raises a number of questions. For a start, how does the translator establish author intent? It also somehow implies that social relations between the characters and socio-economic background are expressed in the same way across both languages.

Assumptions about one style and register in one language do not necessarily hold true for another. For instance, whereas an educated English speaker would avoid the use of 'ain't' in all contexts (except, perhaps, for ironic or comic effect), it is very common – at least in informal contexts – for an educated Arabic speaker to use equivalent grammatically 'incorrect' expressions in everyday conversation. So, while the vocabulary will vary depending on the topic, context and education of the speaker, the phonological, morphological and syntactic features will be very similar across all levels.[112] For instance, there will be very little difference in phonology and syntax of the speech between those of little education and, say, that heard from a discussion among academics who are native speakers of the same variety of Arabic.

This means that when translating from Arabic to English in this case, the translator has to be very conscious of effect and purpose and avoid jumping to conclusions and choosing an inappropriate, unidiomatic register. As a result, it may be necessary to translate the phrase '*mā ᶜandīsh*', which occurs in a number of dialect areas, including Tunisia and Egypt, as 'I haven't got' or 'I ain't got', depending on the speaker.

While the aim is to obtain equivalence in rendering dialect and idiomatic speech, it is often difficult to assess this.

The difficulties attendant upon dealing with the issue of diglossia in translation are legion:

- How does one accurately determine (and distinguish between) levels in the ST? This very basic step is fraught with problems when dealing with Arabic diglossia since, as we have seen, this should be viewed as a continuum rather than as a linear progression of discreet divisions. Matters are further compounded by the degree of variation and differences between the vernaculars and the fact that in many cases registers are a vernacular-specific phenomenon, rather than a generic one.
- Is it fundamentally any different from dealing with shifts in register, which is something that affects all languages and many genres of texts?
- Does every language have the same levels of register?
- Does the issue of diglossia have a similar effect on translations into and from Arabic?
- The assumption of 'dialect/vernacular-for-dialect/vernacular' rendition raises the question of 'which dialect?', i.e. from which country, or region. This risks overtly 'localizing' a text and potentially excluding or, at the very least, alienating large segments of the Arabic-speaking target readership.[113]
- How does one identify, interpret and reproduce the effect of pragmatic and cultural factors?
- How does one deal with gaps in terms of register between the ST and TT?
- How does one ensure consistency in interpreting levels, bearing in mind the other factors that may come into play?

How is the translator to deal with this highly complex issue? Bearing in mind the limitations mentioned above, any strategy has to follow a number of key steps in regard to the ST:

- What is the background of the character?
- What is the context of the utterance (formal vs informal)?
- What are the features of the other characters' speech?
- What is the pragmatic content and intent of the utterance?

It is only then that one can start looking at how to render it into the TL, which register, style, etc. one should use to maximize comprehension, naturalness and idiomaticness, and avoid pragmatic loss.

Let us start with the ways in which diglossia and registers may manifest themselves in a text.

Arabic>English translation

The first step in translating from either language should be to identify register markers, which may appear in spelling, lexis and syntax.

Spelling

Whenever an author or translator wishes to render dialectal speech, the form in which to do so always poses problems in both languages, but especially in Arabic, since there is often not a recognized 'formalized' way in which to render regional speech. Secondly, the Arabic script is unable to render certain commonly used dialectal pronunciations, notable examples being the vowels 'ō' and 'ē', which are generally rendered by و and ي, i.e. 'ū' and 'ī', respectively. Consonant changes reflecting local speech include the following:

- ظ for ض: e.g. مضبوط > مظبوط, 'correct' (ECA)
- س for ث: e.g. ثعلب > سعلب, 'fox' (ECA)
- ز for ذ: e.g. ذبذب > زبزب, 'to swing' (ECA)
- ه for ح: e.g. راح نقول > حنقول > هنُقول, 'we will say' (ECA)
- گ for /g/: e.g. قاعِد > گاعد, progressive particle (Kuw.)
- ق (or ڨ) for /g/: e.g. غاز > ڨاز, 'gas' (Tun.)

Vowel changes include 'clipping', i.e. shortening of a long vowel: e.g. حرامية > حرمية (ECA, 'thieves').

Two important caveats must be made here. First, not all phonological changes are rendered in writing: for instance, even in dialects where ق is realized as a glottal stop (*hamza*), the ق remains written. Assimilations are also customarily unrendered: e.g. جانبي ('next to me') instead of جمبي which is actually heard. Second, there is no recognized way of rendering the vernacular and often one encounters variation: e.g.

هذا > دا / ده
هذه > دي / ده

Third, even if some of the markers are present, they do not in and of themselves enable the reader to identify the 'level of colloquialism'.

Syntax and grammar

When it comes to syntax, the markers that occur in writing are smaller in number than for spelling or lexis. For instance, subject-verb-object order, as opposed to the 'classical' verb-subject-object is no longer a reliable marker since it is also commonly used in several MSAs.[114] Other more reliable markers include the following:

- إللي (for MSA الذي , اللذان , اللذيْن , الذين , التي , اللتان , اللتيْن , اللواتي);
- clipping of the third person plural of the *muḍāri*ᶜ: e.g. يعملوا ('they are doing');
- the negative particle ما (e.g. Eg., Tun., Mor.) or مو (some Gulf dialects) e.g. *mā ᶜandīsh* ('I don't have');
- future particles:

  a ***rāḥ*** or its clitic *ḥā* (also *hā*) (e.g. Eg., Levantine): e.g. حايوافق ('he will agree')
  b ***ghādī*** (Mor.): e.g. غادي نمشي ('I'll go')
  c ***bāsh*** (*bish*) (Tun.): e.g. بش نمشي ('I'll go')
  d ***bi*** (Kuw.): بنروح ('we'll go');

- the progressive particle *ᶜam* (e.g. Levantine): e.g. عم بقلك ('I'm telling you');
- the progressive particle *gāᶜid* (Kuw.): e.g. گاعد يِشْرَب ('he is drinking');

- the progressive particle *ʿammāl* (Eg.): e.g. عمال ياكل ('he keeps on eating').

Whilst the first two items can be found in a multitude of dialects, the others are common only to a number of them.

Lexis

This is the principal code/register switching marker, but unfortunately it is not always straightforward since, as we have seen, there are many common items in the normative and vernacular varieties.

It is clear that the complexities and extreme variation make it a mare's nest for the translator. And while it may be easier in many cases for the native Arabic-speaker, even he or she may be just as stymied by an unfamiliar vernacular. As a result, even the most proficient and experienced Arabic–English translator is reliant much more on native speaker informants than, say, his French>English counterpart. In addition, there is also a shortage of good lexicographical resources for the dialects, as many of them remain insufficiently documented.

One of the biggest problems facing the Arabic>English translator is the already-mentioned lack of register in that MSA is often used in both spoken utterances and narrative discourse. This cannot be simply transposed in English, and the translator therefore has to make a series of value judgements, based on the above steps, in order to 'pitch' the text at the right level. For instance, the sentence *'mādha taqūlīna yā ummī'* needs to be translated in different ways, depending on the setting, character features, etc. If spoken by a thirteen-year-old boy, the translation can hardly be 'What are you saying, oh mother?' Instead, a 'neutral' rendition in (British) English might be 'What're you saying, Mum?' This may be further fine-tuned by adding the pragmatic variable; for instance, if the boy is annoyed at the mother interrogating him about something, one might opt for 'What're you on about, Mum?'

In any event, the translation must be idiomatic and natural speech. Unlike in Arabic, where the issue of dialect complicates matters, there exists a speech register in written English that is, for the most part, not dialect specific.

Another key difference with English>Arabic translation is the fact that the English reader is used to colloquial, or even slang, in translations and is able to 'suspend disbelief', as it were, when the dialogue of a character in an Arabic novel includes the very informal: 'Oh, come off it, mate!' Arabic-speaking readers, on the other hand, are far less willing to accept a British policeman's speech rendered in broad Egyptian colloquial dialect, for instance.

In order to produce an idiomatic translation, all these strategies must be explored by the translator, who has to act accordingly.

English>Arabic translation

The situation in English is, in many respects, more straightforward than it is in Arabic, at least when it comes to identifying the verancular, though not, as we shall see, for translation into Arabic.

To begin our discussion, let us take an excerpt from Twain's *Tom Sawyer and Huckleberry Finn*, in which dialectal features have been highlighted in bold:

'Because it **ain't** in the books so—that's why. Now, Ben Rogers, do you want to do things **regular**, or don't you?—that's the idea. Don't you reckon that the people that made the books **knows** what's the correct thing to do? Do you reckon *you* can learn **'em** anything? Not by a good deal. No, sir, we'll just go on and ransom them in the regular way.'

'All right. I don't mind; but I say it's **a fool way**, anyhow. Say, do we kill the women, too?'

'Well, Ben Rogers, if I **was** as ignorant as you I wouldn't let on. Kill the women? No; nobody ever saw anything in the books like that. You **fetch** them to the cave, and you're always as polite as pie to them; and **by and by** they fall in love with you, and never want to go home any more.'

'Well, if that's the way I'm agreed, but I **don't take no stock** in it. Mighty soon we'll have the cave so cluttered up with women, and fellows waiting to be ransomed, that there **won't be no place** for the robbers. But go ahead, I **ain't** got nothing to say.'

Little Tommy Barnes was asleep now, and when they **waked** him up he was scared, and cried, and said he wanted to go home to his ma, and didn't want to be a robber any more.

So they all made fun of him, and called him cry-baby, and that made him mad, and he said he would **go straight** and tell all the secrets. But Tom **give** him five cents to keep quiet, and said we would all go home and meet next week, and rob somebody and kill some people.

Ben Rogers said he couldn't get out much, only Sundays, and so he wanted to begin next Sunday; but all the boys said it would be wicked to do it on Sunday, and that settled the thing. They agreed to get together and fix a day as soon as they could, and then we elected Tom Sawyer first captain and Jo Harper second captain of the Gang, and so started home.

I **clumb** up the shed and crept into my window just before day was breaking. My new clothes **was** all greased up and **clayey**, and I was dog-tired.[115]

In the novel, the **grammatical** features of the vernacular speech include the following, some of which appear in the above passage:

- auxiliary and copula deletion: e.g. 'I gone home';
- simple past 'done': e.g. 'I done this';
- multiple negation: e.g. 'I ain't got nothing';
- subject-verb non-agreement (esp. 3rd person): e.g. 'he know';
- object pronoun 'them' for subject pronoun: e.g. 'them there days';
- overuse of co-ordinating 'and'.

Some of the **phonological** features of vernacular English speech one may encounter are:

- loss of /r/ after consonants;
- 'h hypercorrection' (the addition of /h/ in word-initial positions before a vowel): e.g. 'helephant';
- consonant cluster reduction: e.g. 'liberry' (for 'library');

- velar nasal deletion in gerund ending *-ing*: e.g. 'singin';
- /ai/ –> /i/: e.g. 'me dad';
- elision: e.g. 'em' (<'them');
- t-glottalling (substitution of glottal stop for /t/ in some contexts): e.g. 'bu'e(r)' ('butter').

As stated above, in the case of Arabic, one is faced with the intractable problem of which dialectal variety to choose. In addition to the alienation aspect mentioned earlier, the use of a particular dialect may make the text difficult, or in some cases impossible, to understand by Arabic speakers from other areas. This may be illustrated by some examples of everyday utterances and the ways in which these are idiomatically rendered in a number of vernaculars from both the Near East and North Africa.

	That should not be a problem.
MSA	لَنْ تَكُونُ تِلْكَ مُشْكِلة. لا يَنْبَغِي أَنْ يَكُونَ ذلِكَ بِمُشْكِلةٍ.
Jordanian	ما في آي مشكلة. هذي مش رح تكون مشكلة.
Syrian (Damascus)	مو المفروض يكون هالشي مشكلة. لازم ما يكون هالشي مشكلة. اذا هيك مو مشكلة.
Palestinian	ما فيه مشكلة.
Saudi (Najd)	ما فيه مشكلة / مهب مشكلة. هادي ماراح تكون مشكلة.
Omani	ما أعتقد أنه هذه مشكلة. المفترض أنها ما تكون مشكلة.
Kuwaiti	مافي أي مشكلة. هل شي المروض مايسببلك مشكلة.
Yemeni	ماشي مشكلة.
Egyptian	مش مشكلة / مفيش مشكلة.
Tunisian	ماكانش مشكلة.
Algerian	ماكانش مشكل / ما فيها باس.
Libyan	هاذيك ماهيش مشكلة.

	You wouldn't have been able to do anything, even if you had been there.
MSA	ما كَانَ بِاسْتِطَاعَتِكَ / بِإِمْكَانِكَ عَمَل شَيْء، حَتى لَوْ كُنْتَ هُناكَ.
Jordanian	ما كان طلع بإيدك تسوي إشي حتى لو كنت موجود. حتى لو كنت هناك، ما كان رح يطلع بإيدك شيَ.
Syrian (Damascus)	ما كنت راح تقدر تعمل شي حتى لو كنت موجود.
Palestinian	ما كان بايدك تعمل اشي حتى لو كنت موجود هناك.
Saudi (Najd)	ما تقدر تسوي شي حتى لو كنت هناك. حتى لو إنك كنت موجود ما كنت حتقدر تسوي شي.
Omani	أصلا ما كنت بتقدر تسوي أي شي إذا كنت هناك. حتى لو كنت هناك، كنت ما أتقدر تسوي شي.
Kuwaiti	حتى لو كنت موجود ماكنت تقدر تسوي شي. حتى لو كنت هناك ماكنت راح تقدر اتسوي شي.
Yemeni	لو كنت هاناك ماكنت عتقدروا تفعلوا شي.
Egyptian	ما كنتش حتقدر تعمل حاجة حتى لو كنت هناك.
Tunisian	ما كنت تنجم تعمل شي حتى لوكنت غادي.
Algerian	ما كنت تقدر ادير والو حتى لو كان كنت ثمّة.
Libyan	ماكنت تقدر إدير شي حتى لو كنت غادى.

As the Arabic translations are all by native speakers of the varieties in question, it is a useful exercise to identify markers (spelling, lexis and syntax) and associated levels. There are a number of similarities in terms of syntax and syntactic devices, as well as in lexis, with a number of items being shared by several dialects. At the same time, some of the examples reveal that there are more discrepancies within a group of geographically close dialects. In other words, distance does not necessarily correlate with intelligibility (or lack thereof). As a result, even using the vernacular within the same broad group might be problematic and the Tunisian sentence would not, in most cases, be fully understood by, for instance, the average Moroccan reader.

Some researchers have identified translating the colloquial as 'the main problem facing the translator of an Arabic work of literature.'[116] In addition to the problem of comprehension, the issue is further complicated by the fact that in the SL literature, there are several schools of thought when it comes to the issue of using the colloquial in dialogue. While authors such as N. Mahfouz avoid it altogether, others (e.g. Y. Idris, E. Kharrat, Y. al-Sibāʕī) opt for varying degrees of the colloquial, while a third group (e.g. T. al-Ḥakīm) employ a simplified form of MSA in dialogue.

In Translation Studies, there would appear to be more of a consensus. In her study of the Arabic translations of Harriet Beecher Stow's *Uncle Tom's Cabin*, al-Sarrani rejects the use of the colloquial out of hand because of 'the challenging specificity of the Arabic colloquial dialect being representative (sic) of the Arabic country it is spoken in.'[117] After discussing the linguistic features of the book and the significance of idiolectal usage, al-Sarrani simply states that writing MSA is standard, whereas 'the Arabic Egyptian colloquial dialect cannot be used to translate the African American dialect in Stowe's text since the African American dialect is presenting a racial group that is part of America, whereas the Egyptian dialect represents the people of Egypt.'[118]

Muhaidat, who analysed Arabic translations of Dickens' *A Tale of Two Cities*, also gave the issue short shrift, simply pointing out the various losses in translation because of the use of Standard Arabic, without giving any suggestions for improvement or how to deal with this.[119] At the same time, the author praised the use by the translator of what she considered vocabulary that is common to both standard and colloquial Arabic. This is, however, a spurious point as it is predicated on the false premise that there is such a thing as a supranational 'spoken Arabic'. One of the examples adduced is *'ukhrus* ('shut up'), which is indeed used in a number of dialects, but not in others, such as Egyptian, where *'uskut* is the common form. It is also worth pointing out that the colloquials are regional, rather than national, due to the considerable differences in dialects spoken in a single country.

Against this kind of polarized backdrop, the choice would seem to be equally polarized – and polarizing; that is, to use the colloquial, or not. In fact, we would contend that this is a simplistic way of approaching the issue as it presupposes that the middle ground does not exist, for reasons outlined above, the main ones being intelligibility and/or acceptance of another dialect on the part of the reader. However, the losses in translation are often so great that it affects idiomaticity, which, in turn, also affects reception of the text. The middle ground would involve the following possibilities:

1 Use of the colloquial of the target readership; this approach can only be used if the target readership is known and the Target Text does not go beyond this group. Though not appropriate for general works of literature, the strategy may be used in, for instance, certain types of persuasive literature aimed at one specific community. Even in this scenario, choices have to be made; for instance, if the text is aimed at a purely Egyptian audience, would it be in the Upper Egyptian (*Ṣaʿīdī*) dialect, or the northern ECA? As it is rarely, if at all, possible and/or practicable to produce translations for each variety within a country, the translator strategy should sensibly involve what may be called the 'prestige' dialect, which would, in any case, be understood by all. In our example, this would be ECA.

2 While vocabulary tends to be dialect specific, here, too, choices can be made by, for instance, modulating the degree of formalcy of lexical items or even introducing verbs such as *shāfa/yashūfu* to mark the colloquial register.

3 The use of supradialectal morphological and syntactic 'colloquialization' markers that the translator can use in dialogue in order to add spoken 'colour'. These may include the following:

a the invariable relative pronoun اللي;
b subject-verb-object order, rather than the CA verb-subject-object order;
c simplification of the plural by the use of the oblique case ين only for masculine sound plurals;
d simplification of the dual by the use of the oblique case: يْن;
e clipping of the third person plural imperfect ending: وا (instead of ون): e.g. يعلموا ('they know');
f the use of *mā* as the negating particle for the perfect (الماضي), rather than the high classical *lam*;
g the avoidance of high-classical items (e.g. *laqad*).

This would allow the translator to mark a sentence like 'the boyscouts who are playing football' off from the SA narrative text:

الكشافون الذينَ يَلْعَبُونَ بِكُرةِ القَدَم
vs
الكشافين اللي يلعبوا بكرة القدم

This strategy enables the translator to introduce the necessary shifts in register without, however, using any specific dialect and thus avoiding the above-mentioned problems that the latter would entail.

At this point, it is useful to look at some examples. The first text is an extract from Rajaa Alsanea's *Banāt al-Riyāḍ* (2005), translated as *Girls of Riyadh* by M. Booth (London, Fig Tree, 2007).

The wedding planner called out to Sadeem, who was hiding behind the curtain with her friend Gamrah. In her singsong Lebanese Arabic, Madame Sawsan informed Sadeem that the wedding music tape was still stuck in the machine and that efforts were being made to fix it.	اتصلت مدام سوسن المختبئة مع قمرة خلف الستار، لتخبرها أن شريط الزفة ما زال عالقاً، والمحاولات جارية لإصلاحه:
'Please, tell Gamrah to calm down! It's nothing to worry about, no one is going to leave. It's only one a.m.! And anyway all the *cool* brides these days start things on the late side to add a bit of suspense. Some never walk down the aisle before two or three a.m.!'	"دخيلك قولي لقمرة تهدي حالها... ما صار شي! لسّاتون الناس مأربزين هون ما حدا فل، وبعدين كليات العرايس الكوول بيتأخروا شوي تيعملوا سسبنس!"
Gamrah, though, was on the verge of a nervous breakdown. She could hear the voices of her mother and her sister Hessah shrieking at the events manager from the other end of the ballroom,	قمرة على وشك الانهيار، وصوت والدتها وأختها حصة اللتين تصرخان في وجه منظمة الحفل يأتي من آخر القاعة منبئاً بفضيحة وليلة سوداء، وسديم ما زالت إلى جانب صديقتها العروس، تمسح عن جبينها قطرات العرق قبل أن تلتقي بالدموع التي تحبسها أطنان من الكحل داخل جفنيها. يملأ صوت محمد عبده المنبعث من جهاز التسجيل القاعة الضخمة، وتصل إشارة البدء من مدام سوسن إلى سديم، التي تلكز قمرة بكوعها: – سَرينا ..

and the whole evening was threatening to turn out to be a sensational humiliation. Sadeem stayed at the bride's side, wiping beads of sweat from her friend's forehead before they could collide with the tears that were held back only by the quantity of kohl weighing down her eyelids. The voice of the famous Saudi singer Muhammad Abdu finally blasted from the amplifiers, filling the enormous hall and prompting Sawsan to give Sadeem the nod. Sadeem poked Gamrah. '*Yalla*,* let's go.' [p. 4]

* *Yalla* can mean 'c'mon' or 'hurry up' or 'let's go'

The novel provides a wonderful case for treatment since it contains a multitude of examples of diglossia and various dialects, even though the author is, herself, Saudi. The source text shifts between MSA, Saudi and Lebanese dialects, Arabized English (the so-called *ᶜarabīzī*) and internet Arabic.

The sample passage provides an example of the mixing of Saudi and Lebanese Arabic. This mixture poses a problem for the translator, whose choices are limited:

- ignore the differences and concentrate on the register, rather than attempting to modulate vernaculars;
- mix English vernaculars to correspond to the Arabic ones;
- provide metatextual pointers.

As discussed above, the most natural solution is to have idiomatic spoken English. In this case, this is used in combination with the third option. Though there is no difference between the English of the wedding planner and that of the other characters, her speech is demarcated by referring to 'her singsong Lebanese Arabic'. Even though there is a loss, the English-speaking reader gets two very important pieces of information that are readily apparent to the Arabic reader: the character is Lebanese and Lebanese Arabic has distinct features setting it apart from Saudi dialects.

The 'Lebaneseness' of the character's speech is clear to the ST reader through the vocabulary used, but as this is not accessible to the English TT reader, it is 'transposed' through referencing the intonation pattern, as a suprasegmental aspect of speech, which is not rendered in the ST, but is implied. In other words, the translator explicated what is implicit.

A second point of interest is the rendition of 'cool', which appears in transliteration in the Arabic text, and is signposted in the ST by the use of italics.

The second example is a translation of a story by the Iraqi author Fu'ād al-Takarlī, *Khazīn al-lāmar'iyyāt*:[120]

She said: 'Who is she? But ... don't you know? She's the daughter of Ali Asghar, a sergeant-major in your uncle's outfit and his aide. Her poor mother was very fond of me. She would visit us and leave Khadija so she could help me out around the house and play with the girls until her mother finished the housework at your uncle's house. How destiny can change things! Did you say that she's the wife of your managing director? Talk about a reversal of fortune!' Afterwards, I needed to restore the hidden balance of the simple and unexciting life I had always wanted. Unfortunately, the memories would not allow me to do so. We were free as birds that summer holiday. My sisters, Khadija and I fooled around and played in our large house to our hearts' content, with the innocence of childhood. The game we used to play most was hide-and-seek.	تقول من كانت؟ ولكنها.. ألا تعلم؟ ابنة رئيس العرفاء "عليٍ أصغر" الذي كان تحت إمرة خالك ومرافقاً له، وأمها المسكينة كانت تأتي تزورني محبة بي، وتبقيها عندنا كي تساعدني وتلعب مع البنات ريثما تكمل هي خدمتها في بيت خالك. ياللقدر! تقول إنها زوجة مديركم العام؟ ياللقدر! كان علي، بعد ذلك، أن أعيد التوازن اللامرئي لحياتي التي أردتها، دائماً، بسيطة ومسطحة. ولكن الذكريات لمٍ تترك لي أن أنجح في هذه المهمة. كنا أحراراً كالطيور، في تلك العطلة الصيفية، أنا وشقيقاتي وخديجة، نمرح ونلعب في بيتنا الكبير كما نشاء وتشاء البراءة والعبث واختلاط الأمور. وكانت تلك اللعبة "الختيلة" الجميلة والمراوغة، هي التي تجذبنا أكثر من الألعاب الأخرى.

This text is an example of the use of MSA in both narrative and dialogue, albeit with some local (lexical) influences (underlined in the text); one can almost hear the characters declaim their lines with full declensions!

This type of style poses another kind of problem for the translator, i.e. the absence of shifts in register. The options in this case are to transfer this to the TT or to employ an adaptation strategy and 'colloquialize' the dialogue in order to make the text more idiomatic and natural. The translator opted for the latter option but made sure not to lower the level inordinately and, for instance, avoided using slang terms that would have been out of place not only with the tenor of the story, but also with the character.

Similar issues also affect the other translation direction, as shown by the following examples. The first one is an extract from the Arabic translation of a Sherlock Holmes story, 'The Second Stain' (*Mughāmarāt Shīrlūk Hūlmz: al-Mushkila al-akhīra. The Adventures of Sherlock Holmes. The Final Problem*, Dār al-Bihār, 2010, p. 276–7):

English	Arabic
[Holmes] 'Well, take my advice. Examine him carefully. Don't do it before us. Ask him how he dare to admit people and leave them alone in this room. Don't ask him if he has done it. Take it for granted. Tell him, you *know* someone has been here. Press him. Tell him that a full confession is his only chance of forgiveness. Do exactly what I tell you!' Soon Lestrade's voice was heard in the passage. 'Sorry to keep you waiting, Mr Holmes. Well, he has confessed all right. Come in here MacPherson. Let these gentlemen hear of your most inexcusable conduct.'	"إعمل بنصيحتي وتحقق منه بعناية، لكن على انفراد. إسأله كيف يجرؤ على إدخال الناس إلى الغرفة وتركهم لوحدهم فيها. لا تسأله إن فعل هذا. بل سلم بالأمر. قال له إنك تعرف أن أحدهم دخل إلى هنا. إضغط عليه. قل له إن اعترافه الصريح الكامل هو خلاصه الوحيد العفو عنه. إفعل ما أقولك!" سمعنا بعد قليل صوت ليستراد في الرواق. "المعذرة على جعلك تنتظر يا سيد هولمز. لقد أقر بما عنده. تعال إلى هنا يا ماكفيرسون. أكلع السيدين على تصرفك المشين."

In this case, the English dialogue does not differ substantially between the characters, all of whom adopt formal speech. This is mirrored in the Arabic text, where the same formal register is used throughout. When a new character – a policeman – is introduced, the register shifts noticeably as the following exchange unfolds:

English	Arabic
'I meant no harm sir, I'm sure. The young woman came to the door last evening – mistook the house, she did.	"لم أشأ إفساد الأمور، أؤكد لك هذا يا سيدي، أتت الشابة ليلة أمس وقالت إنها أخطأت المنزل.
And then we got talking. It's lonesome when you're on duty here all day.	ثم بدأنا نتحدث وأنت تعرف كم من الصعب أن تظل هنا بمفردك تؤدي خدمتك طوال النهار.
She wanted to see where the crime was done – had read about it in the papers, she said.	أرادت أن ترى أين حصلت الجريمة بعد أن قرأت عنها في الصحف على حد قولها.
When she saw that mark on the carpet, down she dropped on the floor as if she were dead.'	لكنها حالما رأت البقعة على السجادة وقعت أرضاً وكأنها ميتة."

Here, there are plenty of colloquialisms:

- intensive auxiliary: 'she mistook the house, she did';

- lexical error: 'it's lonesome' (for 'lonely');
- subject deletion and inversion; 'had read about it in the papers, she said';
- metathesis: 'down she dropped on the floor'.

To the English-speaking reader, all of these provide obvious clues regarding the character's background, social status, education, and so on. If we turn to the Arabic translations, however, we find that all these markers have been 'ironed out' for the sake of a uniform register in which there is no longer a difference in the speech of the policeman and that of Sherlock Holmes, which constitutes both a pragmatic and a cultural loss. This could have been attenuated by using some of the above-mentioned strategies, such as negating the perfect by means of *mā* (instead of *lam*).

The final example, a translation of Dickens' *A Tale of Two Cities*,[121] demonstrates the use of spelling to indicate even clearer shifts in register and dialect (highlighted in bold) between the various characters:

'**Hooroar**, father!' cried young Jerry.	فصاح جيري الصغير: "هورا، هورا يا أبت!"
'What **d'ye** mean? What are you hooroaring at? What do you want to convey to your own father, you young Rip? This boy **is getting too many for me!**' said Mr. Cruncher, surveying him.	و قال مستر كرانشر و هو يصعد طرفه في ابنه و يخفضه: "ماذا تعني؟ علام تصيح هذا الصياح المتهلل؟ مالذي تريد أن تقوله لأبيك أيها الولد السافل؟ لقد ضقت ذرعا بهذا الصبي!
'**Him and his hooroars!** Don't let me hear **no more** of you, or you **shall** feel some more of me. **D'ye** hear?'	ضقت ذرعا به و بصيحاته! حذار أن تسمعني صوتك. بعد الان، و إلا أشعرتك بمزيد من بطشي. أسمعت؟"
'I **warn't doing no** harm,' young Jerry protested, rubbing his cheek.	فاحتج جيري الصغير، ماسحا خده: "أنا لم أوذ أحدا." فقال مستر كرانشر: "أقلع عن ذلك إذن.
'Drop it then,' said Mr. Cruncher; 'I won't have **none of your no harms.** Get **a top** of **that there** seat, and look at the crowd.'	أنا لا أريد أن أرى شيئا من أعمالك اللاموذيه قف على ظهر ذلك المقعد و انظر الى الحشد."

The Arabic text contains no trace of the flavour and local colour of the original. In short, it has been entirely 'sanitized', with all characters speaking in the same formal way. The shifts in register are such that the losses and mismatches between the STs and TTs exceed what is acceptable. Once again, the solution here lies in striking a medium of sorts by amending the MSA register, simplifying it, while introducing some spelling and morphological changes that bring the text closer to what most readers would recognize as a spoken, rather than high-classical register.

EXERCISES

Exercise A

The following is a translation of *A Very Egyptian Tale*, a short story by the famous Egyptian author Yūsuf Idrīs (1927–1991), as it appears in his collected works (*Qiṣaṣ*, 81ff.). Comment on the translation choices in those areas where the two texts vary. Research comparable texts in order to inform your judgement.

Target Text

These brief moments, when a stranger meets another stranger, each of them cursing the bad luck in their own way, and subsequently reconciling with the other, also in their own way.

Let's take that nice cabbie, fat and plump – a father of three university students, who is good at recounting the event and the joke.

'I was driving along, near the Sheraton hotel when, suddenly, at the junction, there was a legless beggar, whose body – or rather what was left of it – was blocking the way. I stopped the car. I was surprised at the amazing agility – like that of a monkey or a reptile – with which this man jumped from the front of the car to my door. He opened it and then slid his torso next to me. He was panting heavily, and said: "let's go, guv'!"[i]

"Go, where?" I said to him: "It's only natural that I give you some alms, but this does not extend to giving you a lift."

He replied: "Listen, I need to go to Shubra El-Kheima or Shubra al-Mizallat.[ii] Please take me there. I am a legit fare,[iii] not a beggar. Quickly, let's get going, I beg you!"

I hesitated somewhat, but it seemed it was urgent. I was finally convinced by the handful of change that he took out of his pocket and showed me, so I decided to take him.

I took the Nile Corniche road, looking for a fare.

His clothes were torn and he looked dirty. Though still a young man, his dishevelled hair added ten years to his age. I started to become suspicious again, and stopped the car. I told him: "What is the deal with you, exactly? I'm not going anywhere until you tell me."

He said: "let's have a Coke."[iv]

He called over to the soft drink seller and paid him ten piasters for two bottles, which we drank. He said: "Listen, guv,[v] I'm a beggar ..."

I said to myself: *That's pretty clear for all to see.*

He continued: "I needed to take a taxi in order to escape from the cop."[vi]

I asked: "You mean the anti-vagrancy police."

He said: "No ... a traffic cop."

I said: "But what is the connection between a traffic policeman and you, a beggar?"

He said: "Work."

I said to myself: "What kind of work could possibly link this guy and the traffic cop?"

He said: "Yes, it's got to do with work."

He then started to tell me the story:

"The day I lost both my legs in a train[vii] accident, God opened the gates of profit to me. Since then, whenever people saw me crawling about on the floor, they would willingly reach into their pockets. I would make fifty to sixty piasters a day. I thought, how wonderful! I began to realize that, suddenly, I had money. My lost legs in fact always constituted a considerable capital and I had to turn them to good use. And so, I became very proficient at selecting my spots. I knew the character of people and passers-by in all districts of Cairo. The strange thing is that those who gave me money were always either very poor or very rich. On the other hand, it appears very difficult to stir compassion in the hearts of those who are in the middle, like yourself. In the course of my profession, I discovered that those who live in Egypt quickly run short on compassion when they are regularly confronted with things. The newcomers are those who still have a heart, and pockets, filled with money and compassion.

Eventually, I found myself on that corner, close to that big hotel, where I got into your car. A first-rate spot and job – near the traffic light; the cars stop when it turns red. But I have to move quickly in order to ply my trade with the drivers before the light turns green and the traffic starts moving again. In fact, I found that the lights didn't stay red long enough for me to get to all the cars. So, one day, I went to the traffic cop who was standing by the light and it didn't take long to strike a deal by which he would keep the light red until I had visited all the cars and signalled him that everything was okay. And then he would change the light."

I said to him: "Why, you little rascal!"[viii]

So, that was the reason that light, and perhaps others, stayed red for so long! I said to myself.

I asked him: "Fifty to sixty piasters every day?"

He replied: "Sure. Fifty to sixty piasters every day."

"How much do you make?"

"It depends, two to three ... maybe a little more, five to six a day if the traffic is heavy."

"So, what happened today? What were you trying to get away from?"

"Today, it's the period where I wish everyone a happy new year, and I'm raking it in hand over fist. So, I said to myself that I was going to try and do a runner before my partner in crime, the traffic cop, arrived."

I pondered the issue and then said: "Okay, but tomorrow the cop is going to get you, Einstein!"[ix]

He looked at me with a boyish smile, full of Egyptian shrewdness and ingenuity, and said: "No, tomorrow, there's another cop, and another arrangement. This was the last day that particular cop works on that spot."

"We've arrived at our destination."

"This is your lucky day, guv'."

The fare was 43 piasters. He gave me fifty piasters, seven piasters' worth of tip, and said: "If you hang around this traffic light for more than ten hours every day, and take me where I need to go, I'll give you fifty piasters."'

Commentary

i The ST has the more culture-specific term of address '*usṭa*', which literally translates as 'teacher' and is usually used for blue-collar professionals (see Parkinson 1985). The British English term 'guv' (short for 'governor') is used in similar contexts (as well as ironically), especially for one perceived to be higher up on the social scale.

ii Rather than formal transliterations, these are the recognized forms of these Cairo suburbs.

iii In line with the register of the character, this highly colloquial phrase is more appropriate than the rather formal 'customer'. The addition of the slang term 'legit' (> legitimate) further underscores this.

iv Although the original has 'Coca Cola', the clipped form is used here in line with TL convention.

v The Arabic *sidi* is more respectful and more formal than the above '*usṭa*'. 'Guv' is used here for the sake of consistency, because it reflects the same relationship between the two characters. Furthermore, a literal translation of 'sir' would be unidiomatic in this context.

vi The Arabic word literally translates as 'soldier'; however, this is also the word used for 'policeman' (alongside *shurṭī*) in Egyptian Arabic. In keeping with the register, 'cop' is preferable here to something formal like 'police officer'.

vii The Arabic *mitrū* can refer to either a metropolitan or an underground train (US: 'subway'). Although 'metro' is the commonly used term for the underground train system, it cannot be used here since it did not exist at the time the story was written (the first section only opened in 1987).

viii The Egyptian Arabic vernacular expression يا ابن الايه literally translates as 'you son of a so-and-so', which can also be rendered as 'why, you little …'.

ix The ST literally has 'oh clever (one)'; the translation provides a common English turn of phrase denoting the same idea.

Source Text

حكاية مصرية جداً

تلك اللحظات القليلة، غريب يلتقي بغريب، وكل منهما يلعن الحظ بطريقته، ويتلاءم أو يتصارح، بطريقته أيضاً .

ذلك السائق الطيب. سمين وملظلظ وأب لثلاثة طلبة في الجامعة، ويجيد رواية الحديث والنكتة .

قال: كنت سائراً قريباً من شيراتون، وفجأة في تقاطع شارعين، وجدت شحاذاً مقطوع الساقين يتعرض بجسده (أو بالأصح بالباقي من جسده) طريق العربة. وقفت. وفوجئت بذلك الإنسان، وبقدرة هائلة كقدرة القرود والزواحف، يقفز من حيث كان أمام العربة إلى حيث الباب المجاور لي ويفتح الأكرة وينزلق بجسده إلى جواري وهو يلهث ويقول: اطلع يا اسطى.

أطلع ازاي. قلت له. معقول أن أعطيك حسنة. أما أن أوصلك حسنة فهو ما لم يسمع به أحد قال: يا اسطى أنا عايز أروح شبرا ْالخيمة أو شبرا المظلات، من فضلك وصلني. انا زبون ولست شحاذاً اطلع بسرعة.. أرجوك .

ترددت قليلاً ولكن إلحاحه الشديد.. ثم قبضة النقود التي أخرجها نصف إخراجة من جيبه أقنعاني أن أطلع. وطلعت. سرت على كورنيش النيل أتأمل الزبون.. ملابسه مقطعة، جسده قذر، شاب لا يزال ولكن شعره منكوش بطريقة تضيف إلى عمره عشر سنين. ولعب الفأر في عبي مرة أخرى فأوقفت السيارة وقلت له: أنت إيه حكايتك بالضبط. مش ماشي إلا لما تقول لي.

قال: تشرب كوكاكولا..

ونادى على بائع الكوكاكولا، ودفع له في الزجاجتين عشرة قروش بسخاء وشربناها. قال: اسمع ياسيدي.. أنا شحات..

قلت في سري: هذا يبدو واضحاً..

قال: وأنا أريد أن آخذ تاكسي مخصوص لأهرب من العسكري

سألته: قصدك شرطة مكافحة التشرد.

قال: لأ.. عسكري المرور.

قلت: وما علاقتك بعسكري المرور وأنت شحات؟

قال: علاقة عمل.

قلت في سري: أي عمل هذا الذي يربط بينك وبين عسكري المرور؟

قال: أيوه.. علاقة عمل.

وأخبرني بالقصة.. قال:

من يوم أن قطعت ساقاي في حادث مترو بدأ ربنا يفتحها عليّ، وبدأ الناس كلما رأوني زاحفاً على الأرض من تلقاء أنفسهم يعطونني، وبدأت أطلع في اليوم بخمسين ستين قرشاً، وأقول نعمة. ولكني بدأت أفهم وأوعى وأعرف أنني أمتلك رأس المال. ساقاي المقطوعتان رأس مال لا بأس به أبداً لا بد أن أشغله. وهكذا بدأت أتقن انتقاء الأماكن، وأعرف طباع السكان والمارة في كل حي من أحياء القاهرة. الغريب أن الذين كانوا «يعطفون» دائماً علي هم: إما الفقراء جداً أو الأغنياء جداً. أما متوسطو الحال من أمثالك فالظاهر أن الرحمة صعبة الوصول إلى قلوبهم تماماً. ولكني أيضاً بطول المزاولة اكتشفت أن الذين يعيشون في مصر تتيبس الرحمة في قلوبهم بعد قليل من كثر ما يرون، أما القادمون الجدد فهم الذين لا تزال قلوبهم، وجيوبهم أيضاً، عامرة بالمال والرحمة.

وهكذا كان لا بد أن أعثر أخيراً على ذلك الركن القريب من الفندق الكبير الذي ركبت معك من جواره. مكان وشغلانة لوكس. الركن إشارة. تقف العربات عند النور الأحمر، في سرعة أكون قد مسحت ركاب العربات الواقفة وسائقيها قبل أن يضيء النور الأخضر وينطلق المرور..

ولكني اكتشف أن الإشارة لا تستمر طويلاً بحيث لم أكن أتمكن من تكملة مسح العربات كلها.

وهكذا في يوم ذهبت إلى العسكري الواقف عند الإشارة ولم يأخذ الأمر سوى كلمتين اتفقت معه بعدهما أن يطيل من فتح النور الأحمر حتى (أمسح) العربات كلها وحين أعطيه أنا (إشارة) من رأسي أن كله تمام يفتح هو (الإشارة).

يا ابن الإيه. هكذا قلت له. وقلت لنفسي أهذا هو السبب إذن في غياب تلك الإشارة وربما غيرها من الإشارات؟.

ووجدتني أسأله: وكنت تعطي العسكري.

قال: طبعاً.. خمسين ستين قرشاً كل يوم.

- أمال أنت بتطلع بكام.

مش كله.. اتنين تلاتة.. ممكن أكثر شوية خمسة ستة في يوم المرور زحمة.

- طيب والنهاردة.. مالك هربان ليه؟ إيه اللي حصل؟

- النهاردة يوم موسم كل سنة وأنت طيب. والشغل كان على ودته، وقلت أهرب قبل ما بيجي العسكري يشاركني فيه.

- ولكن (هكذا قال الأسطى) تفكرت في الموضوع وقلت له:

طب ماهو العسكري بكره ح يقفشك يا حدق.

ونظر لي بابتسامته الشابة الحدقة المصرية الساخرة وقال:

لا.. بكره في عسكري تاني باتفاق تاني.. ده كان آخر يوم للعسكري ده في الحتة دي

قال الأسطى: كنا قد وصلنا المكان.. عندك ياسطى وقفت.. كان الحساب ٤٣ قرشاً. أعطاني ٥٠ قرشاً.. سبعة قروش بأكملها بقشيش وقال لي: لو تبقى كل يوم تعدي على الإشارة دي الساعة عشرة كده وتوصلني ح أديك خمسين قرش.

Exercise B

The following is a translation of George Orwell's *Down and Out in Paris and London*: (مُتَشَرِّداً في باريس ولندن, trans. Saᶜdī Yūsuf, Damascus: Dār al-Madā li 'l-Thaqāfa wa 'l-Nashr, 1997, p. 146). Identify the shifts in register in the Source Text and how these are rendered in the Target Text. Comment on the translation choices and research comparable texts in order to inform your judgement. Finally, produce your own translation and justify your strategies.

None of these old men had any other resource whatever. One of them was talkative, and I asked him how he managed to exist. He said: 'Well, there's ninepence a night for **yer** kip – that's five **an'** threepence a week. Then there's threepence on Saturday for a shave – that's five **an'** six. Then say you **'as a 'aircut** once a month for sixpence – that's another **three'apence** a week. So you **'as** about four **an'** four-pence for food **an' bacca**.'	لَيْسَ لأَيٍّ مِن هَؤُلاءِ الرِّجال مَوْرَدٌ آخَر مِن أَيِّ نَوْع. أَحَدُهُم كانَ يُحِبُّ الكَلامَ، وَقَد سَأَلْتُهُ كَيْفَ يُدَبِّرُ عَيْشَهُ. قالَ: «حَسَناً. هُناكَ تِسْعَةُ بِنْساتٍ كُلُّ لَيْلَةٍ لِلْمَبِيتِ – أَيّ ثَلاثَةُ شِلِناتٍ وثَلاثَةُ بِنْساتٍ في الأُسْبُوعِ. ثُمَّ هُناكَ ثَلاثَةُ بِنساتٍ يَوْمُ السَّبْتِ لِلْحَلاقَةِ – المَجْمُوع خَمْسَةُ شِلِناتٍ وَسِتَّةُ بِنساتٍ – ثُمَّ قُلْ إِنَّكَ تَحْلَقُ شَعْرَ رَأْسِكَ مَرَّةَ شَهْرٍ بِسِتَّةِ بِنْساتٍ وهذا ثَلاثَةُ شِلِناتٍ وبِنْسٌ أُخْرَى في الأُسْبُوعِ، هَكَذا يَكُونُ عِنْدَكَ حَوالِي أَرْبَعَةُ شِلِناتٍ وَأَرْبَعَةُ بِنْساتٍ لِلأَكْلِ وسِواهُ.»

Exercise C

The table below contains a set of highly informal sentences and their renditions in two dialects. Comment on the dialectal variants provided. Which ones come closer to the ST? Why? What about the MSA translations? Are there any alternatives?

	MSA	*Iraqi*	*ECA*
'What the hell are you doing?'	ماذا تَفْعَلُ يا للهَوْلِ/ بِحَق الجَحِيم؟	لك ها اشدَ تسوي؟ خَرة بالسَموات، لك ها اشدَ تسَوي؟	انت بتهبب إيه؟ الله يِخْرَب بيتك! أيه اللي بتعمله ده؟ بحَق جاه النبي! أنت إيه اللي بتعمله ده؟
'I ain't got nothing to do with this.'	لَيْسَ بِذا عَلاقةٍ لِي.	ما إلي أي علاقة بهاي الشغلة	أنا ماليش دَعْوة بِدَه. أنا ماليش أي علاقة بما حَصَل دَه!

'I haven't got a clue what you're talking about!'	لَيْسَ لَدَيّ أي فِكْرَة عَما تَقُولُهُ! لا أَفْهَمُ ما تَتَحَدثُ عَنْهُ البَتة! لا أَعْرَفُ ما الذي تَتَكَلمُ عَنْهُ بالمَرَّةِ!	والله ما أدري عنيش دَتحجي! والله ما عندي أي فكرة عنيش دَ تحجي	ما عَنْدِيش أي فكرة خالص انت بتتكلم عن إيه! أنا مش فاهم بالمرة انت بتتكلم في إيه! إيه اللي بتقوله ده بالزبط؟ أنا مش فاهم انت بتتكلم في إيه!
'He beat the crap out of me and told me to get lost.'	ضربني ضرباً مبرحاً و/ثم قال لي أذهب إلى غير رجعة/ أشرب من البحر.	دمر حياتي وطردني/طردني كلي ورح ولي.	ضربني علقة سُخنة، وطردني. ضربني لما قطعني وقال إمشي ياد انت من هنا. ضربني ويهدلني، وقال لي إياك اشوف وشك العكر ده هنا تاني.
'That's a bloody mess we have gotten ourselves into!'	ما هذا الخَراب الذِي جَعْلناه عَلَى أنْفُسِنا!	لك هاي شلون ورطة تورطنا	يا دي الداهية السودا اللي جبناها لنفسنا! إيه المصيبة السودا اللي وقعنا نفصنا فيها دي؟ يا نهار اسود! إيه اللي عملنا في نفسنا!

3 Legal translation

> And the greatest help to rational legislation is that the laws when once written down are always at rest; they can be put to the test at any future time, and therefore, if on first hearing they seem difficult, there is no reason for apprehension about them, because any man however dull can go over them and consider them again and again.
>
> (Plato, *Laws*)

LEGAL LANGUAGE AND TEXT TYPOLOGY

Is there such a thing as legal language? This is not so much an arresting opening as a question that requires an answer. If so, what is it? Most people will probably recognize some of the elements mentioned in R. Benson's definition:

> There is plentiful evidence that lawyer's language is hocus-pocus to non-lawyers, and that non-lawyers cannot comprehend it. There exist scores of empirical studies showing that most of the linguistic features found in legalese cause comprehension difficulties. Legalese is characterized by passive verbs, impersonality, nominalizations, long sentences, idea-stuffed sentences, difficult words, double negatives, illogical order, poor headings, and poor typeface and graphic layout. Each of these features alone is known to work against clear understanding.[122]

Despite the generic term, legal language is used in a wide variety of contexts and aimed at a wide variety of readerships. And whilst it is considered a technical register of language, that is, a *special purpose language* or *jargon*, legal language – or *legalese* as it is often called – has crept into our daily language use. For one thing, like the law, legal language is inherently *interdisciplinary*, as 'it regulates most areas of human activity'.[123]

Second, legal language is not restricted to professionals of the law – lawyers, judges, scholars, to name but a few – as it is also used to communicate with, and between, laymen. Indeed, is there any aspect of modern life that is not carried out within a legal framework? For instance, anyone reading the warranty form of a newly bought toaster, or the terms and conditions on the back of plane ticket when going on their annual holiday, or filling out any type of official form, is confronted with numerous references to legal concepts, usually with words such as 'liability', 'compliance' that are not generally part of our daily vocabulary. This raises the first difficulty with regard to legal language, i.e. the fact that in many cases it is supposed to be 'all things to all men'.

The question that ensues from this is, of course, whether this is at all possible? In other words, is it reasonable to assume that jargon can be used to communicate effectively and efficiently with those who are outside the professional community? Judging by the complaints levelled by the general public at the opaqueness of legal language, the answer to these questions is probably 'No'!

The second peculiarity of legal language is that in the law, language is both the *medium* and the *object of study*.[124] This sets it apart from other technical languages; for instance, in chemistry, language is the medium, but what is analysed is the chemical process; in law, words are the equivalents of the chemical elements.

Third, legal language is much less subject to change in an ever-changing world, which is another distinguishing factor in comparison with other technical registers of language. This historic constancy means that legal documents (e.g. legislation) may look and sound the same as a similar document written two hundred years ago; in fact, it may be obligatory that it does for the document to have legal validity (e.g. US Act of Congress). It is this compliance aspect that accounts for much of the *formulaicness* of legal texts.

On another level, one could argue that the very word 'legal' needs to be further defined since even literary texts can have legal implications: e.g. as proof in a slander or obscenity trial. Here, we are going to take a more narrow, conventional approach to 'legal language' and 'texts' as those that are inherently part of the judicial process.

One possible, albeit very broad, division of legal texts is based on function, i.e. whether they are prescriptive or descriptive, or, to be more precise, the degree to which they are one or the other.[125] Prescriptive texts are *regulatory* documents, that is, they impose certain things on the parties concerned, whereas lack of compliance with the provisions will normally carry a sanction: e.g. constitutions, treaties, laws and contracts.

The descriptive category includes official requests, affidavits, complaints that do not possess a normative dimension, but still remain legal instruments. The texts in this group, in fact, come in many guises:[126]

- *declarative*, which constitute statements or declarations within a legal context, such as a witness statement or affidavit;
- *directive*, which involve instructing or getting other parties to perform a particular activity: e.g. a lawyer's brief;
- *exhortatory*, which aim to incite action on a particular issue: e.g. petitions;
- *expressive,* which convey a speaker's psychological state or attitude towards something: e.g. closing arguments of a trial;
- *commissive*, which reflect a commitment on the part of the speaker: e.g. marriage ceremony, wills.

These categories are rooted in Speech Act theory, as propounded by J. L. Austin and D. Searle, particularly the *performative* function of language, i.e. it is used to make people do things, which is of particular relevance to many varieties of legal discourse.

There is, however, another category that should be added, which is, in some ways, the odd one out in that these are texts that talk *about* the law, such as textbooks, scholarly articles on jurisprudence; these do not constitute legal instruments in that they are not recognized as documents in law. This category, we shall call *metalegal*. The various constituent components may be represented as follows:

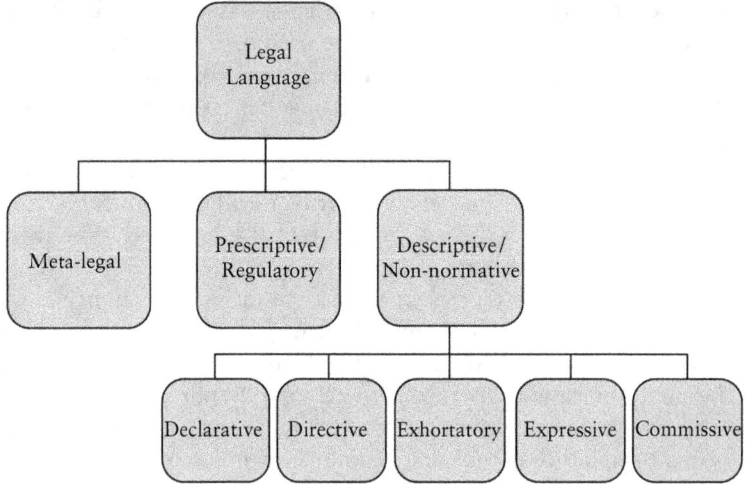

Figure 3.1 Functions of legal language

It is important to state that the chart does not do justice to reality as it is too static a model for a number of reasons. First, it is not uncommon for texts to cut across different categories: e.g. instructions to file a divorce may be both descriptive and prescriptive; a witness statement is both expressive and exhortatory.

Second, from a formal point of view, there are obvious overlaps in legal language features across the various text types. As a result, it is more appropriate to represent the relations between the various subdivisions as a Venn-diagram:

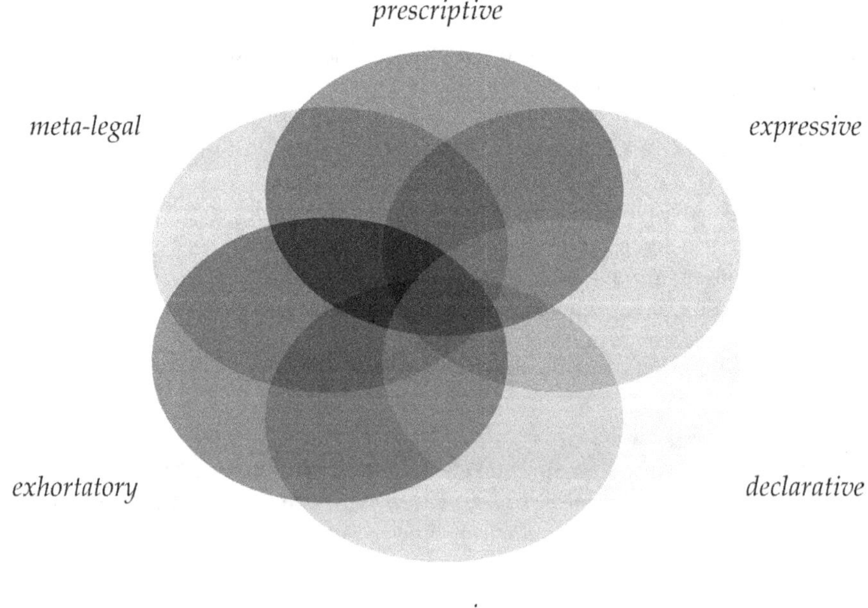

Figure 3.2 Overlaps in legal language features across text types

Another possible subdivision of legal texts is based on *text producers* rather than function: legislative, judicial, legal scholarly texts and private legal texts.[127] The first group contains texts that are drawn up by law-making bodies such as parliaments (e.g. constitutions, treaties, national laws). Judicial texts are produced by other legal authorities (e.g. the courts), whereas legal scholarly texts denote commentaries by scholars or lawyers. The distinctive feature of the fourth variety is the fact that these are legal documents, such as wills or private agreements, drawn up between individuals, usually by lawyers, but often also by individuals.

A link between language use and field of *application* results in a subdivision with the following categories as the constituent components, according to Jean-Claude Gémar: the language of the legislator, judges, the administration, commerce, private law and scholarly writings.[128]

Although legal language has validity as an 'overarching term' in the sense that all these text type categories share a number of universal features, they display sufficiently distinctive features that militate against considering legal language as a single-register variation. Consequently, it is more correct to speak of 'languages of the law'[129] or 'a set of related legal discourses',[130] as is reflected in the above diagrammatic representation of the inputs and overlaps in legal language.

Another complicating factor revolves around the parties involved in legal communication, which has already been hinted at above. Unlike in other types of technical communication, the parties involved in legal communication are not limited to professionals, neither to individuals, nor to organizations. For instance, an organization, such as a company, can enter into a legal relationship with one or several other organizations (e.g. joint venture agreements), individuals (e.g. employment contracts with its staff), national states (e.g. public tender), foreign states (e.g. consultancy agreements), or supranational organizations (e.g. appeals to the Court of Human Rights), as Figure 3.3 demonstates.

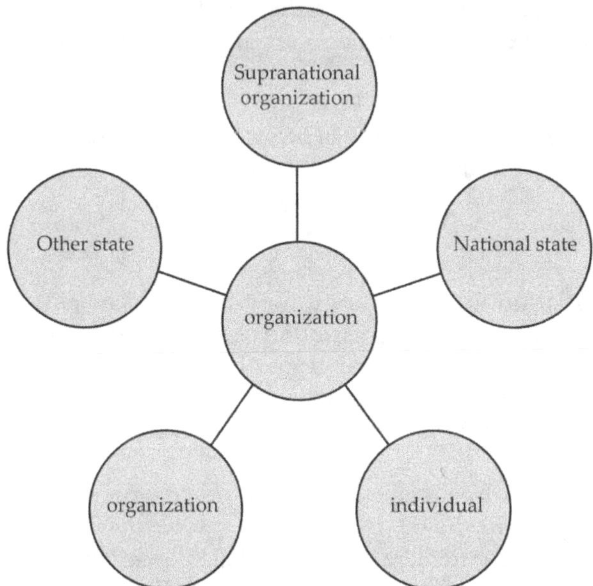

Figure 3.3 Legal relationships of companies

Each of the 'satellites' can be put in the centre of the diagram, as all the parties can enter into legal communication with one another (or several others), through, for instance, a promissory note (one individual to another), a national law (the state with the individuals making up its population), an EU Directive (between a supranational organization and its member states, or even non-member), a treaty (between two states). As a result, the target audience varies according to the documents, and must, of course, be taken into consideration by the translator.

Up until now, we have been talking about *written* documents; but a great deal of legal interaction is *spoken*, with lawyers talking to each other, to their clients, or, in a courtroom, to a judge and/or a jury. Naturally, like in all other areas of language use, oral legal communication is not necessarily the same as that which is written. A number of features that are generally associated with legalese, such as archaicisms and overly long sentences, tend to be toned down, at the very least, in the spoken language.[131] Perhaps more importantly, the spoken language is, by its very nature less formal, and, in the case of the law, this also means that it is less binding, in the absence of written corroborative documentation, as the old Latin adage *verbum volat* ('the [spoken] word flies [away]') makes clear!

Further variation results from geographical differences, with legal language differing even within the same speech community, for historical linguistic or legal-cultural reasons. For instance, though many English-speaking countries share the same legal system, the terminology is often different: e.g. in the USA *to table* a proposal, means 'to shelve' it, i.e. to take off the table, whereas in the UK it means 'to submit for discussion'. A separate historical development of systems that have the same origin also means that certain concepts, and thus the corresponding terminology, are lacking. And while the differences in legal French as used in France and in Canada can easily be explained because the Canadian legal system is English in origin and patterned on a wholly different set of principles, it is perhaps more surprising to find that there are equally dramatic discrepancies between France and Belgium or Switzerland, all of which have legal systems rooted in the French tradition. The same applies to the discrepancies between legal German used in Germany, Switzerland, Austria or Belgium.

Finally, in our global society a great deal of legal language is conducted internationally and, thus, *interlingually*. This is where translation comes in, which will be discussed in the following section.

LEGAL TRANSLATION

The earliest examples of translation in history are those of legal documents, some of which go back to the very dawn of world civilization. As mentioned above, one of the peculiarities of legal language as a special-purpose language or jargon is the fact that it is aimed at a wide range of target audiences, ranging from individuals, to commercial entities and states. The same is true in many cases for translations of legal documents.

Another factor that distinguishes legal translation from other types of technical translation, such as medical translation, is the fact that it is *system-specific*; in other words, it is linked to a particular legal system, rather than being knowledge-based like, for instance, the sciences. However, irrespective of systemic and cultural specificities, one may observe a number of common features in most legal texts. When it comes to legal translation, the concept of faithfulness to the source text is often mentioned as the prevailing consideration, sometimes to the extent of what would, in general or literary translation, be called 'literality', which sometimes extends to copying both repetition and length of sentences. This view is rooted in a number of arguments that have gained currency:

- 'the letter of the law' supersedes all else and leaves no room for interpretation or ambiguity;
- legal language is marked by its emphasis on linguistic precision, which much be rendered in the target language as much as possible;
- the punitive nature of many types of legal texts, with any deviation from the *letter* of the source text being perceived as a deviation, i.e. reinterpretation, of the *meaning*.

Many of these arguments are not as robust as one might think. For instance, one may argue whether translation is not always interpretation, whereas ambiguity is sometimes intentional in legal texts and should, therefore, be maintained in translation! In regard to the second point, can any text be reduced to linguistic precision, which seemingly excludes attention to what this precision conveys, namely *meaning*? Finally, why should the possible implication of a translation necessarily have a bearing on how the meaning is to be rendered in the target language? This is linked to the principle of 'equivalent effect', as the translator not only needs 'to understand [...] what the words mean and what a sentence means, but also what legal effect it is supposed to have, and how to achieve that legal effect in the other language'.[132]

On the other end of the spectrum, one finds the view that the priority of the translator should be 'fidelity to the uniform intent of the single instrument, i.e. what the legislator or negotiators intended to say'. It is, however, important to add to this statement 'and in the *way* they customarily say it'!

As a rule, technical translation – and legal translation is no exception – requires the translator to be familiar with the field; when dealing with the law this in many cases implies a knowledge of several often very different systems. This does not mean that one has to be a lawyer in order to be a legal translator (though it does help!), but that the translator should be fully conversant with the way the law works in both source and target language communities. As mentioned above, this is one of the features that sets legal translation apart from other types of technical translation, where generally the field of knowledge is identical in both source and target languages. For instance, unless one is talking from a historical point of view, there is no such thing as 'French chemistry', 'German chemistry' or 'Arab chemistry'; there is, simply, 'chemistry'.

This situation is exacerbated by the second challenge to the legal translator, namely the above-mentioned interdisciplinarity of law in that it governs all fields of human society and activity. It stands to reason that in order for legal translators to acquit themselves of the task effectively, they should be familiar with the areas of knowledge that form the object of the documents that they are required to translate.

Consider, for instance, the following excerpt from a contract:

Intangible drilling costs and all **operating expenses**, including those accumulated prior to the commencement of **commercial production**, shall be recoverable in the **fiscal year** in which they were incurred.	تكاليف الحفر غير الملموسة وكافة مصروفات التشغيل بما في ذلك ما تراكم منها قبل بدء الإنتاج، تسترد ابتداء من السنة الضريبية التي أنفقت فيها هذه التكاليف والمصروفات.
Capital expenditures for **exploration** shall be recoverable at the rate of twenty (20) per cent per annum based on **amortization** at that **rate**.	النفقات الرأسمالية لعمليات تسترد بمعدل عشرين (20) في المائة في السنة على أساس استهلاكها بهذا المعدل.

The terms in bold are technical terms from the field of business and finance, rather than legal terms. In fact, one could argue that the only recognizably 'legal' aspects of the above passage are the syntactic complexity (see below) and repetition – or parallelism, to be more exact in this case – that are usually associated with texts of a legal nature.

In addition to the in-text terminology, it is also very common for corporate contracts to have technical specifications, drawings, blueprints, etc. appended to them, the translation of which also usually falls upon the legal translator.

'Translating' legal systems

As mentioned above, unlike most other technical languages, law is a system- and culture-specific idiom, which greatly complicates the task of the legal translator.[133] As a result of the different developments in different cultural, social and historical contexts, the language of the law varies, to a lesser or greater degree, across different systems. Depending on the sources and the subdivisions adhered to, specialists traditionally distinguish between five or eight groupings of legal systems, which include religion-based laws such as Islamic and Hindu Law.[134]

The two main legal systems in use today are Common Law (or Case Law) and Civil Law (or Statutory Law). To put it in simple terms, in Common Law systems, laws are developed by judges, whereas Civil Law relies on codified laws sourced from a Constitution and statutes passed by a central law-making body such as a Parliament. Historically, Civil Law is firmly rooted in Roman law, and is the system used in most Continental European countries. Common Law originated in England and remains largely associated with English-speaking countries such as the United States, Canada, Ireland, South Africa, New Zealand and Australia. As mentioned before, legal systems are the result of historical and cultural factors and traditions, and a common underlying heritage does not prevent substantive differences between various countries, as a result of separate developments and mixtures with other legal traditions. Consequently, the picture that emerges is indeed quite confusing at times.

However, this is only part of the story, which can become very confusing at times. For a start, it is important to add that there is no such thing as 'British' law, just as there is no such thing as 'American' or 'US' law; Scotland has its own unique legal system, while the legislation in the USA is split into Federal (= national) Law and State Law, i.e. the legislation that is applied and made in each individual state. While US Federal Law is an example of Common Law, a state like Louisiana is rooted in the civil law system as it was once a French territory (until 1803). For the same reason, the Canadian Province of Quebec has a (French) Civil Law substrate, which one does not find in British Columbia, for instance.

The law is also a *living* being and many areas of it are constantly being amended and updated to meet changing conditions, whether they be social, criminal or constitutional. For instance, state law in Arizona or New Mexico, which are contiguous to Mexico and have large immigrant populations, is gradually being added with features one would associate more with Civil Law. The distinctly Civil Law linguistic features of European Union legislation also go back to the fact that the founding nations of this body were Civil Law Countries, such as France, Belgium and Luxembourg.

Similarly the fact that countries such as Algeria, Morocco, Syria and Tunisia have Civil Law (alongside Islamic Law) is obviously due to the past French influence during the colonial era, while Oman's close ties with the UK have resulted in a legal system rooted in English Common Law.

These differences are highly significant for the translator as each system 'has a vocabulary to express concepts, its rules are arranged into categories, it has techniques for expressing rules and interpreting them'.[135] The more the legal systems differ, the greater the problem. This is further exacerbated by the degree of cultural difference, though it is perhaps somewhat of an exaggeration to say that 'the symbolic and connotational meanings of cultural-specific [sic] legal concepts cannot be translated and thus tend to remain a mystery even when extensive explanations are used.'[136]

Despite the differences between common and civil law systems, they nevertheless share a number of basic concepts that aid translators in their activity. The same cannot be said when one translates concepts from religious law, such as Islamic (or Shariah) Law (شريعة), which is applied in all Arab countries alongside a 'secular' code of law – usually Civil or Common – or, as is the case in Saudi Arabia, for instance, as the sole source of law. The primary sources of Islamic law are the Qur'an and the *Sunnah* – the Prophet Muhammad's words and actions, as reflected, for instance, in the canonical Hadith (sayings of the Prophet) literature. These are supplemented by precepts resulting from consensus among Muslim legal scholars (إجْماع, *ijma'*) and analogical reasoning, known as قِياس (*qiyas*), in which injunctions contained in the Hadith are compared with what is found in the Qur'an with a view to responding to new problems.

The linguistic consequences of the plurisystemic nature of legal translation are situated at two main levels, that is, system-bound terminology and style. The main terminological problems are most prevalent in the following areas, which also apply to Arabic–English legal translation, as the examples indicate:[137]

- words associated with the legal profession: e.g. solicitor, القاضي;
- words associated with courts and their hierarchy: e.g. High Court, tribunal, مَحْكَمة شَرْعية;
- words associated with areas of Law and institutions: e.g. *law of obligation* (Civil Law), *equity* (Common Law), اِجْتِهاد (Islamic Law).

As regards style, there are also significant differences between the various systems in certain areas of law, such as court decisions. The fact that Common Law relies on case law and precedence, means that legal opinions and judgements are generally much longer than in Civil Law since the former needs to refer in detail to past cases to arrive at a rule in the case at hand (good examples for the UK can be found at www.

hmcourts-service.gov.uk/cms/judgments.htm). When it comes to legislation, systems also differ dramatically, with Civil Law statutes stating principles in broad terms, as opposed to the detail and definitions found in Common Law.[138] This may be shown by the following examples:

UK

'BE IT ENACTED by the Queen's [King's] most Excellent Majesty, by and with the advice and consent of the Lords Spiritual and Temporal, and Commons, in this present Parliament assembled, and by the authority of the same, as follows:-'

USA

'Be it enacted by the Senate and House of Representatives of the United States of America in Congress assembled,'

Canada

'Her Majesty, by and with the advice and consent of the Senate and House of Commons of Canada, enacts as follows'

Egypt

Law No 73 of 1956	قانون رقم 73 لسنة 1956 بتنظيم مباشرة الحقوق السياسية وتعديلاته
In the name of the Nation	باسم الأمة
The Council of Ministers	مجلس الوزراء
Having reviewed the constitutional declaration issued on the 10th of February 1953; And in view of the decision issued on the 17th of November 1954 granting the Council of Ministers the powers of the President of the Republic;	بعد الاطلاع على الإعلان الدستورى الصادر فى 10 من فبراير سنة 1953؛ وعلى القرار الصادر فى 17 من نوفمبر سنة 1954 بتخويل مجلس الوزراء سلطات رئيس الجمهورية؛
And having reviewed Decree no. 148 of 1935 pursuant to elections, and the laws amending it; And based on what has been believed by the State Council; And what has been presented by the Minister of the Interior;	وعلى المرسوم بقانون رقم 148 لسنة 1935 الخاص بالانتخاب والقوانين المعدلة له؛ وعلى ما ارتآه مجلس الدولة؛ وبناء على ما عرضه وزير الداخلية؛
Has issued the following law:	أصدر القانون الآتى:

Oman

We, Qaboos Bin Said, Sultan of Oman,	**نحن قابوس بن سعيد - سلطان عمان،**
After perusal of the State Basic Law promulgated by the Royal Decree No.101/96,	بعد الإطلاع على النظام الأساسي للدولة الصادر بالمرسوم السلطاني رقم 101/96
And the Labour Law issued by the Royal Decree No. 34/73 and amendments thereof,	وعلى قانون العمل الصادر بالمرسوم السلطاني رقم 34/73 وتعديلاته،
And in accordance with the public interest,	وبناء على ما تقتضيه المصلحة العامة.
-Have Decreed as Follows-	رسمنا بما هو آت

Bahrain

Legislative decree no.19 of the year 2001 with respect to promulagating the civil code	**القانون المدني** **مرسوم بقانون رقم (19) لسنة 2001 بإصدار القانون المدني**
We, Hamad bin Isa Al Khalifa, Amir of the State of Bahrain	نحن حمد بن عيسى آل خليفة أمير دولة البحرين.
Having reviewed the Constitution, And Amiri Order No.(4) of 1975, And Proclamation No.(46) of 1374 Hijra with respect to the Legally Prescribed Period for Hearing Law suits in the Law Courts, Commercial Transactions and Pearl Divers Debts, And the Contract Law of 1969, And the Civil Wrongs Ordinance of 1970, And the Civil and Commercial Procedures Act promulgated by Legislative Decree No.(12) of 1971, as amended, And the Land Registration Law promulgated by Legislative Decree No.(15) of 1979, And the Law of Custody of Funds Promulgated by Legislative Decree No.(7) of 1986, And Legislative Decree No.(8) of 1987	بعد الإطلاع على الدستور، وعلى الأمر الأميري رقم (4) لسنة 1975، وعلى الإعلان رقم (46) لسنة 1374 هـ بشأن المدة القانونية لسماع الدعاوى في المحاكم والمعاملات التجارية، ودين الغواصين، وعلى قانون العقود لسنة 1969، وعلى قانون المخالفات المدنية لسنة 1970، وعلى قانون المرافعات المدنية والتجارية الصادر بالمرسوم بقانون رقم (12) لسنة 1971 والقوانين المعدلة له، وعلى قانون التسجيل العقاري الصادر بالمرسوم بقانون رقم (15) لسنة 1979، وعلى قانون الولاية على المال الصادر بالمرسوم بقانون رقم (7) لسنة 1986،

Governing the Ownership of Storeys and Flats, And the Law of Evidence in Civil and Commercial Matters promulgated by Legislative Decree No.(14) of the Year 1996, And upon the submission of the Minister of Justice and Islamic Affairs, And having sought the opinion of the Consultative Council, And with the approval of the Council of Ministers,	وعلى المرسوم بقانون رقم (8) لسنة 1987 بتنظيم ملكيات الطبقات والشقق، وعلى قانون الإثبات في المواد المدنية والتجارية الصادر بالمرسوم بقانون رقم (14) لسنة 1996، وبناء على عرض وزير العدل والشئون الإسلامية، وبعد أخذ رأي مجلس الشورى، وبعد موافقة مجلس الوزراء،
Hereby Enact the Following Law:	رسمنا بالقانون الآتي:

When translating between Arabic and English, another language-specific issue rears its head. While English legal style is concise and precise, Arabic legal style is often not devoid of literary flourishes and high-flown prose. One good example of this is the preamble to a number of constitutions of Arab countries, like this one of Egypt:

We, the people of Egypt, who have been toiling on this great land since the dawn of history and the beginning of civilisation;	نحن جماهير شعب مصر العامل على هذه الأرض المجيدة منذ فجر التاريخ والحضارة
We, the people working in Egypt's villages, cities, plants, centres of education, industry and in any field of work which contributes to create life on its soil or which plays a part in the honour of defending this land;	نحن جماهير هذا الشعب فى قرى مصر وحقولها ومدنها ومصانعها ومواطن العمل والعلم فيها، وفى كل موقع يشارك فى صنع الحياة على ترابها أو يشارك فى شرف الدفاع عن هذا التراب
We, the people who believe in our immortal and spiritual heritage, and who are confident in our profound faith, and cherish the honour of man and of humanity; We, the people, who in addition to shouldering the trust of history, carry the responsibility of great present and future objectives whose seeds are embedded in the long and arduous struggle, and which hosted the flags of freedom, socialism and unity along the path of the great march of the Arab nation;	نحن جماهير هذا الشعب الذى يحمل إلى جانب أمانة التاريخ مسئولية أهداف عظيمة للحاضر والمستقبل، بذورها النضال الطويل والشاق، الذى ارتفعت معه على المسيرة العظمى للأمة العربية رايات الحرية والاشتراكية والوحدة

We, the Egyptian people, in the name of God and by His assistance, pledge indefinitely and unconditionally to exert every effort to realise:

نحن جماهير شعب مصر؛ باسم الله وبعون الله نلتزم إلى غير ما حد، وبدون قيد أو شرط أن نبذل كل الجهود لنحقق:

1. Peace to our world

Being determined that peace should be based on justice, and that the political and social progress of all peoples can only be realised through the freedom of these peoples and their independent will, and that any civilisation is not worthy of its name unless it is free from exploitation whatever its form.

(أولا) السلام لعالمنا:

عن تصميم بأن السلام لا يقوم إلا على العدل وبأن التقدم السياسى والاجتماعى لكل الشعوب لا يمكن أن يجرى أو يتم إلا بحرية هذه الشعوب وبإرادتها المستقلة، وبأن أى حضارة لا يمكن أن تستحق اسما إلا مبراة من نظام الاستغلال مهما كانت صوره وألوانه.

2. Union

The hope of our Arab Nation, being convinced that Arab Unity is a call of history and of the future, and a demand of destiny; and that it cannot materialise except through an Arab Nation, capable of warding off any threat, whatever the source or the pretexts for such a threat.

(ثانيا) الوحدة:

أم أمتنا العربية عن يقين بأن الوحدة العربية نداء تاريخ ودعوة مستقبل وضرورة مصير وأنها لا يمكن أن تتحقق إلا فى حماية أمة عربية قادرة على دفع وردع أى تهديد مهما كان مصدره ومهما كانت الدعاوى التى تسانده.

3. The constant development of life in our nation

Being convinced that the true challenge confronting nations is the realization of progress and that such progress does not occur automatically, or through slogans; but that the driving force behind it is the release of the potentials of creativity and inspiration in our people, who have asserted at all times their contribution to civilization and to humanity through work alone.

(ثالثا) التطوير المستمر للحياة فى وطننا:

عن إيمان بأن التحدى الحقيقى الذى تواجهه الأوطان هو تحقيق التقدم، والتقدم لا يحدث تلقائيا أو بمجرد الوقوف عند إطلاق الشعارات، وإنما القوة الدافعة لهذا التقدم فى إطلاق جميع الامكانيات والملكات الخلاقة والمبدعة لشعبنا الذى سجل فى كل العصور إسهامه عن طريق العمل وحده فى أداء دوره الحضارى لنفسه والإنسانية.

Our people have passed through successive experiences, meantime offering rich experiences on the national and international level and being guided by them, which ultimately took shape in the July 23 Revolution of 1952. This Revolution was brought about by the alliance of the working forces of our militant people who were able, through profound and

لقد خاض شعبنا تجربة تلو أخرى، وقدم أثناء واسترشد خلال ذلك بتجارب غنية، وطنية وقومية وعالمية، عبرت عن نفسها فى نهاية مطاف طويل بالوثائق الأساسية لثورة 23 يوليو سنة 1952 التى قادها تحالف القوى العاملة فى شعبنا المناضل، والذى استطاع بوعيه العميق وحسه المرهف، أن يحافظ على جوهرها الأصيل، وأن يصحح دواما وباستمرار

refined consciousness, to retain their original character, but at the same time move forward in a bid to realise full integration between science and faith, between political and social freedom, between national independence and social affiliation; and to participate in the worldwide struggle for the liberation of man, on the political, economic, cultural and ideological levels, and in the struggle against the forces of regression, domination and exploitation.	مسارها وأن يحقق بها تكاملا يصل إلى حد الوحدة الكلية بين العلم والإيمان وبين الحرية السياسية والحرية الاجتماعية وبين الاستقلال الوطنى والإنتماء القومى وبين عالمية الكفاح الإنسانى من أجل تحرير الإنسان سياسة واقتصادا وثقافة وفكرا والحرب ضد كل قوى ورواسب التخلف والسيطرة والاستغلال.
4. Freedom for the humanity of the Egyptian man	**:(رابعا) الحرية لإنسانية المصرى**
Realising that man's humanity and dignity are the lights which guide and direct the course of the great development of mankind for the realisation of its supreme ideal.	عن إدراك لحقيقة أن إنسانية الإنسان وعزته هي الشعاع الذى هدى ووجه خط سير التطور الهائل الذى قطعته البشرية نحو مثلها الأعلى.
Man's dignity is a natural reflection of the nation's dignity, now that the individual is the cornerstone in the edifice of the homeland, the land that derives its strength and prestige from the value of man and his education.	أن كرامة الفرد انعكاس لكرامة الوطن، وذلك أن الفرد هو حجر الأساس فى بناء الوطن وبقيمة الفرد وبعمله وبكرامته تكون مكانة الوطن وقوته وهيبته.
The sovereignty of law is not only a guarantee for the freedom of the individual alone, but is also at the same time the sole basis for the legality of authority.	أن سيادة القانون ليست ضمانا مطلوبا لحرية الفرد فحسب، لكنها الأساس الوحيد لمشروعية السلطة فى نفس الوقت.
The alliance of the active popular powers is not a means for social strife leading towards historical development. In this modern age, it is a safety valve, protecting the unity of working powers in the country and eliminating, through democracy, contradictions.	أن صيغة تحالف قوى الشعب العاملة ليست سبيلا للصراع الاجتماعى نحو التطور التاريخي، ولكنها فى هذا العصر الحديث ومناخه ووسائله صمام أمان يصون وحدة القوى العاملة فى الوطن، ويحقق إزالة المتناقضات فيما بينها فى التفاعل الديمقراطي.
We, the people of Egypt, out of determination, confidence	نحن جماهير شعب مصر تصميما ويقينا وإيمانا وإدراكا بكل مسئولياتنا الوطنية

and faith in all national and international responsibilities, and in acknowledgment of God's right and His Heavenly Messages, and in the right of the country and nation, as well as of the principle and responsibility of mankind, and in the name of the Almighty and His assistance, declare on the 11th of September, 1971 that we accept, and grant, to ourselves this Constitution, affirming our determination to defend and protect it, and asserting our respect for it in letter and spirit.

والقومية والدولية وعرفانا بحق الله ورسالاته وبحق الوطن والأمة وبحق المبدأ والمسئولية الإنسانية وباسم الله وبعون الله، نعلن فى هذا اليوم الحادى عشر من شهر سبتمبر سنة 1971، أننا نقبل ونمنح لأنفسنا هذا الدستور، مؤكدين عزمنا الأكيد على الدفاع عنه وعلى حمايته وعلى تأكيد احترامه.

(Source: www.egypt.gov.eg/english/laws/constitution/default. aspx)

The above text may be compared to those of the USA and Australia, which offer two examples of Common Law legislative prose (Arabic translations are included in the Appendix at the end of this chapter):

We the People of the United States, in Order to form a more perfect Union, establish Justice, insure domestic Tranquility, provide for the common defence, promote the general Welfare, and secure the Blessings of Liberty to ourselves and our Posterity, do ordain and establish this Constitution for the United States of America.

An Act to constitute the Commonwealth of Australia

[9th July 1900]

Whereas the people of New South Wales, Victoria, South Australia, Queensland, and Tasmania, humbly relying on the blessing of Almighty God, have agreed to unite in one indissoluble Federal Commonwealth under the Crown of the United Kingdom of Great Britain and Ireland, and under the Constitution hereby established:

And whereas it is expedient to provide for the admission into the Commonwealth of other Australasian Colonies and possessions of the Queen:

Be it therefore enacted by the Queen's most Excellent Majesty, by and with the advice and consent of the Lords Spiritual and Temporal, and Commons, in this present Parliament assembled, and by the authority of the same, as follows:-

1 This Act may be cited as the Commonwealth of Australia Constitution Act.
2 The provisions of this Act referring to the Queen shall extend to Her Majesty's

3 It shall be lawful for the Queen, with the advice of the Privy Council, to declare by proclamation that, on and after a day therein appointed, not being later that one year after the passing of this Act, the people of New South Wales, Victoria, South Australia, Queensland and Tasmania, and also, if Her Majesty is satisfied that the people of Western Australia have agreed thereto, of Western Australia, shall be united in a Federal Commonwealth under the name of the Commonwealth of Australia. But the Queen may, at any time after the proclamation, appoint a Governor-General for the Commonwealth.

4 The Commonwealth shall be established, and the Constitution of the Commonwealth shall take effect, on and after the day so appointed. But the Parliaments of the several colonies may at any time after the passing of this Act make any such laws, to come into operation on the day so appointed, as they might have made of the Constitution had taken effect at the passing of this Act.

5 This Act, and all laws made by the Parliament of the Commonwealth under the Constitution, shall be binding on the courts, judges, and people of every State and of every part of the Commonwealth, notwithstanding anything in the laws of any State; and the laws of the Commonwealth shall be in force on all British ships, the Queen's ships of war excepted, whose first port of clearance and whose port of destination are in the Commonwealth.

6 'The Commonwealth' shall mean the Commonwealth of Australia as established under this Act.

'The States' shall mean such of the colonies of New South Wales, New Zealand, Queensland, Tasmania, Victoria, Western Australia, and South Australia, including the northern territory of South Australia, as for the time being are parts of the Commonwealth, and such colonies or territories as may be admitted into or established by the Commonwealth as States; and each of such parts of the Commonwealth shall be called 'a State'.

'Original States' shall mean such States as are parts of the Commonwealth at its establishment.

7 The Federal Council of Australasia Act, 1885, is hereby repealed, but so as not to affect any laws passed by the Federal Council of Australasia and in force at the establishment of the Commonwealth.

Any such law may be repealed as to any State by the Parliament of the Commonwealth, or as to any colony not being a State by the Parliament thereof.

8 After the passing of this Act the Colonial Boundaries Act, 1895, shall not apply to any colony which becomes a State of the Commonwealth; but the Commonwealth shall be taken to be a self-governing colony for the purposes of that Act.

9 The Constitution of the Commonwealth shall be as follows:-

Intra-system differences

The legal translator's task is made even more challenging by the already-mentioned differences that occur even within a given system, resulting in often dramatically varying terminologies relating to the legal profession, courts and areas of law.

A typical example for the first is the use in the UK and USA of *lawyer*, *attorney*, *solicitor*, *barrister*, *advocate* and *counselor* and *counsel*, all of which may be rendered into Arabic by مُحام. Does that mean that they are synonyms? Of course not! While *lawyer* and *attorney* (*at law*) are synonyms in the USA, only the former is used in the UK in this sense, as *attorney* in British usage only refers to someone acting on someone else's behalf, and is short for *attorney-in-fact* (وَكِيل), as in *power of attorney* (سَنَد التَّوْكِيل).

The distinction applied in the UK and Australia between *solicitor* and *barrister* is unknown in the USA, as are the terms, while Scotland's generic term is *advocate*. Finally, *counsel* occurs in the phrase *Queen's Counsel*, which denotes a senior barrister, with *counselor* being synonymous with *lawyer*, especially used in the USA. For Arabic, one may cite the example of the عَدْل (pl. عُدُول), which is only used in Morocco, Algeria and Tunisia, and refers to a *qāḍī*'s assistant, often performing what in Continental Europe are duties performed by a notary public (كاتِب عَدْل).

The terminology relating to the courts as well their hierarchical structure is equally diverse within individual systems, as Table 3.1 demonstrates:

Table 3.1 Overview of court systems in the English-speaking world

Canada	*New Zealand*	*England and Wales*	*Scotland*	*Northern Ireland*	*Irish Republic*	*USA*
Supreme Court	High Court	Supreme Court	Supreme Court	Supreme Court	Supreme Court	Supreme Court
Federal Court of Appeal	Court of Appeal	Court of Appeal	Court of Session	Court of Appeal	Court of Criminal Appeal	State Supreme Courts
Federal Court	District Court	High Court (of Justice)	High Court of Justiciary	High Court	High Court	District Court
Provincial/ Territorial Court	Family Court	Crown Court	Sheriff Court	Crown court	Circuit Court	County Court
	Youth Court	Magistrates' Court	District Court	County court	District Court	
		Family Proceedings Courts	Justice of the Peace Courts	Subordinate court		
		Youth courts				
		County Courts				

Equally relevant to legal translation is the converse to what has been explained above; identical terminology either within or across systems does not imply synonymy as the same term may, and often is, used to denote different concepts. In many cases the legal translator must think in terms of *equivalence* rather than mere *lexical* translation since the latter will add to the confusion.

For instance, the New Zealand *High Court* is equivalent to the US or UK *Supreme Court*, while *District Court* has different meanings in the Irish Republic, the USA and

Scotland. This situation poses significant problems to specialized lexicographers, as the following entries from *Faruqi's Law Dictionary* show:

> Supreme Court: محكمة عليا، محكمة تمييز، محكمة نقض وإبرام
> High Court: محكمة العدل العليا
> Court of Appeals: محكمة الاستئناف، محكمة المراجعات
> District Courts: محاكم محلية ذات اختصاص مكاني يقتصر على المنطقة التابعة لها
> Justice of the Peace Courts: محاكم جزئية غير تدوينية

It is difficult to see how the last two, in particular, are of use to translators who would raise more than a few eyebrows in their readership if they rendered the rather circuitous and overgeneralized paraphrases, 'local courts, with special competence limited to the area over which they have Jurisdiction' and 'summary courts, not of record', respectively.

Similarly, Arab countries have developed their own court systems, with their own terminologies and/or specific meanings, as Table 3.2 shows. The translations, which are the ones officially used by the countries concerned, also reveal another interesting feature, betraying the Civil Law origins, i.e. the use of such French calques like *Court of Cassation* and *Court of First Instance.* Neither of these is part of the British or American legal English, except when referring to Continental European bodies. But even here, the pitfalls are many and dangerous; in European Union law, the *Court of First Instance* is, in fact, a Court of Appeal (from decisions of the European Commission).

This diversity is mirrored by an equally large array of terms for legislative bodies in Arab countries, each of which has its own recognized translation, which does not necessarily correspond to the same source language term in another country, nor, of course, does an identical Arabic term imply that the legal body functions in the same way! The following is an overview of the names for legislative bodies in the Arab world:

Country	*Official Translation*	*Arabic Term*
Algeria	National People's Assembly	المَجْلِس الشَّعْبِيّ الوَطَنِيّ
Kuwait	National Assembly	مَجْلِس الأُمَّة
Bahrain	Council of Representatives	
Iraq		
Jordan		
Morocco	House of Representatives	
Yemen		مُجْلِس النُّواب
Lebanon	National Assembly	
Tunisia	Chamber of Deputies	
Libya	General People's Congress	
Egypt	People's Assembly	
Syria	People's Assembly	مَجْلِس الشَّعْب

Sudan	National Assembly	المَجْلِس الوَطَنِيّ
Sudan	Council of States	مَجْلِس الوِلايات
UAE	Federal National Council	المَجْلِس الوَطَنِيّ الاِتِّحادي
Palestine	Legislative Council	المَجْلِس التَّشْرِيعِيّ الفَلَسْطِينِيّ
Algeria	Shura Council	
Egypt	Advisory Council	
Qatar		
Oman		مَجْلِس الشُّورَى
Saudi Arabia	Consultative Council	
Yemen		
Jordan	Senate	مَجْلِس الأَعْيان
Morocco	Assembly of Councillors	مَجْلِس المُسْتَشارِين
Tunisia	Chamber of Councillors	
Oman	State Council	مَجْلِس الدَّوْلة

Legal style, too, may vary within the same legal system, with different genres of documents being subject to their own specific styles. Applying this to the categories mentioned above, practice teaches us that *declarative*, *commissive* and *exhortatory* texts – which may be called *operative legal* documents[139] – have in common a very formulaic style, combined with a very rigid structure. The expository prose of *expressive* and *directive* text types, on the other hand, tends to be far less formulaic than the previous group.

Similarly, the influence of the spoken language should not be disregarded either, as many documents that have legal force reflect spoken language, typical examples being witness statements and affidavits.

All of the previous applies to both Arabic and English legal documents. The formatting and structure of legal documents will be discussed next.

LAYOUT AND PRESENTATION

In most cases, the layout of legal documents tends to be fixed, to some degree or another, depending on the type of document, with the above-mentioned operative documents, such as a will or birth certificate, being subject to much more precise predetermined guidelines than, for instance, contracts. Equally rigid in both structure and language are statutes. For instance, the above example of a UK Act of Parliament is identical in each case, with the short title of the act (with the Chapter number) preceding the full title of the Act and followed by the formula of enactment. An act is further divided hierarchically in Parts, Chapters, cross-headings and numbered sections (or paragraphs), as shown in Figure 3.4.

Table 3.2 Overview of the court systems in the Arab world

Country	مَحْكَمة الصُلْح	مَحْكَمة البِداية	مَحْكَمة إبْتِدائية	مَحْكَمة الدَّرَجة الأُولَى	مَحْكَمة الإسْتِئناف	مَحْكَمة التَّمْيِيز	مَحْكَمة التَّعْقِيب
Jordan	Magistrates' Court	Court of First Instance	–	–	Court of Appeal	Court of Cassation	–
Tunisia	–	–	Court of First Instance	–	Court of Appeal	–	Court of Cassation
Morocco	–	–	Court of First Instance	–	Court of Appeal	–	–
Egypt	–	–	Court of First Instance	–	Court of Appeal	–	–
Lebanon	–	–	–	Court of First Instance	Court of Appeal	Court of Cassation	–
Syria	–	–	Court of First Instance	–	Court of Appeal	–	–
Oman	–	–	Court of First Instance	–	Court of Appeal	–	–
Saudi Arabia	–	–	Court of First Instance	–	–	Court of Cassation	–
Kuwait	–	–	Court of First Instance	–	Court of Appeal	Court of Cassation	–
United Arab Emirates	–	–	Court of First Instance	–	Court of Appeal	Court of Cassation	–

مَحْكَمة النَّقْض	المَحْكَمة العُلْيا	المَحْكَمة الخاصّة للعَدْل	مَحْكَمة ناحِية	مَحْكَمة جُزْئِية	مَحْكَمة جَزائِية	مَحْكَمة الأُسْرة	مَحْكَمة شَرْعِية
–	–	–	–	–	–	–	Shariah Court
–	–	–	District Court	–	–	–	–
–	Supreme Court	Special Court of Justice	–	–	–	–	Shariah Court
Court of Cassation	–	–	–	Court of Limited Jurisdiction	–	Family Court	Shariah Court
–	–	–	–	–	Criminal Court	–	Shariah Court
Court of Cassation	–	–	–	–	–	–	Shariah Court
–	Supreme Court	–	–	–	–	–	Shariah Court
–	Supreme Court	–	–	–	–	–	Shariah Court
–	–	–	–	–	–	–	Shariah Court
–	–	–	–	–	–	–	Shariah Court

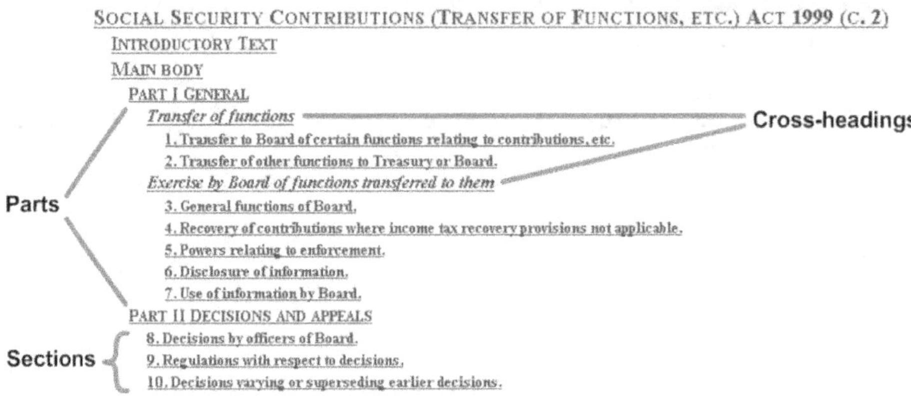

Figure 3.4 Hierarchical division of Acts (www.statutelaw.gov.uk/help/Main_Body_and_Schedules.htm)

However, depending on the country, there are some differences; for instance, Australian legislative texts apply a Chapter–Part–Division–Section hierarchy, whereas in the USA the terms 'Section' and 'Title' (see the example below) correspond to the English (UK) 'Part' and 'Chapter'.

Public Law 110–114
110th Congress

An Act

To provide for the conservation and development of water and related resources, to authorize the Secretary of the Army to construct various projects for improvements to rivers and harbors of the United States, and for other purposes.

Be it enacted by the Senate and House of Representatives of the United States of America in Congress assembled,

SECTION 1. SHORT TITLE; TABLE OF CONTENTS.

(a) SHORT TITLE.—This Act may be cited as the "Water Resources Development Act of 2007".

(b) TABLE OF CONTENTS.—The table of contents for this Act is as follows:

Sec. 1. Short title; table of contents.
Sec. 2. Definition of Secretary.

TITLE I—WATER RESOURCES PROJECTS

Sec. 1001. Project authorizations.
Sec. 1002. Small projects for flood damage reduction.
Sec. 1003. Small projects for emergency streambank protection.
Sec. 1004. Small projects for navigation.
Sec. 1005. Small projects for improvement of the quality of the environment.
Sec. 1006. Small projects for aquatic ecosystem restoration.

Sec. 1007. Small projects for shoreline protection.
Sec. 1008. Small projects for snagging and sediment removal.
Sec. 1009. Small projects to prevent or mitigate damage caused by navigation projects.
Sec. 1010. Small projects for aquatic plant control.

The situation in Arabic also differs between countries, as Table 3.3 makes clear.

Table 3.3 Differences in legal terminology across Arab countries

Translation/Equivalent	*Egypt*	*Morocco*	*Syria*	*Tunisia*
Preamble	مقدمة	توطئة	مقدمة	توطئة
Chapter/Part	باب	باب	باب	باب
Section/Chapter	فصل	قسم	فصل	فصل
Article	مادة	فصل	مادة	مادة
Paragraph	فقرة	فقرة	فقرة	فقرة
Clause/subsection	بَنْد	بَنْد	بَنْد	بَنْد

The question that arises is how format, presentation and layout should be 'translated', if at all? In other words, should the structure reflect target language guidelines and traditions, or comply with the ST layout? The degree of relevance of this aspect depends on a number of factors, such as text type (e.g. a contract vs a birth certificate) and function (e.g. sworn translation). With the advent of word processing software, and the ease with which layout can be manipulated to produce an exact copy of the source text, the prevailing school of thought is that both ST and TT should, as much as possible, be structured similarly. In the case of forms, certificates and the such, this also applies to font sizes and type (italics, bold), underlining, and so on.

In Arabic–English translation, script direction poses an interesting challenge in some cases, particularly in headings of forms, certificates, etc. As these are often clearly marked in the source text, some translators choose to leave them in their original place, presumably on the assumption that not doing so might confuse the reader since these parts of the document may be readily recognizable, such as text boxes, logos, etc. The current trend is to apply the direction rigidly, so that everything is in mirror image, so to speak, as shown in the following two examples of BA degree certificates, the first from a Libyan university, the second from one in the Yemen. Note the use of square brackets ([]) in order to make metatext such as signatures and official stamps stand out from the core information on the certificate.

Arabic and English have different ways of putting text into relief, due to typographical reasons. For instance, the fact that Arabic does not have capital letters is usually compensated by a change in font. The translator has to be wary, however, of transferring this into English, where the mixing of fonts is usually frowned upon. In the first sample text, for instance, the heading contains no fewer than three different fonts, as well as sizes, both of which are 'translated' by the same font, with hierarchy being marked by capitalization and/or bold. The use of bold, too, requires attention, particularly as Arabic tends to overuse it; in English, on the other hand, it is restricted to headings, titles, etc., or to signpost truly vital information.

الجماهيرية العربية الليبية الشعبية الاشتراكية العظمى

جامعة التحدي

سرت

إن الدراسة ليست غاية في حد ذاتها
وإنما الغاية هي خلق الإنسان النموذجي الجديد

التاريخ: ....
الموافق: ....
الرقم الإشاري: ....

إفادة تخرج

تفيد جامعة التحدي بأن الطالب/ المقيد بكلية الآداب والتربية قسم :/اللغة العربية تحت رقم قيد ( ) وبصفة قيد:/ نظامي قد أنهى جميع المقررات الدراسية اللازمة للحصول على الإجازة الجامعية الأولى (ليسانس) تخصص/ لغة عربية، بتقدير عام (ممتاز) للعام الجامعي 200 /200 إفرنجي.

<u>أعطيت له هذه الإفادة لاستعمالها فيما يخوله القانون</u>

مسجل كلية الآداب والتربية

أمين اللجنة الشعبية لكلية الآداب والتربية

مسجل عام الجامعة

Figure 3.5 Graduation certificate from Libya

Great Socialist People's Libyan Arab Jamahiriya

Education is not an aim in itself, but the aim of the new model citizen

Al-Tahadi University
Sirt

Date: ...
Corresponding to: ...
Reference No: ...

[STAMP: Great Republic
Al-Tahadi University]

GRADUATION CERTIFICATE

Al-Tahadi University hereby attests that the student .... is enrolled in the Faculty of Literature and Education, English Section, with the number ...., as a regular student, has completed all the necessary study requirements to be awarded the first University degree (*Licence*), with a major in Arabic, with the mention of 'Excellent' for the Academic Year 200./200.. A.D.

This certificate was provided to him to use pursuant to the law

[signature]

Registrar of the Faculty of Literature and Education

[signature]

Secretary of the People's Committee at the Faculty of Literature and Education

الجمهورية اليمنية
جامعة عمران
الرقم الجامعي: __/_200

بسم الله الرحمن الرحيم

شهادة تخرج

تشهد جامعة عمران – كلية __التربية والعلوم التطبيقية_ **بأن الطالب** ________ // ________
المولود في ________ **بتاريخ** __198 م__ **وجنسيته** __يمني

حاصل على درجة: بكالوريوس في التربية **تخصص** لغة إنجليزية //__

في دور: يونيـــو **عام** __200م (ألفين_وثمانية)_ميـلاديـــة//__________

بتقدير عام: جيد جداً مع مرتبة الشرف **وبمعدل:** (89%)______________

صدرت بتاريخ: ____/_/_200م______________________________

مسجل الكلية ______________ **عميد الكلية** ______________

المسجل العام ______________ **نائب رئيس الجامعة** ______________

Figure 3.6 Graduation certificate from Yemen

IN THE NAME OF ALLAH, THE COMPASSIONATE, THE MERCIFUL

THE REPUBLIC OF YEMEN [PHOTO STAMP: AMRAN UNIVERSITY – bottom half ILLEGIBLE]

AMRAN UNIVERSITY

UNIVERSITY No: .....

GRADUATION CERTIFICATE

Amran University, the Faculty of Education and Applied Sciences of Hajja

Certifies that the student: ....

Born in: ... on: ...

Of Yemeni nationality has been awarded the degree of **BACHELOR OF EDUCATION,**

Major: **ENGLISH**

in the June examination session of the year 200...

with the mention **'VERY GOOD'**, which corresponds to 89%

Date of issue: .../.../200.

FACULTY REGISTRAR DEAN OF THE FACULTY

[SIGNATURE] [SIGNATURE]

GENERAL REGISTRAR VICE-CHANCELLOR OF THE UNIVERSITY

[SIGNATURE] [SIGNATURE]

[STAMP: UNIVERSITY OF YEMEN AMRAN UNIVERSITY]

LEXIS AND TERMINOLOGY

Generally speaking, legal terminology refers to any term that is used in a legal context with a specific meaning, denoting legal concepts. Like all specialized terminology, the terms tend to be in a one-to-one relationship with the concept to which they refer. In other words, a legal concept is generally rendered by one term, and one term only. However, anyone working with legal terminology cannot fail to be struck by the frequent occurrences of **polysemy**, i.e. one word containing several distinct technical meanings.

Let us, by way of example, examine the meanings of the word 'law'. According to *Black's Law Dictionary*,

> Law, in its generic sense, is a body of rules of action or conduct prescribed by controlling authority, and having binding legal force. That which must be obeyed and followed by citizens subject to sanctions or legal consequences is a law. Law is a solemn expression of the will or the supreme power of the state.

Many of these elements can be found in *Faruqi's Law Dictionary*:

> أحكام مقننة تضعها وتصدرها السلطات التشريعية في البلاد لما ترى وجوب مراعاته.
> 'Fixed rules laid down and issued by the legislative bodies of a country when this is necessary for its citizenry.'
>
> مجموعة المبادىء والأسس والأنظمة والقواعد التي تطبقها مراجع القضاء في الدولة على ما يطرح أمامها من شؤون أو منازعات.
> 'The body of principles, rules and regulations that are applied by legal scholars in a country to matters or disputes that are brought before them.'

According to the *Oxford English Dictionary*, 'law' has the following meanings:

1 'A rule of conduct imposed by authority' or 'One of the individual rules which constitute the 'law' of a state or polity':

   e.g. 'There is no "**law**" that forbids the eating of meat.'
   لا يَتَواجِدُ أيٌّ **قانونٍ** ضِدَّ أكْلِ اللَّحْمِ.

2 'The body of rules, whether proceeding from formal enactment or from custom, which a particular state or community recognizes as binding on its members or subjects. (In this sense usually *the law*)':

   e.g. 'The **law** forbids torture under any circumstances.'
   يَمْنَعُ **القانون** التَّعْذِيبَ عَلَى الإطْلاق.

3 '(Usually *the law*.) The profession which is concerned with the exposition of the law, etc.', and 'with more or less of personification, an agent uttering or enforcing the rules of which it consists':

   e.g. 'The **law** was on the heels of the fugitive.'
   كانَت **الشُّرْطة** تتَعَقَّب الهارِب.

4 'One of the branches into which law, as an object of study or exposition, may be divided':

e.g. 'commercial **law**', **قانون تجاري**
'civil **law**', **قانون مدني**

5 'In the sciences of observation, a theoretical principle deduced from particular facts':

e.g. 'the **laws** of nature', **النَّوامِيس الطَّبِيعِيَّة**

In the above examples the Arabic word قانون (pl. قَوانِين) is the usual translation of the English 'law', except for the metaphorical uses in 3) and 5), with the former being rendered by 'police' (شُرْطة).

However, anyone looking up 'law' in an Arabic dictionary, will find any, or, if it is a good dictionary, all of the following:

قانُون, law (generic);
شَرْع, Islamic law;
الحُقُوق, law as an academic subject (NOTE: this is usually written with a capital in English: e.g. 'He studied Law in London');
نامُوس (pl. نَوامِيس), natural law;
مَرْسُوم (pl. مَراسِيم), decree, act, edict, regulation;
شَرِيعة, Islamic law;
تَشْرِيع, legislation;[140]
دُسْتُور, regulations, statutes, but also the most commonly used word for 'constitution';
ضابِط (pl. ضَوابِط), general moral rule.

The most striking thing in the list is, of course, the fact that a number of terms are specific to Islamic law, and should, therefore, never be used to refer to 'secular' law in any context. When it comes to the adjective 'lawful', the number of terms drops dramatically: only قانُونِيّ and شَرْعِيّ are used in the 'secular' sense, whereas the 'religious' term is حَلال, which, once again, should not be used in a non-religious context.

This lack of one-to-one translations poses serious problems to practitioners. Consider, for instance, the core terms in international legislation and their varied translations shown below:

English	*Example*	*Arabic*
	قَرار	
resolution	enabling resolution; Security Council resolution (UN)	قرار الإذْنِ/ – السَّماحِ؛ قرار مَجْلِسِ الأَمْنِ
award	arbitral award	قرار المُحَكَّمينَ؛ قرار التَّحْكِيم

adjudication	court adjudication	قرار المَحْكَمةِ
decision	judicial decision	قرار قَضائيٍّ
order	board order	قرار المَجْلِسِ
indictment	public indictment	قرار اِتِّهامٍ عَلَنِيٍّ
ruling	sanctions ruling	قرار تَطْبِيقِ جَزاءَات

لائحة

indictment	sealed indictment	لائحة اِتِّهامٍ سِرِّيَّةٍ
regulation	Council Regulations	لائحة المَجْلِسِ
bill	true bill	لائحة اِتِّهامٍ صَحِيحةٍ
rule	administrative rule	لائحة إدارِيَّةٌ

قاعدة

database (قاعدة البيانات)	United Nations Landmine Database	قاعدة بَياناتِ الأُمَمِ المُتَّحِدةِ للأَلْغامِ الأَرْضِيَّةِ
rule	substantive rule, legislative rule, gag rule	قاعدة مَوْضُوعِيَّةٌ، قاعدة آمِرةٌ
base	patrol and observation base, missile base	قاعدة الدَّوْرِياتِ وَالمُراقَبةِ; قاعدة دَوْرِيَّة وَمُراقَبَة / قاعدة قَذائفَ، قاعدة لإنْطلاقِ القَذائفَ
data	Interim Terrain Data	قاعدة البيانات المؤقتة للأراضي
norm	zero emission norm	قاعدة الإنْبِعاثِ المَعْدُومِ (الصِّفْرِيِّ) 0
regulation	Temporary Regulation	قاعدة مُؤَقَّتة
jus	*jus sanguinis*, *jus soli*	قاعدة حَقِّ الدَّمِ، قاعدة حَقِّ الأَرْضِ
lex	*lex specialis*	قاعدة التخصيص

مرسوم

decree	supreme/royal/emergency decree	مرسوم سامِي، مَلَكِيٌّ، طَوارِئ
ruling	Ruling on the General Amnesty	مرسوم العَفْوِ العامِّ

As stated above, dictionaries often offer little solace. Let us imagine the translator faced with the Arabic renderings of the English phrase *to comply with*:

1 أطاع
2 طاوَعَ
3 اِسْتِكانَ
4 اِمْتَثَلَ
5 ذَعِنَ
6 أَذْعَنَ
7 قَبِلَ
8 اِسْتِجابَ
9 راعى

For a start, no Arabic speaker would consider these words to be synonyms. For instance, no. 3 means 'to surrender, to yield to someone', and never occurs in the legal context of complying with a regulation, rule or law. When one adopts a 'back-translation' approach, i.e. looks up the above in *Hans Wehr's Arabic–English Dictionary*, one finds that only 1–2 and 8–9 have 'comply' as one of the translations.

That is not to say that the meanings of the others fall outside the semantic field of 'obeying' or 'submitting to', which are used in the entries of translations 4–5 and 7. Let us now imagine that our translator then encounters the phrase *in compliance with*; he or she will find that none of the above is actually applicable since this phrase is customarily translated by عَمَلاً ب!

We shall now take a closer look at the specific features of the legal lexicon, both in English and Arabic.

Features of English legal language[141]

The following are features that may be considered typical of English legalese, and they reveal the specific history of the legal system, which, in its formative period, was heavily infused with words coming from abroad.

Archaicisms

Old English and Middle English words that have fallen into disuse in general English are used: e.g. *aforesaid*, *heretofore*, *witnesseth*.

Foreign words

1 **Latin** words and phrases: the early Latin heritage can be traced back to a number of events in English history. The first was Julius Ceasar's invasion of Britain in 55 BC, which marked the beginning of Roman occupation that would last until AD 410. Two centuries later, Pope Gregory I sent Christian missionaries, who were trained in Latin. Finally, when in 1066 the (Norman) French invaded the British Isles, they brought with them a legal system that was founded on Roman law, and thus contained a lot of Latin terms. Examples of

Latin terms are: *mens rea* (نِية جَرمِيّة), *sub iudice* (أمام القاضي), *viva voce* (شَفَوِياً).

2 Old/Norman French: the Norman French invasion ushered in not only new political changes, but also, and more lastingly, a social as well as linguistic upheaval. The French of the new rulers quickly became the language of the elite, though English remained the language of the common people. Though by the end of the twelfth century some of the nobility were native English speakers, French continued to be used in Parliament, the courts and public proceedings. In fact, it would not be until 1362 that English would be used for the first time at the opening of Parliament! This explains the huge number of words of French origin in the English legal language. We can distinguish two types:

   a anglicised forms, i.e. those that have been 'naturalized' in the sense that their form and pronunciation no longer make them recognizably foreign: e.g. *crime* (جَرِيمة), *verdict* (قرار);
   b phrases and words that have retained their original French form: e.g. *sans frais* (دُونَ نَفَقة), *tort* (جَرِيرة شَخْصِية).

Binomial pairs/doublets

The use of two (or sometimes more) often synonymous words joined by the conjunction *and* – known as *binominal expressions* or *conjoined phrases*[142] or *doublets*, which we have already encountered in Chapter 1 – are very prominent in legal prose and add to its formulaic nature. All these sets serve as fixed expressions, legal idioms if you will, and as such there is no room for creativity on the part of the authors.

Below are some common examples and their Arabic translations, which are decidedly simpler, with the English multi-word item being consistently rendered by a single word in Arabic.

made and signed	تُحَرِّرُ
to have and to hold	يَمْلُكُ
by and between; between and among	بَيْنَ
true and correct	صَحِيح
goods and chattles	مَنْقُولاتٌ
ordered, adjudged, and decreed	يُقَرِّرُ
all and every	كُلٌّ
requisite and necessary	ضَرُورِيٌّ
part and parcel	جُزْءٌ لا يَتَجَزَّأ
last will and testament	وَصِيةٌ

terms and conditions	شُرُوط
bind and obligate	يُلْزِمُ
cancel, annul and set aside	يُلْغِي
give, devise and bequeath	يَهَبُ
free and clear	خالِي
null and void	خالِص
	باطِل
claims and demands	مُطالَباتٌ

While in the fixed phrases above the Arabic translator does not provide a word-for-word translation, the latter would be required in other cases, such as خالِص ومُطْلَق ('free and clear'). In the opposite direction, things are not straightforward either; when the English translator sees بين does he or she simply put 'between' or go with the technical 'by and between' or 'between and among'? Opinions sometimes vary on this, depending on whether or not one talks to proponents of 'plain English' in legal documents.

In practice, most documents reveal that translators make the sensible decision to comply with target language expectations of a particular style. This includes, for better or for worse, formulaic expressions, no matter how superfluous they are.

Polysemy

The concept of polysemy refers to a given word having multiple related meanings. For instance, the English word *bed* refers to something we sleep on, the bottom of a river or sea, and an area set aside for the growing of plants (*flowerbed*). There are many cases of polysemy in English legal language, which are of great importance to the translator since the same word in the overwhelming majority of cases is rendered in different ways, depending on its specific meaning in the context. For instance, *to seize* ('to grab') is used in the following legal senses:

1 'to impound' (goods): e.g.

> 'The customs official **seized** the goods that could not be exported.'
> قامَ الجُمْرُكِيُّ بِحَجْزِ البَضائعَ المَمْنُوعِ إسْتِيرادِها

2 'to arrest': e.g.

> 'The police **seized** the thief as he left the crime scene.'
> قَبَضَت الشُّرْطَةُ اللِصَّ عِنْدَ خُرُوجِهِ مِن مَوْقِعِ الجَريمةِ

3 'to be seized of': to reserve the right to reconsider a matter; with regard to the United Nations Security Council, it refers to the fact that no other organ of the United Nations may legally take up a matter, as under Article 12 of the UN Charter: e.g.

'[The Council] [d]ecides to remain seized of the matter.'
يُقَرِّرُ أَنْ يَبْقى المَسْأَلَةُ قَيْد نَظَرِهِ الفِعْلِيّ

Features of Arabic legal language

Islamic terms

Though every area of legal language contains cultural terms since the law is developed in a particular cultural context, there are certain areas that have a higher proportion than others. In Arabic legal terminology, the first that comes to mind is, of course, the vocabulary related to Islamic law, for which no ready equivalents may be available in English. Specialized Islamic legal terminology cuts across a number of areas: legal concepts, institutions, the legal profession, etc. The possible strategies open to the translator are:

- TL **equivalent**: e.g.

  طلاق بائن, 'irrevocable divorce'
  حُجَّة, 'certificate'
  مَهْر, 'dowry'

- **paraphrase** of the original, i.e. a so-called 'exegetic' translation in which the term is essentially explained: e.g.

  القاضي, 'Islamic Judge'
  عِدَّة, 'legally prescribed waiting period before marrying'
  ثَيِّب, 'deflowered woman'
  دُخُول, 'consummation of marriage'

- **borrowing** of the original term: e.g.

  فقيه, *faqih*
  رِباء, *riba'*
  حجاب, *hijab*
  وقف, *waqf*

That is not to say that the same option can be used at all times; indeed, the strategy to a large degree depends on the context, target readership (e.g. laymen versus scholars), and text type (e.g. an employment agreement vs marriage contract).

As a result, in some cases it is more appropriate to render حجاب as 'headscarf', or عدة as *idda*. For instance, the English version of a marriage contract between Muslims will contain more borrowed technical terms than a trading contract between companies.

Some of the terminology within Islamic law may also differ across Muslim regions, and even countries: for instance, religious endowments are known as وَقْف (pl. أَوْقاف) in the East, and as حَبْس (pl. حُبُوس) in North African countries.

Another salient feature of Arabic legal documents is the use of religious formulae such as the prefatory بسم الله الرحمن الرحيم, for which there are currently a number of competing translations:

> 'In the Name of God/Allah, the Compassionate the Merciful';
> 'In the Name of God/Allah, the Most Merciful, the Most Compassionate';
> 'In the Name of God/Allah, the Most Beneficent, the Most Merciful'.

In the past, this opening formula, which is uttered at the start of any activity in order to beg God's indulgence, tended not to be translated in general legal documents. Today, however, increasingly, one finds it included. In any event, it should not be excluded from certificates, forms, etc.

Titles

The use of titles, terms and references of address differs considerably between Arabic and English. The following guidelines may be given: when it involves non-technical documents, the aim should be to produce as natural a translation as possible into English, which means either toning down or even omitting titles, functions and hyperbolic salutation formulae.

For instance, in Arabic it is common to list several functions of personalities each time their name is mentioned and it would be anathema to simply mention a name without a title, as is common in English: e.g. 'Margaret Thatcher did not agree with the policy.' What makes legal translation special in this respect is that it is more literal than general translation, and titles should in many cases be retained and English equivalents provided, as shown in the following examples:

His Majesty, Sultan Qaboos bin Said [the Exalted, the Beloved – May God preserve, guard and protect him!] agreed with Saudi Arabia's new initiative.	اتفق عاهل البلاد جلالة السلطان قابوس بن سعيد المعظم المفدي – حفظه الله ورعاه – على المبادرة السعودية الجديدة.
Last night, His Majesty, King Abdallah [II], opened the Fifth International Conference on Royal Medical Services.	افتتح جلالة الملك عبد الله الثاني المؤتمر الدولي الخامس للخدمات الطبية الملكية.
The Custodian of the Two Holy Mosques, King Abdullah bin Abdulaziz Al Saud [May God protect him] chaired the Cabinet session.	رأس خادم الحرمين الشريفين الملك عبدالله بن عبد العزيز آل سعود –حفظه الله– الجلسة التي عقدها مجلس الوزراء.

[His Excellency] Shaykh Mohammad Bin Rashid Al Maktoum [May God guard and protect him!], the Emir of Dubai, Vice-President of the UAE and Prime Minister has issued a resolution regarding some consumer goods circulating in the United Arab Emirates.	أصدر صاحب السمو الشيخ محمد بن راشد آل مكتوم نائب رئيس الدولة رئيس مجلس الوزراء حاكم دبي، رعاه الله، قراراً بشأن بعض البضائع والمنتجات الاستهلاكية التي يتم تداولها في دولة الإمارات العربية المتحدة.

This issue is perhaps even more delicate when translating into Arabic as the translator has to take care to apply the reverse, and add the appropriate titles and formulae in order to comply with target culture readership expectations and ensure acceptance of the text.

Common features of Arabic and English legal language

Specialized terms/jargon

At the core of legal jargon are words and phrases that are peculiar to legalese. These include denominations for courts (e.g. *District Court*), the legal profession (e.g. *solicitor*, *barrister*), as well as expressions like *pursuant to* or terms denoting concepts such as *liability* (مَسْؤُلِية), or processes such as *to remand* (أعادَ الدَّعْوَى/المُدَّعَى عَلَيْه).

The importance of specialized terminology is borne out, for instance, by the following list of top twenty words drawn from the Leeds legal corpus (http://smlc09.leeds.ac.uk/query-ar.html), all of which are technical terms: المادة; القانون; المحكمة; المتهم القضاء; الدعوى; حقوق; قرار; الدستور; الجنائية; القضائية; النيابة; الحكم; الجرائم; التحقيق; الأمن; الشرطة; التعذيب; يجوز; السلطة.

Mention has already been made above of the intra-system and intra-lingual differences, which also affect Arabic: for instance, 'Graduation Certificate' is rendered in a variety of ways, depending on the country: إفادةُ التَّخَرُّج (Lybia), وَثِيقةُ التَّخَرُّج (Saudi Arabia), شهادةُ التَّخَرُّج (e.g. Tunisia, Oman), whereas ظاهِر ('decree, edict') is used only in Morocco.

Homonyms

A number of legal terms in both English and Arabic are words that are in general use, but with completely different meanings. This is an example of homonymy, which refers to words that have the same form, but completely unrelated meanings. These are, of course, of particular interest to the translator since they pose potential traps. Let us consider the following words, for instance.

Term	*General Meaning*	*Translation*	*Technical Meaning*	*Translation*
consideration	attention	إعْتِبار	amount of money	مَبْلَغ
brief	concise	مُوجَز	type of legal document	مذكرة بحيثيات القضية

instrument	tool	أداة	document	وَثِيقة
motion	movement	حركة	official request	طَلَب

Repetition

The discussion of binomial sets already demonstrated the propensity in legal language for repetition. But while these involved parallel pairs of near-synonyms, there is a general point to be made as well; whereas in non-technical, or non-specialized English of most types, repetition is frowned upon, it is the norm in legalese, primarily in order avoid any kind of ambiguity or confusion. So, for instance, each reference to 'the Company' will be made in exactly the same way, rather than through variants such as 'the Corporation', 'the Firm', or 'the Business', since these might, in theory, refer to other entities.

In practice, this means that, rather than using pronouns or synonyms, legal professionals will prefer to use the same word, lest it leave room for discussion or dispute. The use of repetition is not limited to these fixed expressions, but affects legal writing in general.

At the heart of this lies a concern to cover all contingencies since any omission, however small, may result in legal consequences such as altering liability. In legal language, nothing is taken for granted; there is no exclusion or inclusion by default, so to speak. For instance, the fact of stating that the agreement is about foodstuffs only does not preclude the lawyer from specifically stating that it *excludes* non-food, even if one should logically conclude this from the previous. This attention to extreme precision of expression also explains the use of such phrases like *including but not limited to*, or *shall not be deemed to limit*.

Let us consider the following examples from contracts:

Employer is responsible for the risks of war, hostilities, invasion, acts by foreign enemies, rebellion, revolution, military uprising, coups-d'état, toppling of the regime, civil war, riot, commotion or disorder, [...]	يتحمل صاحب العمل تبعات الحرب وأعمال العدائية والغزو وأعمال الأعداء الأجانب والتمرد والثورات وعصيان الجيش أو اغتصاب السلطة أو الحرب الأهلية أو الشغب أو الاضطراب السياسي أو الفوضى

Each Establishment shall be operated pursuant to a License Agreement between the Licensor and Licensee which shall be executed not less than ninety (90) days prior to the opening of the Establishment. The License Agreement for each Establishment shall be substantially in the form of the License Agreement attached as Schedule Four.	يتم تشغيل كل منشأة بموجب عقد ترخيص بين المرخص والمرخص له يجري في موعد أقصاه تسعون (90) يوماً قبل افتتاح المنشأة. ويكون عقد الترخيص الخاص بكل منشأة من الناحية الجوهرية في شكل عقد الترخيص المرفق في الملحق الرابع (4).

The first extract contains a large number of expressions which, in everyday English, would probably be rendered less exhaustively and reduced to a simple ‘war and civil unrest’. Indeed, what is the difference between ‘war’ and ‘hostilities, invasion, act by foreign enemies’? In the second passage, full noun phrases are translated at every occurrence, rather than just the head noun (e.g. ‘Agreement’) or reference (through pronouns).

Collocations

As discussed in Chapter 1, collocations may constitute a significant problem to translators, as their translation is not always straightforward. Whereas in some cases a collocation is rendered through a collocation in the target language, in others, it is rendered by a single verb: for instance, رَفَعَ الدَّعْوَى ضِدَّ ... أمامَ ... is translated as ‘to file a complaint against (someone) in (a court)’ or, simply, ‘to sue someone’. The choice of the colligates is rarely transparent and getting it wrong often has a dramatic impact on meaning, as shown by the examples below, which rely on occurrences from the BYU arabiCorpus (http://arabicorpus.byu.edu/) and the Leeds (legal) Arabic Corpus (http://smlc09.leeds.ac.uk/query-ar.html):

Example	*Preposition*		*Verb*
طَرَف ثالِث	ضِدَّ against (someone)		رَفَعَ (يَرْفَعُ)
محكمة بيروت	أمام before (a court)		
لُبْنان السنة الماضِية	في in (e.g. a country, district)	دَعْوَى to bring a lawsuit, to sue, to file/lodge a complaint	أقامَ
كُلّ من بريطانيا	على against		
ديوان المظالم بالرياض ضِدّ وزارة الثَّقافة	إلى to		
			اِرْتَكَبَ
الإنسانية	ضِدّ against		اِقْتَرَفَ
		جَرِيمة to commit, perpetrate, carry out a crime	أَدَّى
			اِجْتَرَمَ / أَجْرَمَ / جَرَمَ (يَجْرِمُ)
	إلى/ على against		
			جَنَى (يَجْنِي)

صحفي يمني	ضِدّ against	حُكْم	نَفَّذَ to execute
اثنين من المتهمين بالإعدام	عَلَى against		صادَقَ عَلَى to confirm, to ratify
المَسْأَلة	في in (e.g. a lawsuit, case)		صَدَرَ (يَصْدِرُ) to be promulgated, to be published
			أَبْرَمَ to confirm
			أَصْدَرَ to issue, to publish, to pronounce, to pass
			اِسْتِصْدَرَ to obtain, to cause to be pronounced
			أَلْغَى to rescind, to annul
			طَعَنَ (يَطْعَنُ) فِي to appeal against, to impeach
			طالَبَ to demand
			رَفَضَ (يَرْفِضُ) to reject

The traps for the translator are legion here; for instance, the fact that 'to carry out' collocates with 'crime' and is a translation of ارتكب, etc. does not mean that one can simply apply back-translation as the Arabic verbs for 'to carry out', such as, نَجَزَ (يَنْجُزُ) أَنْجَزَ or نفَّذ are not commonly found with 'crime'; rather, they tend to collocate with such words as مَشْرُوع ('project'), اِخْتِبار ('testing') and بَرْنامَج ('programme').

Recognized translations

Interlingual legal translation is an ever increasing field, concomitant with the unstoppable globalization that affects every human activity and science. International organizations and transnational agreements require multilingual documents. In addition, there is a trend towards the translation of even national laws by many countries in the Arab world, which reveals the level of contact and extent of dealings with countries and business entities outside the region.

One of the consequences of this 'localization' is the concomitant creation of precedent, with which subsequent translations then have to comply, even if the translation is not as sound as it could be. This complicates the work of the legal translator since the use of a given term or phrase may be determined less by semantics than by conventions of the specific target language context.

This does put the onus of background research onto the translator and establish whether there are any recognized translations in use in the target context. For instance, the Omani Ministry of Justice refers to itself as 'Ministry of Legal Affairs', which is a translation of وزارة الشؤون القانونية, while in most other Arab countries وزارة العدل is used. In official documents, the translator, whether in Arabic or English, must use the Omani term for the Ministry, just as وزارة الخارجية is to be translated, depending on the country, as 'Foreign Office' (UK), 'State Department' (USA) or 'Ministry of Foreign Affairs' (all others).

Recognized translations also affect more mundane documents such as certificates, which are often the 'bread and butter' of the full-time freelance translator. Once again, the 'translation by example' is important as failing to do so may result in the TT being rejected, for instance in the case of sworn translations.

In addition to a linguistic sensitivity, there are ideological or political motives that drive the need for a 'localized' version. Figures 3.7 and 3.8 show some examples of educational certificates from two different countries (Saudi Arabia and Palestine).

SYNTAX

It is a legal document that has the dubious honour of having the longest sentence recorded in an official document, running to an astounding 516 words, which rightly invoked the wrath of the 'Plain English Campaign' (www.plainenglish.co.uk/examples/long-sentences.html). And while sentence length is probably the most distinctive feature of legal language, there are many other syntactic features that are typical of legalese. Many of them can be found in the opening paragraph to UK Acts of Parliament.

> **An Act to amend the Weeds Act 1959 in relation to ragwort, and for connected purposes. [20th November 2003]**
>
> **BE IT ENACTED by the Queen's most Excellent Majesty, by and with the advice and consent of the Lords Spiritual and Temporal, and Commons, in this present Parliament assembled, and by the authority of the same, as follows:—**

In addition to the use of the **formulaic subjunctive** ('Be it enacted'), one observes subject-verb inversion, the use of lengthy sub-clauses, the postposition of adjectives (e.g. 'Lords Spiritual'), and the high incidence of the coordinating conjunction 'and' (e.g. the yoked binomial pair 'by and with the advice and consent of').

KINGDOM OF SAUDI ARABIA
Ministry of Higher Education
TAIBAH UNIVERSITY
Deanship of Admission and Registration

المملكة العربية السعودية
وزارة التعليم العالي
جامعة طيبة
عمادة القبول والتسجيل

Graduation Certificate وثيقة تخرج

Taibah University certifies that
[NAME]

تشهد جامعة طيبة
أن

رقم السجل (_ _ _ _ _)

Nationality SAUDI ARABIA — الجنسية السعودية

Was Awarded The BACHELOR — قد حصلت على درجة البكالريوس

In ENGLISH — من قسم اللغات والترجمة

From the faculty of EDUCATION AND HUMANITIES — كلية التربية والعلوم الإنسانية

With An Accumulative Grade Point Average 4.89 EXCELLENT — بمعدل 4.89 وتقدير عام امتياز

مع مرتبة الشرف الأولى

In the FALL *Semester / Year* 2005 – 2006 — في الفصل الدراسي الأول للعام الدراسي 1426هـ 1427هـ

The Degree is Approved by the University — تم منح الدرجة من مجلس الجامعة في الجلسة رقم الثانية لعام 1426هـ

Council on / /20 — بتاريخ: 1426/12/25 هـ

رقم الوثيقة:

Issue date / /20 — حررت في 1427/01/22 هـ

عميد القبول والتسجيل
Dean of Admission and Registration

أي كشط أو تعديل يلغي الوثيقة

Figure 3.7 Graduation certificate from Saudi Arabia

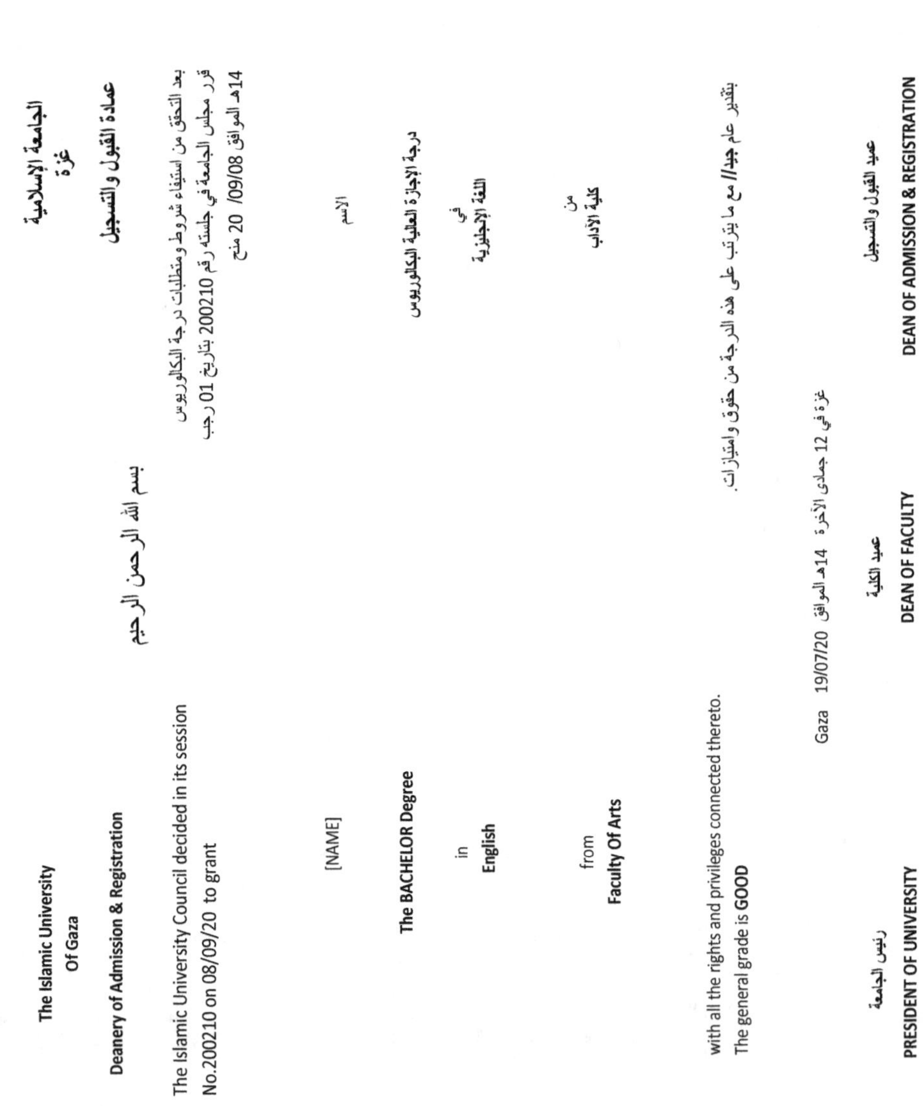

The Islamic University
Of Gaza

Deanery of Admission & Registration

الجامعة الإسلامية
غزة

عمادة القبول والتسجيل

بسم الله الرحمن الرحيم

The Islamic University Council decided in its session No.200210 on 08/09/20 to grant

بعد التحقق من استيفاء شروط ومتطلبات درجة البكالوريوس
قرر مجلس الجامعة في جلسته رقم 200210 بتاريخ 01 رجب
14هـ الموافق 08/09/ 20 منح

[NAME]

الاسم

The BACHELOR Degree

درجة الإجازة العالية البكالوريوس

in
English

في
اللغة الإنجليزية

from
Faculty Of Arts

من
كلية الآداب

with all the rights and privileges connected thereto.
The general grade is **GOOD**

بتقدير عام **جيد//** مع ما يترتب على هذه الدرجة من حقوق وامتيازات.

Gaza 19/07/20 غزة في 12 جمادى الآخرة 14هـ الموافق

رئيس الجامعة
PRESIDENT OF UNIVERSITY

عميد الكلية
DEAN OF FACULTY

عميد القبول والتسجيل
DEAN OF ADMISSION & REGISTRATION

Figure 3.8 Graduation certificate from Palestine

That is not to say that all of these features will be found in all legal documents and language, as there are differences across types of legal documents, and the above highly formulaic and traditional example may be contrasted with the language used in treaties and conventions, for instance, where 'as a rule, drafters [...] make a conscious effort to express the intent of the parties in general terms, using a simple and straightforward style with uncomplicated syntax that can be easily understood and translated into other languages.'[143]

Let us now take a closer look at the main syntactic features legal language and the challenges they pose to translators. Our case study will be the Preamble to the Human Rights Charter.

Preamble	**الديباجة**
Whereas recognition of the inherent dignity and of the equal and inalienable rights of all members of the human family is the foundation of freedom, justice and peace in the world,	لمّا كان الاعتراف بالكرامة المتأصلة في جميع أعضاء الأسرة البشرية وبحقوقهم المتساوية الثابتة هو أساس الحرية والعدل والسلام في العالم.
Whereas disregard and contempt for human rights have resulted in barbarous acts which have outraged the conscience of mankind, and the advent of a world in which human beings shall enjoy freedom of speech and belief and freedom from fear and want has been proclaimed as the highest aspiration of the common people,	ولما كان تناسي حقوق الإنسان وازدراؤها قد أفضيا إلى أعمال همجية آذت الضمير الإنساني. وكان غاية ما يرنو إليه عامة البشر انبثاق عالم يتمتع فيه الفرد بحرية القول والعقيدة ويتحرر من الفزع والفاقة.
Whereas it is essential, if man is not to be compelled to have recourse, as a last resort, to rebellion against tyranny and oppression, that human rights should be protected by the rule of Law,	ولما كان من الضروري أن يتولى القانون حماية حقوق الإنسان لكيلا يضطر المرء آخر الأمر إلى التمرد على الاستبداد والظلم.
Whereas the peoples of the United Nations have in the Charter reaffirmed their faith in fundamental human rights, in the dignity and worth of the human person and in the equal rights of men and women and have determined to promote social progress and better standards of life in larger freedom,	ولما كانت شعوب الأمم المتحدة قد أكدت في الميثاق من جديد إيمانها بحقوق الإنسان الأساسية وبكرامة الفرد وقدره وبما للرجال والنساء من حقوق متساوية وحزمت أمرها على أن تدفع بالرقي الاجتماعي قدماً وأن ترفع مستوى الحياة في جو من الحرية أفسح.

Whereas Member States have pledged themselves to achieve, in cooperation with the United Nations, the promotion of universal respect for and observance of human rights and fundamental freedoms,	ولما كانت الدول الأعضاء قد تعهدت بالتعاون مع الأمم المتحدة على ضمان إطراد مراعاة حقوق الإنسان والحريات الأساسية واحترامها.
Whereas a common understanding of these rights and freedoms is of the greatest importance for the full realization of this pledge,	ولما كان للإدراك العام لهذه الحقوق والحريات الأهمية الكبرى للوفاء التام بهذا التعهد.
Now, therefore,	
The General Assembly,	فإن الجمعية العامة
Proclaims this Universal Declaration of Human Rights as a common standard of achievement for all peoples and all nations, to the end that every individual and every organ of society, keeping this Declaration constantly in mind, shall strive by teaching and education to promote respect for these rights and freedoms and by progressive measures, national and international, to secure their universal and effective recognition and observance, both among the peoples of Member States themselves and among the peoples of territories under their jurisdiction.	تنادي بهذا الإعلان العالمي لحقوق الإنسان على أنه المستوى المشترك الذي ينبغي أن تستهدفه كافة الشعوب والأمم حتى يسعى كل فرد وهيئة في المجتمع، واضعين على الدوام هذا الإعلان نصب أعينهم، إلى توطيد احترام هذه الحقوق والحريات عن طريق التعليم والتربية واتخاذ إجراءات مطردة، قومية وعالمية، لضمان الاعتراف بها ومراعاتها بصورة عالمية فعالة بين الدول الأعضاء ذاتها وشعوب البقاع الخاضعة لسلطانها.

Sentence complexity

The above text is a good example of the kind of sentence that is common in legislation. The first issue is that of **fronting**, i.e. the moving to the front of the sentence parts which would ordinarily be found elsewhere; in this case, it involves a long series of conjoined introductory clauses introduced by *Whereas*, followed by an adverbial (*Now, therefore*), and then the main clause (*The General Assembly* ...).

Each of the introductory clauses also has a number of embedded sub-clauses, which, themselves, act as main clause to other clauses (e.g. 'Whereas it is essential, if man is not to be compelled to have recourse, as a last resort, to rebellion against tyranny and oppression, that human rights should be protected by the rule of Law').

The passive

The passive is employed much more in legal English than it is in general English, whereas, as a rule, Arabic does not favour passive constructions, regardless of the text type or language register. For a start, it is grammatically incorrect to have a passive (appropriately called المَجْهُول, 'the unknown') in Arabic with specification of the agent, as in: 'The door was opened by John'. According to the rules of Classical Arabic, this would have to be turned into an active: يَفْتَحُ جُون الباب. Legal texts reveal the following strategies when rendering English passives into Arabic:

- passive voice verb form;
- active voice;
- use of reflexive forms, such as V (passive of Form II), VII and VIII (passive of Form I);
- dummy verb تَمَّ/يَتِمُّ (followed by المَصْدَر);
- nominalization.

As a result of contacts with European languages, new passive constructions have emerged in some fields (especially the media); the main innovation is the use of the passive voice with the agent expressed, using phrases such as بِواسِطة ('by means of'), مِن قِبَل,مِن طَرَف ('on the part of'). Despite being widely considered sub-standard usage, this calque can now be found frequently in legal documents. On the whole, the passive voice is quite rare in Arabic legal texts, as it is elsewhere, not least because the absence of vowelling results in ambiguity. The following examples illustrate some of the possibilities for rendering the English passives:

If a judgement, writ or warrant of attachment shall be entered or filed …	إذا تم إيداع حكم أو أمر أو إذن
Any certificate representing shares of Licensee shall be endorsed as follows	أية شهادة تمثل أسهم المرخص له يجب أن يؤشر عليها النحو التالي
The work shall be performed by the subcontractor	يتم تنفيذ العمل بواسطة المقاول
The following obligations shall be discharged by the affected Party	يؤدي للطرف المتضرر الالتزامات التالية
The proposed budget shall be reviewed by the Committee	تقوم اللجنة بمراجعة الميزانية المقترحة
After the director is dismissed, the company will withdraw.	بعد عَزل المدير ستنسحب الشركة من المشروع

Modality: *shall* and *may*

In terms of verbs, one of the most striking features of legalese is the use of the modal verbs *shall* and *may*. Particularly the former deviates in usage from everyday English, where it has become very rare and has been crowded out by *will*. In traditional prescriptive grammar, *shall* as a future auxiliary is to be used with the first persons, *will* with other persons: 'I/we shall', but 'you/they will'.

In legal English, *shall* is *never* used as a future auxiliary, rather as a modal denoting **obligation**, and serves the same function as *must*. The use of *may* in legal contexts also differs somewhat, in comparison with general English. Though both share its basic meanings of possibility and permission, its negative *may not* is used as a negative command, which usage is uncommon in everyday English, except in the most formal register.

The use of *shall* and *may* in legislation depends on whether it involves **commands/ permission** or **declarations**, i.e. with *performative* meaning. In the latter case, a simple present is to be used. In the former, a distinction is made between whether the command is *positive* or *negative*, i.e. whether one has to, or is allowed to do something, or is forbidden to do something or it is not required. These uses are represented diagrammatically in Figure 3.9.[144]

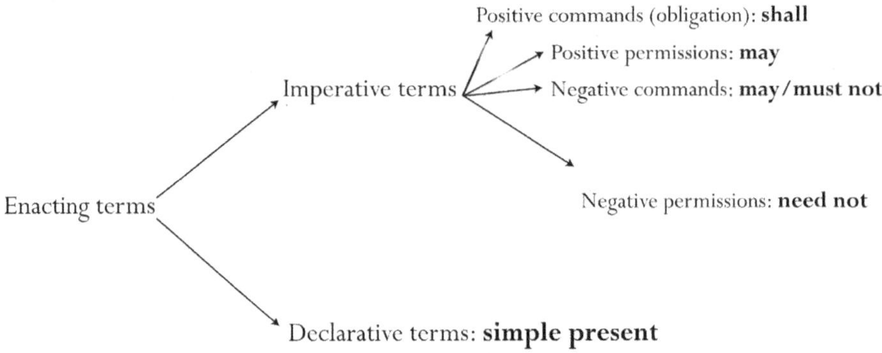

Figure 3.9 The use of *shall* and *may* in legislation

e.g.

> 'This form **shall** (or **must**) be used for all ...'
> 'This Directive **shall** enter into force on ...'
> 'This document **may not** be used ...'
> 'This additive **may be** used in ...'
> 'This test **need not** be performed.'
> 'This Regulation is (hereby) repealed.' (with 'shall' it would be *ordaining*)
> 'A committee is (hereby) established.' (with 'shall' it would be *ordaining*)

In non-enacting terms, *shall* should not be used when objective necessity is referred to, as in 'This sample **must** be pure'.

When translating legal obligation into Arabic, the following are possible:

- عَلَى
- وَجَبَ (يَجِبُ) عَلَى
- لا بُدَّ لَهُ أَن/مِن
- يَنْبَغِي عَلَى أَن

In many cases, however, the English *shall* is not rendered by any of these in Arabic legal texts; instead, the imperfect (المضارع) is employed: e.g.

'... and reaffirming that these human rights instruments **must** be respected in the Occupied Palestinian Territory, including East Jerusalem' (E/CN.62009//L.2/Rev.1)	وإذ يؤكد من جديد وجوب احترام صكوك حقوق الإنسان هذه في الأرض الفلسطينية المحتلة، بما في ذلك القدس الشرقية،
'... and emphasizing that the civilian population **must** be protected' (E/CN.62009//L.2/Rev.1)	وإذ يؤكد على وجوب حماية السكان المدنيين
'*Reiterates* that all Member States, including Eritrea, **shall** comply fully with the terms of the arms embargo [...]' (UN SRes 1907, 2009)	**يؤكد من جديد** أن علي جميع الدول الأعضاء، بما فيها إريتريا، أن تمتثل تماما لأحكام حظر توريد الأسلحة ...
'*Decides* that all Member States **shall** immediately take the necessary measures to prevent [...]'	**يقرر** أن تتخذ جميع الدول الأعضاء فورا التدابير اللازمة لمنع ...
'*Decides* that Eritrea **shall not** supply, sell or transfer directly or indircctly from its territory or by its nationals or using its flag vessels or aircraft any arms or related materiel, and that all Member States **shall** prohibit [...]' (UN SRes 1907, 2009)	**يقرر**ألا تقوم إريتريا ببيع أو توريد أو نقل أي أسلحة أو أعتدة ذات صلة بصورة مباشرة أو غير مباشرة من إقليمها أو بواسطة رعاياها أو باستخدام السفن أو الطائرات التي ترفع أعلامَها وأن تحظر جميع الدول الأعضاء الحصول <على>
'*Decides* that these measures [...] **shall not** apply ...'	**يقرر** ألا تسري هذه التدابير المفروضة ...
'*Reiterating* that all actions undertaken by United Nations entities within the framework of the monitoring and reporting mechanism **must** be designed to support [...]' (S/RES/1882 (2009)	**ويكرر التأكيد على** أن جميع الإجراءات التي تتخذها كيانات الأمم المتحدة في إطار آلية الرصد والإبلاغ يجب أن تستهدف دعم ...

'*Decides further* that the provisions in the above paragraph [...] **shall** be reviewed at the request of the Government [...] and further decides that [...] the provisions of paragraph 22 of resolution [...] shall continue to apply [...]' (S/RES/1905 (2009)	**يقرر كذلك** مراجعة أحكام الفقرة الواردة أعلاه... وذلك بناء على طلب (...) ويقرر كذلك أن تظل أحكام الفقرة 22 من القرار...
'Each State Party **shall** adopt such measures as may be necessary' (*UN International Convention for the Suppression of Terrorist Bombings*)	تتخذ كل دولة طرف التدابير اللازمة
'each State Party **shall** notify the Secretary-General of the United Nations'	تخطر كل دولة طرف الأمين العام للأمم المتحدة
'Each person [...] **shall** be entitled to'	يحق لأي شخص
'The rights referred to [...] **shall** be exercised in conformity with the laws and regulations of the State [...]'	تمارس الحقوق المشار إليها ... وفقا لقوانين وأنظمة الدولة...
'The provisions [...] **shall** be without prejudice to the right of any state party having a claim to jurisdiction'	لا تخل أحكام الفقرتين 3 و4 بما تتمتع به أي دولة طرف قررت ولايتها القضائية
'States Parties **shall** carry out their obligations'	يفي الدول الأطراف بالتزاماتها
'If necessary, the offences **shall** be treated [...]'	إذا اقتضت الضرورة، تعامل الجرائم ...
'States [...] **shall** afford one another the greatest measure of assistance.'	تتبادل الدول ... أكبر قدر من المساعدة
'The offences set forth in article 2 **shall** be deemed to be included as extraditable offences.'	تعتبر الجرائم المشار إليها في المادة 2 بقوة القانون من الجرائم التي تستوجب تسليم المجرمين
'The contractor shall not purchase products or services without prior approval from the owner.'	يتعهد المقاول بعدم شراء منتجات أو خدمات بدون موافقة مسبقة المالك
'the percentage of the price to be deducted **shall be** [...]'	تكون نسبة الخصم من سعر كما يلي ...

The declarative 'do'

Legal English uses *do* in the same way that it occurs in general usage, i.e. as an *auxiliary*, used in interrogative and negative sentences (e.g. 'Do you accept?'), as a *main verb* (e.g. 'I did it for you'), and as an emphasizer (e.g. 'I do like you!'). But while this last usage is restricted to real emphasis in everyday English, legalese uses *do* in affirmative sentences without there being any intended emphasis, merely a statement, as, for instance, in the preamble to the United States of America Constitution above ('We the People [...] *do* ordain [...]').

The function of this kind of *do* is similar to that of a word like *hereby* and is used only with *performative* verbs, i.e. those in which the statement, itself, performs a legal act. In other words, by saying that you ordain something, it is, in fact, ordained. An example from everyday life would be the statement of a promise.

For the purposes of translation into Arabic, it is important to state that this *do* is never rendered into Arabic; instead the main verb is simply rendered by an imperfect (المضارع): e.g.

The Distributor does agree that he is responsible for the cost of reassembly.	يوافق الموزع على أن يكون مسؤولاً عن تكلفة إعادة التجميع
The project was disrupted.	انقطع المشروع

RESOURCES

The Arabic–English legal translator is faced with a relative scarcity of resources, both in terms of Arabic translating and explanatory dictionaries and terminological resources in the legal field, and, often those that exist are either very difficult to obtain and/or not very effective for daily use by translators. The following may be mentioned:

Abū Sulaymān, F., F. Shāmī, F. ᶜAlwān (2007): *al-Muᶜjam al-qānūnī Faransī–ᶜArabī–Inklīzī. Dictionnaire Juridique. Juridic Dictionary*, Cairo: Dār al-Kutub al-ᶜIlmiyya.

Al-ᶜArbī, Lūkarfī (2007): *al-Muᶜjam al-qānūnī wa 'l-idārī li 'l-ᶜaqār ᶜArabī–Inklīzī*, Beirut: al-Dār al-ᶜArabiyya li 'l-ᶜUlūm Nāshirūn.

Armstrong, M. C. & S. H. Amin (1990): *Arabic–English Dictionary of Legal Terms*, Jeffersonville, IN: Royston Publishers.

Faruqi, Harith Suleiman (1988): *Faruqi's Law Dictionary: English–Arabic/Arabic–English*, 2 vols, Beirut: Librairie du Liban.

Maṭar, Līn Ṣalāḥ (2008): *Qāmūs qānūnī muzdawij mufaṣṣal ᶜArabī–Inklīzī/Inklīzī–ᶜArabī maᶜa mulḥaq thunā'ī, 3 maᶜājim fī muᶜjam wāḥid*, Beirut: Manshūrāt al-Ḥalabī al-Ḥuqūqiyya.

Mawsūᶜāt al-muṣṭalaḥāt al-qānūniyya, al-Wasīṭ fī 'l-qānūn wa 'l-daᶜāwā wa 'l-muᶜjam al-qānūnī ᶜArabī–Inglīzī–Faransī, Cairo: Sharikat al-ᶜArīs li 'l-Kumbjūtir, 2007 [electronic only].

Mu'min, Akram (2005): *Muᶜjam al-muṣṭalaḥāt al-qānūniyya maᶜa masrad muṣṭalaḥāt al-sharīᶜa al-Islāmiyya*, Beirut: Dār al-Ṭalā'iᶜ li 'l-Nashr wa 'l-Tawzīᶜ wa 'l-Taṣdīr.

Murād, ᶜAbd al-Fattāḥ (2000): *al-Muᶜjam al-qānūnī rubāᶜī al-lugha, Faransī–Inglīzī–Īṭālī–ᶜArabī-sharᶜī*, n.p.

—— (2000): *Muᶜjam Murād al-qānūnī wa 'l-iqtisādī wa 'l-tijārī, Faransī–ᶜArabī-sharᶜī*, Cairo: al-Dār al-ᶜArabiyya li 'l-Nashr wa 'l-Tawzīᶜ.

Qalᶜajī, M., Ḥāmid Ṣādiq Qunaybī, Quṭb Muṣṭafā (2007): *Muᶜjam lughat al-fuqahā', ᶜArabī–Inklīzī–Faransī. A Dictionary of Islamic Legal Terminology, Arabic–English–French*, Beirut: Dār al-Nafā'is.

Wahab, Ibrāhīm Ismāᶜīl (1963): *al-Qāmūs al-Qānūnī: madanī, jinā'ī, idārī, tijārī, duwalī: Inklīzī–ᶜArabī*, Baghdad: Sharikat al-Ṭabᶜ wa-al-Nashr al-Ahliyya.

al-Wasīṭ fi 'l-qānūn wa 'l-daᶜāwā, al-muᶜjam al-qānūnī Inglīzī–ᶜArabī/ᶜArabī–Inglīzī, Cairo: Sharikat al-ᶜArīs li 'l-Kumbjūtir, 2002 [electronic only].

There are some bilingual English–Arabic legal readers of sorts, which may provide some interesting insights into Arabic>English legal translation, but not necessarily the other way around in the sense that the translations are intended for students of Arabic, and would not always pass muster in English-language legal documents:

Mansoor, M. (1967): *Arabic Legal and Documentary Reader*, 2 vols, Leiden: E. J. Brill.

Shunnaq, A., B. Hatim & R. Buckley (1995): *The Legal Translator at Work: A Practical Guide*, Irbid: Dar Al-Hilal for Translation & Publishing.

In fact, the Arabic–English legal translator's main tools of the trade are secondary sources, which are essentially databases or corpora of legal documents which can be used as models. A good example are the websites of most ministries in Arab countries, which contain databases of relevant laws.

In addition, there are a number of online glossaries – especially those of supranational organizations like the UN and its subsidiaries, whose sites constitute a treasure trove of texts since Arabic is one of the official languages. The result is that an Arabic version – whether source or target text – of documents can generally be found without too much trouble.

The list below contains some useful online resources:

Terminology († = includes Arabic)

http://unterm.un.org/ (United Nations Multilingual Terminology Database [UNTERM])†

http://muqtafi.birzeit.edu/legalLexicon/legal_lexicon2.aspx †

http://dictionary.law.com/ †

http://glossary.ar.eea.europa.eu/ (European Environment Agency, Environmental Terminology and Discovery Service [ETDS])†

www.un.org/en/documents/index.shtml (UN documentation centre)†

www.mcgill.ca/maritimelaw/glossaries/marlaw/ (Glossary of International Conventions and National Laws)†

www.law.cornell.edu/wex/index.php/Contracts (WEX: legal dictionary and encyclopaedia)

www.hg.org/law-dictionary.html (list of legal lexicographical resources, both online and printed)

Legislation

www.lawsociety.org.uk/home.law (Law Society of England and Wales)
www.asil.org/treaty1.cfm (American Society of International Law)
www.australianlawonline.gov.au/accesspoint (Australian Law)
www.loc.gov/law/find/global.php (Library of Congress legal resources)
www.worldbank.org/ (World Bank)
http://laws.justice.gc.ca/en/index.html (Canada)
www.comlaw.gov.au/ (Australia)
www.legislation.gov.uk (UK statute law database)
www.loc.gov/law/help/guide.php (Library of Congress' Guide to online law)
www.lexadin.nl/wlg/legis/nofr/legis.htm (World Law Guide)
www.egypt.gov.eg/english/laws/default.aspx (Egypt)
www.iort.gov.tn/WD120AWP/WD120Awp.exe/CONNECT/SITEIORT (Tunisia)
www.economy.gov.lb/index.php/serviceSubCat/20/4/ (Lebanon)
www.wasmia.com/lawkw.htm (Kuwait)
www.wasmia.com/lawqr.htm (Qatar)
www.wasmia.com/lawbh.htm (Bahrain)
www.wasmia.com/lawom.htm (Oman)
www.wasmia.com/lawae.htm (UAE)
www.wasmia.com/lawksa.htm (Saudi Arabia)
www.wasmia.com/lawjo.htm (Jordan)
www.justice.gov.ma/ar/legislation/legislation.aspx?ty=2 (Morocco)

APPENDIX

ديباجة دستور الولايات المتحدة الأمريكية

نحن شعب الولايات المتحدة، نرسي و نؤسس هذا الدستور للولايات المتحدة الأمريكية، من أجل تشكيل اتحادٍ مثالي، وتحقيق العدالة، وضمان الاستقرار الداخلي، وتوفير سبل الدفاع المشترك، وتعزيز الرفاهية الشاملة، وتأمين نعمة الحرية لأنفسنا ولأجيالنا القادمة.

ديباجة الدستور الاسترالي

قانون تأسيس الكومنولث (الاتحاد) الأسترالي

التاسع من يوليو من عام 1900م

لقد وافق شعوب كل من الولايات التالية، نيو ساوث ويلز وفيكتوريا وجنوب استراليا وكوينزلاند وتسمانيا، بعون الله سبحانه و تعالى وتوفيقه، على أن يتحدوا في كومنولث (اتحاد) فيدرالي واحد، لا ينفصل، تحت حكم / رعاية (تاج) المملكة المتحدة لبريطانيا العظمى وايرلندا، و بموجب هذا الدستور قرروا ما يلي:

وحيث أنه من الملائم (في مصلحتنا) الدخول في كومنولث (اتحاد) مع المستعمرات الأسترالية الأخرى وممتلكات الملكة:

على ذلك ، يُسن هذا القانون من قبل جلالة الملكة المعظمه، بعد بمشورة و موافقة مجالس الشيوخ الدينية و الدنيوية و مجلس العموم، في هذا البرلمان المجتمع حالياً، وبالسلطة المخولة إليه، على النحو التالي:

1 يشار إلى هذا القانون على أنه النص القانوني لدستور الكومنولث (الاتحاد) الاسترالي.

2 أحكام هذا القانون التي تشير إلى الملكة تنطبق على ورثة جلالتها و خلفائها في حكم المملكة المتحدة.

3 سوف يكون من حق الملكة، بمشورة مجلسها الخاص (برفي كانسل)، ان تعلن في بيان انه، منذ التاريخ المحدد هنا، وبعد يوم واحد على هذا القانون، أن شعوب نيو ساوث ويلز، وفيكتوريا، وجنوب أستراليا وكوينزلاند وتسمانيا، وأستراليا الغربية ، بشرط أن تكون جلالتها على قناعة بأن شعب أستراليا الغربية قد وافق على ذلك، سوف تتوحد في كومنولث (اتحاد) فيدرالية تحت اسم كومنولث استراليا. و لكن يحق للملكة، في أي وقت بعد البيان، ان تعين حاكماً عاماً للكومنولث.

4 و سوف يتكون الكومنولث، و يعد دستور الكمنولث (الاتحاد) سارياً، منذ اليوم المحدد هنا. و لكن يجوز لبرلمانات المستعمرات المتعددة في الرابطة في أي وقت بعد تمرير هذا القانون ان تضع أي من هذه التشريعات على ان تدخل حيز التنفيذ في اليوم المحدد لذلك، كما يمكن جعلها من الدستور و الذي تم تفعيله بتمرير هذا القانون.

5 هذا القانون، و جميع القوانين التي وضعها البرلمان للكومنولث (الاتحاد) بموجب الدستور، سوف تكون ملزمة للمحاكم والقضاة والشعوب في كل الولايات وفي كل مكان على ارض الكومنولث، على الرغم من أياً ما كان في قوانين أية ولاية، وسوف تسري قوانين الكومنولث على جميع السفن البريطانية وسفن الملكة الحربية باستثناء تلك التي يكون ميناء اقلاعها والتي يكون ميناء رسوها في الكومنولث.

6 سوف تشير كلمة "الكومنولث" الى كومنولث استراليا على النحو المنصوص عليه بموجب هذا القانون.

سوف تشير كلمة "الولايات" الى اي من مستعمرات نيو ساوث ويلز ونيوزيلندا وكوينزلاند وتسمانيا وفيكتوريا وغرب أستراليا وجنوب استراليا، بما في ذلك الاقليم الشمالي لجنوب استراليا، وهي في الوقت الحاضر جزء من الكومنولث، و مثل هذه المستوطنات أو الاقاليم التي قد يتم قبولها و المعترف بها كاحد ولايات الكومنولث (رابطة الدول)، و اي من أجزاء الكومنولث (رابطة الدول) سوف تسمى "ولاية".

سوف تشير كلمة "الولايات الأصلية" الى هذه الولايات التي كانت احد أجزاء الكومنولث وقت إنشائه.

7 على ذلك يصبح قانون المجلس الفيدرالي (الاتحادي) لأستراليا، لعام 1885، لاغياً و لكن بما لا يؤثر على أي من القوانين التي أقرها المجلس الفيدرالي (الاتحادي) لأستراليا و المعمول بها وقت إنشاء الكومنولث.

يمكن الغاء أي من هذه القوانين في أي من الولايات من قبل برلمان الكومنولث، أو فيما يخص أي مستعمرة من غير الولايات من جانب البرلمان الخاص بها.

8 بعد اقرار هذا القانون لن يصبح قانون حدود المستعمرات، لسنة 1895، ساريا في أي من المستعمرات التي تصبح ولاية من ولايات الكومنولث، إلا ان الكومنولث سيعتبر مستعمرة ذات حكم ذاتي لأغراض هذا القانون.

9 و سوف يكون دستور الكومنولث على النحو التالي:

SAMPLE TEXTS WITH COMMENTARY

Arabic>English

Example 1

عقد زواج عرفي

إنه في يوم الموافق / /

بعون الله اجتمع كل من وبحضور الشهود العدول المبين اسمائهم بباطن هذا العقد:

أولاً : السيد / المقيم /

مواليد : / / بجهة / ويحمل بطاقة ش / ع

اسم الأم / (طرف أول زوج)

ثانياً : الآنسة / المقيمة /

مواليد : / / بجهة / وتحمل بطاقة ش / ع

اسم الأم / (طرف ثاني زوجة)

وقد اتفقا وهما بكامل أهليتهما للتعاقد والتصرفات القانونية على الآتي :

تمهيد

لما كان الطرف الأول يرغب الزواج من الطرف الثاني وقد وافقته على ذلك على يد الشهود العدول المبين أسمائهم بهذا العقد وعلى الصداق المسمى بينهما وعلى مذهب الإمام أبي حنيفة النعمان.

وقد طلبها من الحاضرين تحرير هذا العقد.

البند الأول

يعتبر التمهيد السابق جزء لا يتجزأ من هذا العقد.

البند الثاني

طلب الطرف الأول من الطرف الثاني الارتباط بها على كتاب الله وسنة رسوله بقوله لها أريد الزواج منك على كتاب الله وسنة رسوله وعلى مذهب الإمام أبي حنيفة النعمان والصداق المسمى بيننا ووافقته الطرف الثاني على ذلك بقولها له قبلت الزواج منك.

البند الثالث

قبل الطرفان هذا الارتباط الشرعي بارتباطهما بالميثاق الغليظ على صداق قدرة جنيه دفع منه بمجلس العقد مبلغ وقدرة جنيه والباقي يحل في أقرب الأجلين (الوفاة أو التطليق) وذلك بعد إقرار الطرف الثاني بخلوها من الموانع الشرعية التي تحول بينها وبين الزواج وأنها بكر لم يسبق لها الزواج / وإقرار الطرف الأول (بأنه في عصمته أو ليس في عصمته) زوجة أخرى ومسئوليتهم القانونية عن جميع البيانات المدونة بهذا العقد وفي حالة ظهور ما يخالف ذلك يحق للطرف الأخر اللجوء إلى القضاء للإقتضاء حقه من الطرف المخالف.

البند الرابع

قبل الطرفان هذا الزواج وعلم كل طرف حقوقه وواجباته تجاه الطرف الآخر وتم علمهم أن لهذا الزواج حقوق شرعية لا حق لأي منهم التنصل منها وهو الاعتراف بهذا الزواج والإقرار به أمام الناس وامام جهة رسمية أو قضائية وجعله في قوة السند التنفيذي الواجب النفاذ.

البند الخامس

يلتزم الطرف الأول تجاه الطرف الثاني بإعداد المسكن الشرعي الملائم وفقا لحالته المادية والاجتماعية والقيام بجميع واجباته الشرعية تجاه الطرف الثاني.

البند السادس

يلتزم الطرف الثاني بلإشهار بهذا الزواج وأن يكون زواجاً أبدياً وليس مؤقتا وتم تنبيههم بأن شروط صحة هذا الزوج هو الإشهار والإعلان ولا يكون مؤقتاً ووافقوا على ذلك.

البند السابع

يقر الطرفان بأن من حق أي منهما اللجوء إلى القضاء للإقرار بصحة هذا الزواج والتصديق عليه أمام المحكمة أو إثبات محتواه ومضمونه في وثيقة زواج رسمية على يد مأذون منذ تاريخ هذا العقد حماية لحقوق كل طرف تجاه الطرف الآخر. ولا يحق لأي طرف النكول والتقاعس عن التزامه تجاه الطرف الآخر.

البند الثامن

يحرر هذا العقد من نسختين بيد كل طرف نسخة للعمل بموجبها عند الاقتضاء.

والله خير الشاهدين

الطرف الأول الطرف الثاني

الشهود

الشاهد الأول الشاهد الثاني

CIVIL MARRIAGE[i] CONTRACT

On this the ... day of .... A.H., corresponding to .../.../... C.E.[ii]
With the help of God the Almighty, have appeared in the presence of witnesses of reputable background and sound character,[iii] whose names are stated in the present contract, the following:

Mr ..... residing at ...
Born on ... , in ... , holder of Identity Card/Family Record Document[iv] No ...

Of the one part (hereinafter referred to as 'groom'[v]);
AND

Miss ..... residing at ...

Born on ... , in ... , holder of Identity Card/Family Record Document No ...
Of the second part (hereinafter referred to as 'bride')

Being legal capable and competent[vi] have hereby agreed the following:

PREAMBLE[vii]

Whereas the groom wishes to enter into marriage with the bride, who has accepted this in the presence of witnesses whose names are mentioned in the contract, for a dowry fixed between them and in accordance with the principles of the Hanafi School of Islamic Jurisprudence.[viii]

ARTICLE 1

The preceding Preamble shall constitute an integral part of the present agreement.

ARTICLE 2

The groom hereby requests to enter into a bond with the bride, in accordance with the Holy Quran[ix] and the Sunna of the Prophet Muhammad, by saying, 'I wish to marry you, in accordance with the Holy Quran, the Sunna of the Prophet Muhammad and the Hanafi School of Islamic Jurisprudence, and in exchange of the dowry fixed between us.' The bride hereby agrees to this by saying, 'I accept to marry you.'

ARTICLE 3

Both parties accept this legal bond that unites them by an inviolable vow, for a dowry in the amount of .... Egyptian Pounds, with the amount of .... Egyptian Pounds being paid upon entering into the contract, the remainder falling due upon the demise of the groom, or divorce, whichever occurs the earlier, and following the acknowledgment by the bride that she is free from any legal impediments that can come between both parties, and that she is a virgin, has not previously married, whereas the groom acknowledges – irrespective of whether or not he is in a state of matrimony[x] with another wife – the legal responsibilities and all the statements recorded in the present agreement. In case anything should emerge that runs counter these statements, either party is entitled to seek redress and demand his/her right from the offending party before the courts.

ARTICLE 4

Both parties accept this marriage, and each party is aware of its rights and duties towards the other, as well as of the fact that this marriage is legally valid and that neither of them has the right to renege on his/her legal responsibilities in respect of it, and each acknowledges this marriage in front of other people and the official or legal authorities, who are fully empowered to enforce the present contract.

ARTICLE 5

The groom pledges to the bride that he shall prepare the appropriate legal residence, in accordance with his financial and social circumstances, status in society, and legal duties towards the bride.

ARTICLE 6

The bride pledges to announce this marriage, that it is indefinite,[xi] not temporary. Both parties have been apprised of the conditions of legality of this marriage to be made public, and of the fact that it is not temporary, and both have agreed to it.

ARTICLE 7

Both parties agree that either of them may resort to legal action in order to establish the legal validity of the present marriage and have it certified before the court or its contents authenticated in an official marriage document drawn up by a marriage registrar,[xii] to take effect as from the date of the present contract, with each party's rights being safeguarded in respect of the other. Neither party shall be allowed to shirk from[xiii] or neglect their obligations towards the other.

ARTICLE 8

The present marriage contract has been executed in duplicate, each copy being signed by each party and valid in law.

AS GOD IS OUR WITNESS[xiv]

First Party ('groom')	Second Party ('bride')

THE WITNESSES

First Witness	Second Witness

i عُرْف > عُرْفِي, 'tradition' or 'custom' marriage is peculiar to Islam; in fact, it constitutes a type of marriage agreement that does not involve the same duties and rights as a 'standard' marriage. The translation 'civil' (as opposed to 'religious') is not entirely satisfactory, as some of the provisions in the document clearly refer to the basis in religion, whereas the fact that 'civil marriage' sounds familiar to the English-speaking reader is also a disadvantage in that it might be considered equivalent to 'common law marriage', which concept is entirely different from عرفي. The 'customary marriage', i.e. rooted in 'custom', should be avoided partly for the same reason, partly due to its ambiguity. The culture-specificity of the term makes it an obvious candidate for borrowing, i.e. transliteration: '*urfi* marriage'. The advantage to using this term is that it conveys to the reader that the marriage in question is an Islamic type of marriage, and that it has no counterpart in Western law.

ii The specification of the year is added for the purposes of the non-Muslim readership.

iii عَدْل can be both an adjective ('honest', 'upright') and a noun (pl. عُدُول) which, in Islamic legal terminology, denotes a 'person of good reputation'. The translation here is a commonly used phrase in legal English, and covers both meaning and scope of the original.

iv The abbreviations ش and ع stand for شَخْصِيّة ('personal') and عائلية; the بطاقة عائلية is a document (not dissimilar from the French *livret de famille*) commonly found in Arab countries and contains information regarding the civil status and family composition of the individual. As this concept is unknown to the reader, a paraphrase is the most logical approach.

v The literal translation of زَوْج is 'husband' or '(male) spouse'; 'groom' (and later on 'bride' for زوجة) was chosen by analogy with English-speaking documents. Moreover, at the time of the writing of the document the two parties are not, of course, 'husband' and 'wife'. The omission of 'first/second party' is justified since reference to the parties tends to be monosemic in English-speaking legal documents, i.e. it is not common to find 'hereinafter referred to as … or ….').

vi Rather than translating بكامِل أهْلِيتِهِما للتَّعاقد والتَّصَرُّفات القانونية literally ('with full competence to enter into contracts and legal actions'), the TT uses the customary legal expression in English.

vii Though there is no introductory subheading in the ST, these opening clauses fulfil this function and are generally subsumed under a 'Preamble' heading in English legal texts.

viii The ST descriptive phrase – the religious school (or *madhhab*) of the Imam Abu Hanifa al-Nu'man – would be devoid of meaning to the TT reader; instead, an explanatory gloss involving compression of the original conveys the necessary elements.

ix The use of 'Quran' avoids any ambiguity associated with كتاب الله ('the Book of God') both particularizes and embeds the term in the cultural context, whereas the addition of 'Holy' renders the 'godly' or 'divine'.

x عِصْمَة has a variety of meanings, ranging from protection, to modesty and virtuousness. In a marriage context, however, it collocates with عصمة النِكاح to give 'the bond of marriage', or, as is the case here, في عصمة ..., meaning 'to be under custody', i.e. married to someone.

xi أبَدِي literally means 'eternal, everlasting'; the term is used here within a religious context, and cannot be rendered in the same way in English, where 'indefinite' or 'for an indefinite period (of time)' are the obvious translations.

xii مَأْذُون (literally 'one granted permission') is an official in Islamic law (also known as مَأْذُون شَرْعِي) authorized by a religious judge (قاض) to perform civil marriages.

xiii نَكَلَ, 'to break, renege on an agreement'; however, نُكُول is also a technical term in Islamic law meaning 'refusal to testify in court'.

xiv Literally, والله خَيْر الشّاهِدِين means 'God is the best witness'; the present translation is a cultural and pragmatically equivalent phrase in English.

Example 2

الجامعة العربية المفتوحة

Arab Open University

شهادة تخرج

تشهد الجامعة العربية المفتوحة/ فرع مصر/ بأن الطالب// //

قد أنهى الامتحان النهائي لدرجة البكالوريوس في // إدارة الأعمال // بتقدير عام **جيد**، ومعدل تراكمي: ٢,٣٩ وذلك في نهاية الفصل الدراسي الثاني من العام الأكاديمي ٢٠٠٧/٢٠٠٨.

وقد تحررت هذه الإفادة بناء على طلبه لتقديمها إلى من يهمه الأمر.

علماً بأن الجامعة العربية المفتوحة تم تأسيسها بموجب قرار السيد رئيس جمهورية مصر العربية رقم ٢١٦ لسنة ٢٠٠٣ وموافقة مجلس الشعب المصري بجلسته في ديسمبر عام ٢٠٠٣، وقد صدر قرار المجلس الأعلى للجامعات رقم (١٤٩) بتاريخ ٢٠٠٨/١٠/٢٣ بمعادلة درجة البكالوريوس في إدارة الأعمال التي تمنحها الجامعة بدرجة البكالوريوس في التجارة (إدارة الأعمال) التي تمنحها الجامعات المصرية الخاضعة لقانون تنظيم الجامعات رقم ٤٩ لسنة ١٩٧٢ ولائحته التنفيذية.

شؤون الطلاب	<الاسم>
الاسم:	مدير عام الجامعة العربية المفتوحة / فرع مصر

ARAB OPEN UNIVERSITY

GRADUATION CERTIFICATE

The Egyptian branch of the Arab Open University certifies the student [NAME] has completed the final examination for the degree of Bachelor in Business Administration with the general mention of 'GOOD' and a Grade Point Average of 2.39 at the end of the second semester[i] of the academic year 2008–9.

This certificate has been drawn up at the request of the student for whom it may concern.

Whereas the Arab Open University was set up by decree No. 216, 2003, issued by the President of the Egyptian Arab Republic and endorsed by the Egyptian People's Assembly[ii] in its Session of December 2003;

Whereas the High Council for Universities issued Resolution No. 149, on 23.10.2008 regarding the equivalence of the degree of Bachelor in Business Administration awarded by the University with the degree of Bachelor in Trade (Business Administration), awarded by Egyptian Universities governed[iii] by the Universities Act[iv] No. 49, of 1972, and its implementing regulation.[v]

Student Affairs

Name:

[STAMP] [ILLEGIBLE]

[STAMP] ARAB OPEN UNIVERSITY

[STAMP] [ILLEGIBLE][vi]

[SIGNATURE] [ILLEGIBLE]

Date: 16.01.2008

Head of the Arab Open University – Egyptian Branch

i Although فصل is also used for 'term', the reference to the final examination would seem to indicate that here it means 'semester', since final examinations would be organized in the third (and final) term of the academic year.

ii Recognized translation of this political body (also see above).

iii Example of transposition, with the actor and acted upon being reversed, i.e. 'governed by' rather than 'subject to'.

iv Idiomatic translation, rather than a more literal 'Law/Act organizing universities'.

v Recognized translation of a technical term (see Wehr).

vi Despite being illegible, the presence and position of stamps must be indicated in the translation, as this is a certified translation of an official document.

Example 3

Press Act	**قانون الصحافة**
Dahir[i] N° 1-02-207 of 25 Rajab 1423 A.H. / 3rd October 2002 C.E. relating to the promulgation of Act N° 77-00 amending and completing Dahir N°1-58-378 of 3 Jumada I, 1378 A.H./15 November 1958, and forming part of of the Press and Publishing Act. PRAISE BE TO GOD! His Majesty, King Mohammed VI let it be known by the present Dahir – may God elevate and strengthen its contents! – In view of the Constitution, in particular Articles 26 and 58 that His Sharifian Majesty has decided the following: Shall be issued and published in the Official Gazette, in accordance with the present Dahir, Act N° 77-00 amending and completing Dahir N°1-58-378 of 3 Jumada I, 1378 A.H./15 November 1958 pertaining to the Press and Publication Act, with the advice and consent of the Chamber of Councillors and Assembly of Representatives. Drawn up in Marrakech, on 25 Rajab 1423 A.H./ 3 October 2002.	ظهير شريف رقم 1-02-207 صادر في 25 من رجب 1423 (03 أكتوبر 2002) بتنفيذ القانون رقم 77.00 المغير والمتمم بموجبه الظهير الشريف رقم 1-58-378 الصادر في 3 جمادى الأولى 1378 (15 نونبر 1958) بشأن قانون الصحافة والنشر. الحمد لله وحده، محمد بن الحسن بن محمد بن يوسف الله وليه يعلم من ظهيرنا الشريف هذا، أسماه الله وأعز أمره أننا: بناء على الدستور ولاسيما الفصلين 26 و58 منه؛ أصدرنا أمرنا الشريف بما يلي: ينفذ وينشر بالجريدة الرسمية، عقب ظهيرنا الشريف هذا، القانون رقم 77.00 المغير والمتمم بموجبه الظهير الشريف رقم 1-58-378 الصادر في 3 جمادى الأولى 1378 (15 نوفمبر 1958) بشأن قانون الصحافة والنشر، كما وافق عليه مجلس المستشارين ومجلس النواب. وحرر بمراكش في 25 من رجب 1423 (3 أكتوبر 2002).
Act N° 77-00 pertaining to the Press and Publication Act.	**قانون رقم 77.00 بشأن قانون الصحافة والنشر**
CHAPTER I: PRESS, PRINTING, PUBLISHING AND DISTRIBUTION OF BOOKS	**الباب الأول** في الصحافة والطباعة والنشر وترويج الكتب
<u>Article 1</u> The freedom to publish newspapers, and to print, publish and distribute books is guaranteed under the present Act. All citizens have a right of access to information. All the media have a right of access to all sources of information, and to acquire information from various sources, except if the information is confidential, in accordance with the law.	**الفصل الأول** إن حرية إصدار الصحف والطباعة والنشر وترويج الكتب مضمونة طبقا لهذا القانون. للمواطن الحق في الإعلام. لمختلف وسائل الإعلام الحق في الوصول إلى مصادر الخبر، والحصول على المعلومات من مختلف مصادرها ما لم تكن هذه المعلومات سرية بمقتضى القانون.

These liberties shall be exercised in accordance with the constitutional principles, legal provisions and ethical principles of the profession. The media shall communicate information truthfully and faithfully.

تمارس هذه الحريات في إطار مبادئ الدستور وأحكام القانون وأخلاقيات المهنة، وعلى وسائل الإعلام أن تنقل الأخبار بصدق وأمانة.

Article 2
All printed material made public shall contain the name of the printing press and its address, except if it involves so-called 'civil publications', such as visiting cards, invitations, etc.
Any printed material that does not contain the information provided for in the preceding paragraph shall not be allowed to be distributed.
Any breach of the provisions contained in the present article shall be punishable by a fine of between 2,000 and 15.000 Moroccan[ii] Dirhams.

الفصل الثاني
يشار في كل مطبوع معروض للعموم إلى اسم المطبعة وعنوانها باستثناء المطبوعات المعروفة بمطبوعات المدن كبطائق الزيارة والدعوات وما يشابهها.
ويمنع توزيع المطبوعات التي لا تحمل البيانات المنصوص عليها في الفقرة السابقة.
وكل مخالفة لهذا الفصل يعاقب عنها بغرامة تتراوح بين 2.000 و15.000 درهم.

CHAPTER II: PERIODICAL PRESS

Part 1: Right to Publication, Management, Ownership and Registration[iii]

الباب الثاني
في الصحافة الدورية
القسم الأول
في حق النشر والإدارة والملكية والتصريح

Article 3
All newspapers or periodical publications shall be published without let or hindrance, subject to compliance with the formalities set forth in Article 5 of the present Dahir.

الفصل الثالث
يمكن نشر كل جريدة أو مطبوع دوري بحرية بعد القيام بالإجراءات المقررة في الفصل الخامس من ظهيرنا الشريف هذا.

Article 4
All newspapers or periodical publications shall have a publishing director, who shall be of age, be resident in Morocco, be in possession of all civil rights, without having been deprived of such rights as a result of a court decision. If the provisions of Article 39 of the Constitution apply to the director of the publication, the publishing company shall appoint a deputy director

الفصل الرابع
يكون لكل جريدة أو مطبوع دوري مدير للنشر.
ويشترط في مدير النشر أن يكون راشدا وقاطنا بالمغرب ومتمتعا بحقوقه المدنية غير محكوم عليه بأية عقوبة تجرده من حقوقه الوطنية.
إذا كان مدير النشر ممن تطبق لفائدتهم مقتضيات الفصل 39 من الدستور، تعين مقاولة النشر مديرا مساعدا

who is not subject to the provisions of the aforesaid Article 39 and who complies with the conditions set forth in the preceding paragraph. The provisions of the preceding paragraph shall apply if the director of the publication is a member of the government. The appointment of a deputy director shall take place within one month following the date on which the director of the publication is subject to the provisions of Article 39, or becomes a member of the government. All duties and responsibilities imposed upon the director of the publication under the present Act shall also apply to the co-director. If the appointment of the deputy director does not take place within the prescribed period, the authority charged with communicating with the director of the newspaper or periodical publication shall, by means of a letter sent through the mail by recorded delivery,[iv] put the director in default and call upon him/her to comply with the above provisions within one month following the notice of default. Failure to appoint a deputy director within the period provided in the preceding paragraph shall result in the suspension of the newspaper or periodical publication. This suspension shall be issued by a decree, following a recommendation by the competent authority. In addition to the provision contained in the third paragraph, the employment agreement for the deputy director of the publication shall state that the latter will assume all of the legal duties imposed upon the director of the newspaper of periodical publication, in the way set forth by the present Act. A true and certified copy of the original contract shall be submitted to the competent authority in accordance with the relevant provisions.	لنشر لا تسري عليه مقتضيات الفصل 39 السالف الذكر ويستوفي الشروط المنصوص عليها في الفقرة السابقة. وتطبق مقتضيات الفقرة السابقة إذا كان مديرا النشر عضوا في الحكومة. يجب أن يتم التعيين المذكور داخل أجل شهر يبتدئ من التاريخ الذي أصبح فيه مديرا النشر يستفيد من مقتضيات الفصل 39 المذكور أو عضوا في الحكومة. تسري على مدير النشر المساعد جميع الالتزامات والمسؤوليات الواجبة على مدير النشر بموجب هذا القانون إذا لم يتم تعيين مدير النشر المساعد داخل. الأجل المقرر توجه السلطة المكلفة بالاتصال إلى مدير الجريدة أو المطبوع الدوري إنذارا برسالة مضمونة مع إشعار بالتوصل قصد التقيد بالأحكام السابقة داخل أجل شهر واحد يبتدئ من تاريخ تبليغ الإنذار. ينتج عن عدم تعيين مدير النشر المساعد داخل الأجل المنصوص عليه في الفقرة السابقة إيقاف الجريدة أو المطبوع الدوري، ويصدر الإيقاف المذكور بمرسوم يتخذ باقتراح من السلطة الحكومية المكلفة بالاتصال. علاوة على الحالة المنصوص عليها في الفقرة الثالثة أعلاه يجوز التنصيص في عقد العمل المتعلق بمدير النشر المساعد على أن هذا الأخير يتحمل جميع الالتزامات القانونية الملقاة على عاتق مدير النشر أو المطبوع الدوري كما هو منصوص عليها في هذا القانون. تبلغ نسخة مشهود بمطابقتها لأصل العقد المذكور إلى الإدارة وفق الأشكال المحددة بنص تنظيمي.

i (Pl. ظَهائِر), relating to a root meaning 'to appear', this word generally means 'helper, aid', but is used here in its peculiarly Moroccan acceptation of a type of decree or edict. For interpretation purposes, it makes sense, therefore, to use a transliteration of the term, which is also used in other-language versions of Moroccan laws.

ii The addition of 'Moroccan' is justified in the translation in order to remove any possible ambiguity for an English-speaking reader.

iii تصريح has a variety of meanings, such as 'declaration', 'permit' and 'permission', but in view of the information provided later on, 'registration' is the most appropriate.

iv Despite being much longer and more convoluted, this is the commonly used phrase in legal English documents.

Example 4

Employment Contract	**عقد عمل**
This Agreement made and entered into this ... day of ... A.H., corresponding to .../.../20... CE, by and between ....., having its Head Office in the city of Alexandria, represented by ...., of the one part, hereinafter referred to as 'employer';[i] AND Mr. .... born at .... on ..., residing at .... , holder of Identity Card No. ..., .. issued at .... on ..., of ... nationality, of the other, hereinafter referred to as 'employee'.	انه في يوم ..... من شهر .... سنة ..14 هـ الموافق .../.../..20 قد تم الاتفاق بين كل من: أ- شركة .... و مركزها القانوني في الاسكندرية و يمثلها في هذا العقد رئيس الشركة. (الطرف الأول) ب- السيد / .... المولود في .... بتاريخ / / 19 و المقيم حالياً في .... و الثابت الشخصية بموجب البطاقة الشخصية / العائلية رقم .... الصادرة في / / 19 و المتمتع بالجنسية .... (الطرف الثاني)
<u>PREAMBLE</u>	
This Contract has been concluded between the two parties for the purpose of performing the work specified below to the standard required by employer, as shown in the attached job description.	تحرر هذا العقد بين الطرفين لأداء العمل الموضح بيانه بعد في هذا العقد بالكيفية و المستوي المقررين والموضحين بوصف الوظيفة المرفق بهذا العقد.
Accordingly, employee agrees to enter into this contract on the understanding that he is fully capable of discharging his duties to the standards required by employer and, therefore, undertakes to	و بناء علي ذلك يوافق الطرف الثاني على أنه على علم تام بهذا و على قدرته الكافية انجاز جميع الواجبات العمل بالكيفية و المستوي اللذين يتطلبهما الطرف الأول، و من ثم فإنه يتعهد بالوفاء بالالتزامات المذكورة في هذا العقد.

fulfil the obligations contained herein. Both parties hereto covenant and agree as follows:

ARTICLE 1

Employer agrees to employ employee as from .... in the capacity of ... , provided that employer shall have the right to assign to employee any other services and duties within the nature of employee's qualifications.

1- يوافق الطرف الأول علي استخدام الطرف الثاني اعتباراً من .... لشغل وظيفة .... علي أن يكون للطرف الأول الحق في ان يعهد إلي الطرف الثاني بأي عمل أخر يتفق مع طبيعة مؤهلاته.

ARTICLE 2

The monthly salary agreed upon is ... Egyptian Pounds,[ii] payable monthly by the company at the end of each calendar month. Employer shall deduct from such salary, which shall be deemed to include any supplementary allowances, all sums deductible by law from Employee's salary, including taxes, fees, contributions or any other levies imposed by law on employee.

2- المرتب الشهري المتفق عليه هو .... جنيه مصري (فقط .... جنيه مصري) تدفعه الشركة شهرياً في نهاية كل شهر ميلادي. التالي و سيستقطع الطرف الأول من المرتب السابق ذكره بما فيه من علاوات إضافية أيا كانت كافة المبالغ التى يقضي القانون بخصمها من مترب الطرف الثاني نظير الضرائب و الرسوم و الاشتراكات التى يفرضها القانون علي الطرف الثاني.

ARTICLE 3

Employee shall be deemed to have been appointed subject to a three-month probationary period, during which, or upon expiration thereof, employer shall be entitled to terminate or annul the present agreement without any prior notice or payment of any compensation or remuneration. Upon expiration of the probationary period and unless employer has availed himself of his right to cancel this contract, employee shall be deemed to be employed for an indefinite period effective from the date of employment.

3- يعتبر الطرف الثاني معيناً تحت الاختبار لمدة ثلاثة شهور و في خلال هذه الفترة أو عند انتهائها يكون الطرف الأول الحق في إنهاء أو فسخ هذا العقد فوراً دون حاجة إلي إخطار سابق و دون دفع أي مبلغ بصفة تعويض او مكافأة و عند انتهاء مدة الاختبار و مالم يكن الطرف الأول قد استعمل حقه في فسخ هذا العقد يعتبر الطرف الثاني معيناً في خدمة الطرف الأول لمدة غير محددة اعتباراً من تاريخ التعيين.

ARTICLE 4

Employee shall devote the whole of his time and attention to employer's business during working hours, in accordance with the provisions set forth in Labour Act No. 91.

4- يتعهد الطرف الثاني بأن يكرس كل وقته و جهده لأعمال الطرف الأول أثناء ساعات العمل المقررة في القانون رقم 91.

ARTICLE 5 Employee shall not without written permission from the company engage in any work for the account of a third party, with or without remuneration, even outside official working hours, or participate, directly or indirectly, in any activity in direct conflict with employer's interest, or in any corporation involved in transactions with employer.	5- يحظر على الطرف الثاني بدون إذن كتابي من الشركة أن يؤدي عملاً بغير بأجر أو بدون أجر و لو في غير أوقات العمل الرسمية، أو أن يشترك بصفة مباشرة أو غير مباشرة في أي عمل لدي أية جهة تتعارض مصالحها مع مصالح الشركة أو يكون لها معاملات مع الشركة.
ARTICLE 6 Employee undertakes to comply with all orders and instructions issued to employee by employer's Management and shall accurately implement the Company's regulations and always maintain good conduct, behaviour and reputation.	6- يلتزم الطرف الثاني بأن يراعي كافة الأوامر و التعليمات التى تصدر إليه من إدارة الشركة، كما يلتزم بأن ينفذ بدقة أحكام لوائح الشركة و تعليمتها و أن يحافظ على حسن السير و السلوك و السمعة الطيبة.
ARTICLE 7 Executed in duplicate, each of which when executed and delivered shall constitute an original of this Agreement.	7- تحرر هذا العقد من نسختين تشكل كل منها عند تحريرها وإرسالها نسخة أصلية لهذا العقد.

i The referent 'employer' (and 'employee') is used, rather than 'First Party' (and 'Second Party') since this is the usual term in English employment contracts.

ii The use of فقط is omitted as this has a mere formulaic usage in Arabic when referring to payments.

English>Arabic

Example 1

ZANUSSI-ELECTROLUX GUARANTEE CONDITIONS

We, Zanussi-Electrolux, undertake that if within 12 months of the date of purchase this ZANUSSI-ELECTROLUX appliance or any part thereof is proved to be defective by reason only of faulty workmanship or materials, we will at our discretion repair or replace the same FREE OF ANY CHARGE for labour, materials or carriage on condition that:

- The appliance has been correctly installed and used only on the electricity or gas supply stated on the rating plate.
- The appliance has been used for normal domestic purposes only, and in accordance with the manufacturer's operating and maintenance instructions.
- The appliance has not been serviced, maintained, repaired, taken apart or tampered with by any person not authorized by us.

All service work under this guarantee must be undertaken by a Service Force Centre.
Any appliance or defective part replaced shall become the Company's property.

- This guarantee is in addition to your statutory and other legal rights.
- Home visits are made between 8.30 am and 5.30 pm Monday to Friday. Excluding bank holidays. Visits may be available outside these hours in which case a charge will be made.

شروط الضمان لمنتجات شركة زانوسي الكترولكس

نحن شركة زانوسي الكترونكس، نتعهد في حال وجود أي عيب تصنيعي أو مادي خلال مدة 12 شهراً من تاريخ شراء هذا المنتج، بأن نقوم بإصلاحه أو إستبداله مجاناً وبدون أي تكاليف(مادية) [i] سواء للأيدي العاملة أو المواد المستخدمه أو لأجور النقل شريطة أن:

* يكون قد تم تركيب المنتج بصورة صحيحة وانه تم تشغيله بالكهرباء أو الغاز كما هو مبين في لوحة الإرشادات الخاصة بالشركة.[ii]
* يكون قد تم استعمال المنتج للاستخدامات المنزلية العادية فقط ووفقا لتعليمات التصنيع والصيانة.
* لم يتم صيانة أو إصلاح أو فك المنتج من قبل أي شخص لا تخوله الشركة.[iii]

* يجب أن تجرى جميع أعمال الصيانة الواردة في هذا الضمان من قبل "سيرفيس فورس سنتر" (مركز الخدمات التابعة للشركة).[iv]
* يصبح أي جهاز أو جزء عاطل تم إستبداله ملكاً خاصاً بالشركة / ترجع ملكية أي جهاز أو جزء عاطل منه يتم استبداله، إلى الشركة.

* يعد هذا الضمان إضافة إلى حقوقك القانونية الأخرى.
* تخصص أوقات الزيارات المنزلية فيما بين الساعة الثامنة والنصف صباحا والخامسة والنصف مساء من يوم الاثنين إلى الجمعة ماعدا عطل البنك[v]، مع إمكانية القيام بزيارات خارج هذه الأوقات مع إضافة تكلفة الخدمة.

WHAT IS NOT COVERED	ما لا يشمله الضمان
• Damage or, calls resulting from transportation, improper use or neglect; the replacement of any light bulbs or removable parts of glass or plastic.	* أي ضرر ناتج عن سوء النقل أو الإستخدام أو الإهمال، كما أن الضمان لايشمل أي استبدال سواء لمصابيح الإضاءة أو لقطع الزجاج و البلاستيك.
• Costs incurred for calls to put right an appliance which has been improperly installed or calls to appliances outside the United Kingdom.	* في حالة طلب إعادة تركيب الجهاز بطريقة صحيحة بعد أن قد تم تركيبه بطريقة خاطئة أو أي تكاليف لتلبية طلبات خارج المملكة المتحدة.
• Appliances found to be in use within a commercial environment, plus those which are the subject of rental agreements.	* المنتجات التي يكتشف انها تستخدم لأغراض تجارية بالإضافة إلى المنتجات المخصصة للتأجير.
• Products of Zanussi-Electrolux manufacture which are not marketed by Zanussi-Electrolux.	* منتجات مصنع زانوسي الكترونكس التي لم يتم تسويقها من قبل الشركة نفسها / المنتجات (المزعمة إنها) لشركة زانوسي الكترونكس ولكن لم يتك تسويقها من قبل الشركة نفسها.
EC Countries – the standard guarantee is applicable but is subject to the owner's responsibility and cost, to ensure the appliance meets the standards set the country to which the product is taken. Proof of purchase may be required.	* الدول الأوروبية: إنّ هذا الضمان قابل للتطبيق ولكنه خاضع لمسؤولية المالك والتكلفة ليتم التأكد من أن المنتج مطابق لمواصفات الدولة المأخوذ إليها الجهاز و ربما يتم طلب وثيقة إثبات الشراء.

i The intention behind the use of capital letters in 'FREE OF ANY CHARGE' is best maintained in the Arabic by underlining the phrase: مجانًا وبدون أية تكاليف مادية. The addition of مادية is desirable stylistically – the noun without an adjective in this context sounds incomplete.

ii To avoid any ambiguity, the phrase is best translated this way, rather than as: وأنه قد تم تشغيله بالكهرباء أو الغاز فقط كما هو مبين في لوحة الإرشادات.

iii Or: غير مخول من قبلنا.

iv 'Service Force Centre' is the official name of Zanussi's in-house repair facility. As such, it should be transliterated, i.e. سيرفيس فورس سنترر, rather than translated.

v The temptation to translate 'bank holidays' literally as عطل البنك/البنوك should be avoided! Whereas initially it did, of course, refer to the closing of banks only, today it simply denotes a 'public holiday', hence the translation of العطل العامة.

EXERCISES

Exercise A

Comment on the translation choices in the agreement below in those areas where the two texts vary. Research comparable texts in order to inform your judgement. In addition, discuss which of the variants given in places (demarcated by '/') is/are the more appropriate, and why.

RENTAL AGREEMENT	**عقد إيجار**
THIS AGREEMENT made this the … day of …, by and between …. hereinafter called 'the Landlord'; of the one part and … hereinafter called 'the Tenant', of the other.	تم إبرام هذا العقد في يوم---------------------- من شهر -------------- سنة -- / هذا اليوم المصادف ---------------- بين كل من / بين ------ / بين المدعو -------- المشار إليه فيمابعد بـ / المدعو هنا بـ المالِك / المؤجِر وبين / بين المدعو ----------- والمشار إليه فيما بعد / المدعو هنا بـ المُستَأجِر،
The Landlord hereby agrees to rent to the Tenant the real property located in the City of … State of …, described as follows: Commencing on the 1st day of … and monthly thereafter until the … day of …, at which time this agreement is terminated. The Landlord rents the premises to the Tenant on the following terms and conditions:	وبهذا يوافق المالك على أن يؤجر للمستأجر العقار الثابت / البيت / المسكن / العين / المأجور الواقع في مدينة ------ في ولاية --------------- بالمواصفات التالية: وذلك إبتداءاً من اليوم الأول من ------- وشهرياً بعدها حتى اليوم --------- من ------ ويكون في هذا الوقت قد انتهى العقد / ويكون هذا تاريخ نفاذ العقد. يقوم المالك بأيجار المأجور للمستأجر وفقاً للأحكام والشروط التالية:
1. Rent	**1 – الأيجار/ بدل الأيجار / الأجرة**
The Tenant agrees to pay the Landlord as base rent the sum of $… per month, due and payable monthly in advance on the first day of each month during the term of this agreement. Rent must be received by 5:00 p.m. If the rent has not been received by 9:00 a.m. on the second of the month, then a seven-day notice will be posted.	يوافق المستأجر أن يدفع للمالك أجرة أساسية إجمالي قدرها ------ دولاراً في الشهر، تدفع مقدماً في اليوم الأول من كل شهر خلال فترة هذا العقد. تسلم الأجرة قبل الساعة الخامسة مساءاً، وإذا لم تسلم الأجرة قبل الساعة التاسعة صباحاً من اليوم الثاني من الشهر، فأن المستأجر سيتسلم إخطاراً مدته سبعة أيام لدفع الأجرة.
2. Payment of Rent	**2 – دفع الإيجار / دفع بدل ألأجرة / دفع الأجرة / كيفية أداء البدل/ طريقة دفع الأجرة / تسديد رسم الإيجار**
Monthly rent payments may be paid by check until the first check is dishonored and returned unpaid. Time is of the essence and no excuses will be accepted.	يتم / يجوز تسديد/ دفع رسوم الإيجار بواسطة

Rent shall be made payable to …
and hand delivered (or sent by mail at the Tenant's risk) to the Landlord at … Any rents lost in the mail will be treated as if unpaid until received by the Landlord.

الشيكات / شيك مصرفي إلى أن يتعذر صرف الشيك فيرجع غير مسدد. يجب الالتزام بمواعيد / بأوقات التسديد ولن تقبل أية أعذار، فالوقت هو الجوهر في الدفع. ويدفع الإيجار لـ ——————————————
———— ويسلم باليد (أو يرسل / يتم إرساله بالبريد على مسئولية المستأجر) للمالك على العنوان ————————————
—————، وتتم معاملة رسوم الإيجار التي يتم فقدها عند إرسالها بالبريد على أنها غير مدفوعة إلى أن يتسلمها المالك.

3. Use

3 – الاستخدام

The Tenant agrees to use the premises only as a residence for self, and those persons identified below. By no means may the Tenant allow any additional persons, whose names are not mentioned in the present agreement, to reside in the property. The Tenant agrees to assume all responsibility for actions taken by any person entering the property.

يوافق المستأجر على استعمال العقار كمكان للإقامة لشخصه وللأشخاص التالين / وللأشخاص المدون أسمائهم أدناه:————
ولا يجوز للمستأجر بأي حال من الأحوال السماح لأشخاصٍ آخرين بالسكن ما لم يذكر أسمائهم في العقد، ويتحمل المستأجر مسؤولية كل فعل يصدر عن الأشخاص الذين يقيمون أو يدخلون العقار/ المأجور / السكن

4. Pets

4 – الحيوانات الأليفة

No pet shall be brought onto the Premises (even temporarily) without the express written permission of the Landlord. If a pet has been on the Premises at any time during the Tenant's occupancy (with or without the Landlord's consent), a charge may be made for de-fleaing, deodorizing, and/or shampooing, and/or damages occasioned by the pet.

لا يُسْمَح بإدخال الحيوانات الأليفة الى العقار (حتى بشكل مؤقت) إلا بموافقة خطية واضحة من المالك. وفي حال تم إدخال أي حيوان إلى العقار في أي وقت خلال سكن المستأجر فيه (بموافقة المالك أو من دونها)، فإنه قد يتم تغريم المستأجر بنفقات تتعلق بأجهزة التنظيف وإزالة الروائح والبراغيث وأية أضرار أخرى قد تنجم من الحيوانات / أو أية خسائر تسببها هذه الحيوانات.

5. Non-assignment of Rental Agreement

5 – عدم إحالة عقد الإيجار إلى طرف آخر

The Tenant agrees not to assign this agreement, nor to sub-let any part of the property, nor to allow any other person to live therein without first requesting permission from the Landlord and paying the appropriate surcharge.

يوافق المستأجر على عدم إحالة عقد الإيجار أو تأجير جزء من العقار أو السماح لأي شخص بالإقامة فيه دون طلب إذن/ موافقة خطية مسبقة من المالك، وكما يترتب على المستأجر دفع الأجور الإضافية المترتبة على ذلك.

6. Repair Policy

The Tenant acknowledges that the said property is in good condition. The Tenant shall use customary and due diligence in care of the premises. Any and all repairs made at the instruction of the Tenant shall be carried out by a competent professional and in compliance with all applicable codes and regulations.

6 – سياسة التصليح / التصليحات/ أحكام الصيانة والتصليح

ينبغي على المستأجر العناية بالعقار/ على المستأجر أن يذل ما بوسعه للإعتناء بالعقار وأن يبذل الجهود المطلوبة في ذلك. ويجب أن تكون جميع الأصلاحات التي يقوم بها المستأجر مطابقة لجميع المعايير والمواصفات كما يجب أن يقوم بها حِرَفي كفوء و مختص.

7. Security Deposit

The Tenant has deposited with, and the Landlord acknowledges receipt of, $... as a security deposit. This security deposit is to guarantee the return of the premises to the Landlord in the same or better condition as when accepted by the Tenant, reasonable wear and tear excepted, and to satisfy any obligations of the Tenant unfulfilled at the termination of this rental agreement, as specified herein. If any provision of this rental agreement is breached, the security deposit is forfeited. The security deposit shall be applied to indemnify the Landlord against damage and/or loss of value as a result of the Tenant's actions, mistakes, or inaction during the term of occupancy. The security deposit may not be applied by the Tenant as and for payment of any rent due the Landlord.

7 – وديعة الأمان / عربون الضمان / مقدم السكن المدفوع للضمان

لقد قام المستأجر بإيداع مبلغ من المال قدره ______ دولاراً أمريكياً / كوديعة أمان لدى المالك والذي يقر بدوره بأستلامها. تضمن الوديعة بإعادة العقار للمالك كما كان أو أفضل مما كان عليه عندما يتم استلامه من المستأجر، ويستثنى من ذلك الاستهلاك المعقول للأجهزة والأغراض. كما تضم الوديعة إيفاء المستأجر بأية واجبات لم يتمها عند أنتهاء عقد الإيجار هذا كما هو محدد في هذا العقد. عند الإخلال بأي من أحكام عقد الإيجار هذا فإن المستأجر يخسر حقه في استرجاع وديعة الأمان، ويكون وديعة الأمان بمثابة ضمان للمالك ضد أي ضرر و / أو خسارةٍ مادية جَرَاءَ أي فعلٍ أو خطأ يرتكبه المستأجر أو تراخ من قِبَلِهِ في أداء واجباته طوال فترة إقامته. ولا يمكن للمستأجر أن يستعمل وديعة الأمان كرسم إيجار مستحق للمالك.

8. Tenant Insurance

The Tenant agrees to purchase renter's insurance at their own expense, sufficient to cover themselves and their property from damage or injury caused

8 – تأمين المستأجر

يوافق المستأجر على دفع تكاليف الحصول "التأمين على المستأجر" الذي يجب أن يكون كافياً لحماية المستأجر / والذي يضمن حماية نفسه وممتلكاته من الأضرار الناجمة عن

by fire, theft, burglary, and breakage, and electrical connections and hereby relieves the Landlord of all risks that may be insured thereunder.

الحريق والسرقة والسطو والكسر والتوصيلات الكهربائية، وبناءاً على ذلك يعفى المالك من عبء الأخطار/ المخاطر التي يغطيها التأمين.

9. Alterations

9 – التغييرات / التبديلات

Tenant shall make no alterations, decorations, additions or improvements in or to the premises without the Landlord's prior written consent, and then only by contractors or mechanics approved by the Landlord. The Tenant specifically agrees that no tacks, nails, screws, etc. will be driven into the walls, nor will they be marred or torn by glue or tape. They also acknowledge that they will be responsible for and pay any damage done by rain, wind, hail, tornadoes, hurricanes, etc., if this damage is caused by leaving windows open, allowing stoppage and/or overflow or water and/or sewage pipes, broken windows or doors, torn screens, broken door and window locks, etc. or any damage caused while the Tenant has occupancy.

لا يجوز للمستأجر أن يقوم بأية تغييرات أو تزيينات أو إضافات أو تحسينات للعقار بدون موافقة خطية مسبقة من المالك، وعندها يتم ذلك على أيدي متعهدين/ متعاقدين وميكانيكيين محترفيين يوافق عليهم المالك. ويوافق المستأجر تحديداً على عدم دق مسامير صغيرة أو كبييرة أو براغي أو غيرها في الجدران وعلى أن لا يشوهها أو يثقبها باستخدام الصمغ أو الأشرطة اللاصقة. كما ويتعهد المستأجر بتحمل المسئولية الكاملة وعليه تبعاً لذلك بالدفع مقابل أي أضرار تحدث بسبب المطر، الرياح، البرد، الزوابع، الأعاصير .... الخ، إذا حدث ضرر بسبب إهمال المستأجر للنوافذ بتركها مفتوحة مفسحا المجال للإنسداد بسبب المياه أو الفيضان، إنسداد المجاري، تكسر النوافذ أو الأبواب أو أقفالها .. الخ، أو أي ضرر يحدث أثناء فترة شغل المستأجر للعقار.

10. Utilities

10 – المنافع / المرافق العامة

The Tenant will be responsible for payment of all utilities, garbage, water and sewer charges, telephone, gas or other bills incurred during their residency.

تقع مسئولية جميع المرافق على المستأجر/ المستأجر مسئول عن جميع المرافق التي يستخدمها / سيكون المستأجر مسئولاً عن جميع المرافق التي يستخدمها، مثل النفايات، المياه، رسوم المجاري، الهاتف، الغاز وجميع الفواتير التي يتكبدها خلال إقامته في العقار.

11. Full Disclosure

11 – الإقرار الشامل / الاقرار الكامل

The Tenant signing this rental agreement hereby states that all questions about this rental agreement have been answered, that they fully understand all the provisions of the

إن المستأجر الذي يوقع على هذا العقد يقر بأن كل الأسئلة حول هذا العقد قد تمت الأجابة عليها،

agreement and the obligations and responsibilities of each party, as spelled out herein. They further state that they agree to fulfill their obligations in every respect or suffer the full legal and financial consequences of their actions or lack of action in violation of this agreement. Signature by the Tenant on this rental agreement is acknowledgment and he/she has received a signed copy of the rental agreement.	وانه قد فهم تماماً كل أحكام و بنود العقد وجميع الشروط والمسئوليات لكل جزء وكما هو موضح هنا بالتفصيل. ويقر أيضاً بأنه وافق على الإيفاء بالتزاماته من كل ناحية أو أن يتحمل كل التبعات القانونية والمالية لأفعاله أو لتقصيره أو لانتهاكه لهذا العقد. وتوقيع المستأجر على هذا العقد إقرارٌ بأنه قد استلم نسخة موقعة من عقد الإيجار.
Accepted this day of In witness whereof, the Tenant and Landlord have duly signed this agreement in duplicate.	قُبِلَ هذا العقد في يوم ------ من شهر ---- من العام --------
SIGNATURES Landlord Tenant	توقيع المالك ------------- توقيع المستأجر

4 Arabic–English translation technology

INTRODUCTION

Over the past decades, the nature and performance of translation work has changed dramatically as a result of the increased use of technology. As a result, it is impossible to discuss contemporary translation practice without devoting attention to the technologies that are currently in use. However, it is the very speed by which technology advances that risks making any discussion of it obsolete by the time it is published, as another more powerful technology supersedes existing ones. Similarly, names may change, websites migrate and companies merge. Hence, this overview is very much of a snapshot of the moment.

The aim here is not to provide an exhaustive overview of the use of computers in translation; rather, it is, like the rest of the book, a practical guide for translators. In the course of this chapter, a number of issues related to computer-aided translation will be discussed, and relevant tools evaluated for use to the translator working between English and Arabic. As this is a vast field, the emphasis will be on resources that are widespread, with a preference for those that are available free of charge.

COMPUTER AIDED TRANSLATION (CAT)

This term, and its variants **Computer-assisted Translation** and **Machine-assisted Human Translation** (MAHT), covers a wide variety of software tools that are employed to assist translators in their work. In most cases, it refers to **Translation Memory** (TM) tools, i.e. software that stores the user's previous translations in a resident (= in the computer) database, which the program draws on for suggestions when new texts are being translated. Naturally, this does little more than automate what professional translators were already doing by, for instance, cutting and pasting terminology, etc. from previous translations that they had saved electronically.

At present, there is a wide range of competing commercial products that are also enabled for Arabic, the most widely used being SDL Trados, MultiTrans, MetaTexis, LogiTerm, Wordfast, Star Transit and Déjà Vu. The principle is very simple; with every translation that is entered the database that can be 'mined' (exploited) is enlarged, and as a result it becomes more and more effective over time. In addition, these programs can be used to generate subject-specific dictionaries and glossaries as they incorporate a Terminology Management (confusingly also sometimes abbreviated to 'TM') component. The fact that it is equally possible to load existing translations and originals into the memory by linking (or 'aligning') the source and target texts makes this an invaluable resource. This allows the translator to create Translation Memory databases from existing translation files. Say, one has been translating washing machine manuals for two years and kept all the source and translation files. The program will immediately compile a huge database by linking the appropriate source and target segments, which can be words (e.g. titles), phrases, sentences or paragraphs. Figure 4.1 displays an example of Arabic–English alignment in Déjà Vu.

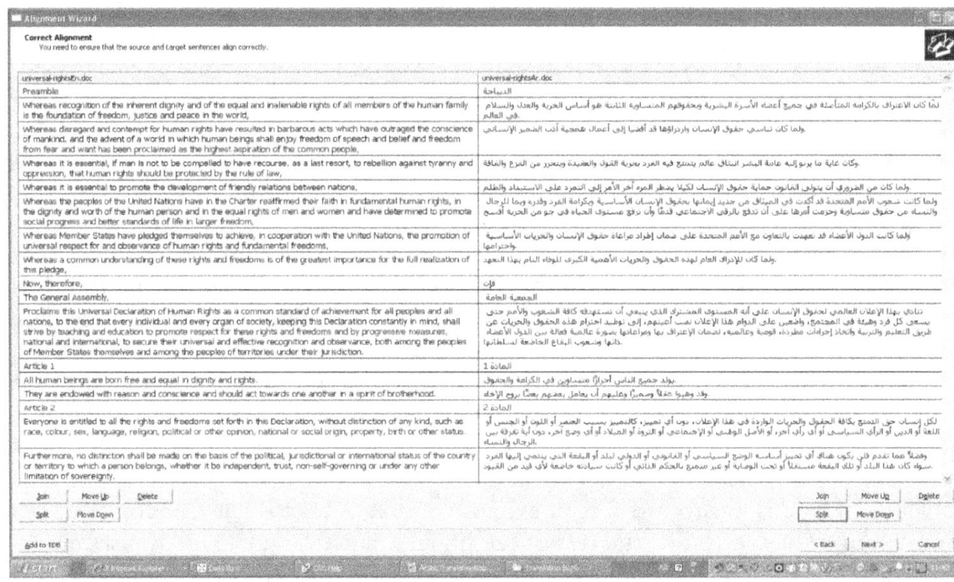

Figure 4.1 Example of Arabic–English text alignment in Déjà Vu

The alignment process is based on so-called sentence delimitation or ‘chunking’ rules that determine how the text in a specific language should be segmented. Many of these rules are common to many languages, with punctuation (e.g. full stop, exclamation and question marks) and layout features (e.g. blank spaces, indentation) being common triggers.

It’s not just a translator’s own files, of course, that can be lined up. For instance, imagine a translator who starts working in the telecommunications industry; by loading past translations of manuals that are available online, he or she will have ready-made translational and terminological databases to draw upon, even before the first assignment comes in. Naturally, the robustness of a program is measured by the extent to which all the segments are properly aligned.

TM-based CAT tools have become ever more sophisticated and the solutions suggested by the software go far beyond identical texts, as individual segments are recognized and predictions are made, based on past translations. As a result, the time savings can be vast. This type of software is most useful for professional translators who are active in a single field. Indeed, the more varied the number of fields one works in, the more varied and the less effective the database is. For instance, if one routinely translates legal or technical documents in the same area, the pre-translation prowess will be such that the memory will, in some cases, provide ‘exact matches’ for 90 per cent of the ST, with the translator merely having to do some minor post-editing, i.e. revision. In many cases, however, the programs will return so-called ‘fuzzy matches’ (segments in which differences are minimal).

It is also worth bearing in mind the time-honoured computing adage 'Rubbish in – Rubbish out'; that is to say, a database is only as good as the translations that have been stored in it and in some cases the outcome is a reduplication of errors! Though the resource is next to pointless for those who are starting out and have nothing to put into the database, there is already a return – however minimal – from the second translation onwards!

The program also holds an attraction to translators' corporate clients, who often insist that the work is provided in a format that allows them to load it into their own Translation Memory systems. Another side-effect of the spread of TM software is that translators receive a 'pre-edited' text, replete with suggestions generated by their principals' memory databases. Rather than being asked to translate the whole ST, translators are, in effect, reduced to editors and revisers. One of the main consequences – or aims! – of this is, naturally, a reduction in the amount of text that can be charged for.

The use of translation software by the end-users has not only resulted in a loss of control by translators of their resource, but also in their choice of tools in that they may be compelled to abide by their clients' software (often at great expense), which has become the norm for those who do agency work or deal directly with corporate end-users. Things have reached their logical conclusion with the increased use of web-based translation, which precludes translators even from building up their own resources as the TT is entered online, with everything being controlled by the clients' system. This is a key component in *localization*, i.e. the translation/adaptation of product information to local markets, which requires the utmost degree of uniformity and precision in terms of terminology, equivalents, etc.

It would seem that the only group of professional translators for whom CAT has little or no added value are the literary translators, though some might churlishly argue that this is not surprising since it is a hobby rather than a profession in view of the low returns.

The term CAT also sometimes covers **Machine Translation** (MT) and **Automatic** (or **Automated**) **Translation** (AT), which, strictly speaking, refers to computerized translation. Rather than relying on memory databases, MT software uses encoded linguistic information in order to generate translations automatically. A very good example of MT are online services such as **Google Translate**, which will be discussed later on.

ONLINE TRANSLATION TOOLS

Many of the most useful tools in modern day-to-day translation practice are to be found online. These range from dictionaries and automatic translation tools to corpora and terminological databases. Below, only those resources that are relevant to Arabic>/<English translation will be discussed.

ONLINE DICTIONARIES

From the outset, it is important to define 'online dictionary' in this context. The term is used to denote various types of resources, such as digitized dictionaries that are available for download but which, on the whole, tend not to be searchable in the form of a database. More often than not it involves works that have been (illegally) scanned in a picture format and, though still useful as a resource, offer little added value to its printed counterparts (other than the fact that they are free). More rarely, the term sometimes refers to electronic dictionaries that are available for purchase online. In this section we shall concentrate on the 'true' online dictionaries, i.e. those that are searchable databases.

There is currently a plethora of free dictionary sites, but Arabic is lagging somewhat behind the more common European languages and not every dictionary offers it. What is more, those online dictionaries that offer Arabic and English do not always provide translations in both directions. The main dictionaries that offer **English>Arabic** are:

Babylon: www.babylon.com/define/98/English-Arabic-Dictionary.html
Dicts Info: www.dicts.info/ud.php?l1=Arabic&l2
al-Misbar: www.almisbar.com/salam_trans.html
Ectaco: www.ectaco.co.uk/English-Arabic-Dictionary/
Firdaus: www.firdaous.com/en/0023.htm
Maajim: www.maajim.com/translate/
World Star: www.stars21.com/dictionary/English-Arabic_dictionary.html

The following site can be used for **Arabic>/<English** translations:

Lingvosoft: www.lingvosoft.co.uk/English-Arabic-Dictionary/

In addition to online translating dictionaries, there are also a number of explanatory dictionary sites, the main one being Maajim (www.maajim.com), which contains all the great classical **Arabic–Arabic** dictionaries: *Lisān al-ᶜArab*, *Tāj al-ᶜArūs*, *Muḥīṭ al-Muḥīṭ*, *al-Wasīṭ*). For **English–English** resources, users are spoilt for choice, with all the major dictionary publishers (Oxford, Longman, Webster's) having an online presence, though full services are often available only on subscription.

It is important to stress, however, that very few of the online translating dictionaries can compete successfully with their (high-quality) printed counterparts, for a number of reasons:

- the number of entries (or *lemmas*, to use the term employed by lexicographers) tends to be considerably lower;
- despite their online mode, they tend to be updated less;
- the absence of additional information such as collocations, examples;
- the absence of technical terms.

However, the main issue with online dictionaries from the translator's point of view is the fact that, unlike printed published dictionaries, the reliability of online sites may be questionable at times, not least because there is usually no listing of authorship, sources, methodology, etc. As such, one should proceed cautiously and bear in mind the principle of *caveat emptor* ('buyer beware!').

The same comment is true for another recent development in online translation services, the translators' forums. Whilst most translators would probably frown upon using a term they were given by somebody they bumped into in the street, many seem to be quite happy to accept a translation from a perfect stranger online! Even if a translation obtained in this way turns out to be correct, it does not detract from the fact that the practice, itself, is dubious and should be avoided by serious professionals, except, perhaps, for some additional checking purposes or as a means of obtaining further references.

A relative newcomer to the field, Almaany (www.almaany.com/), offers translations in both directions and also includes a considerable amount of technical terminology. More importantly, Almaany is particularly valuable to the translator as search results are contextualized, as shown by the example in Figure 4.2.

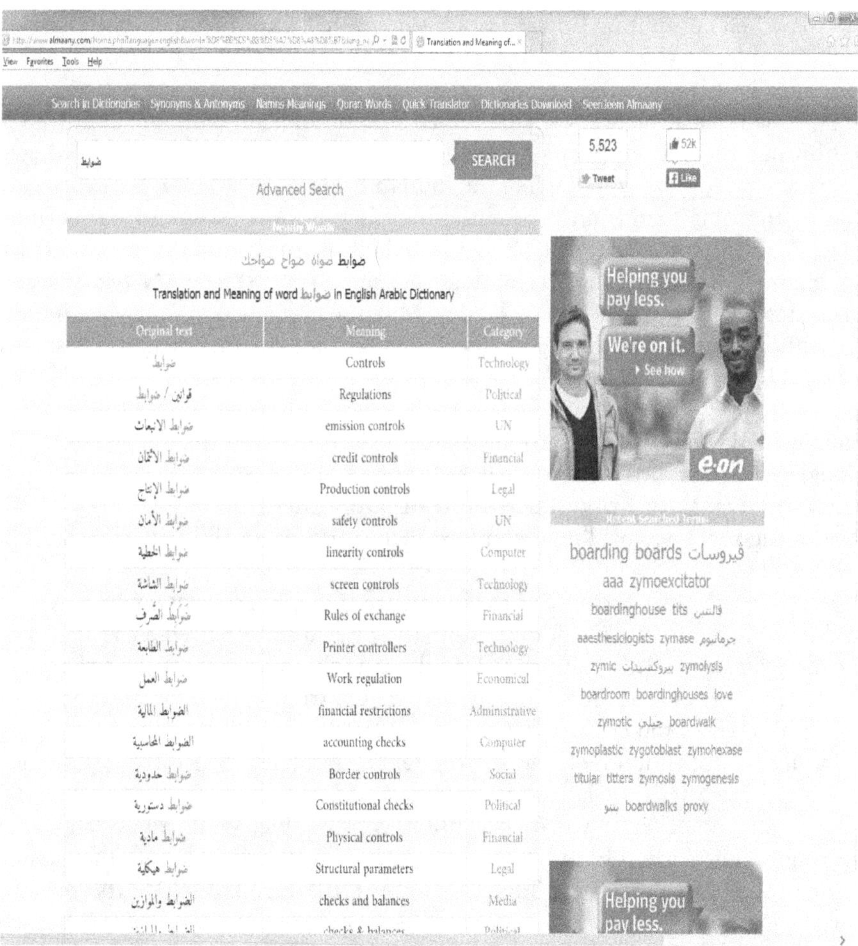

Original text	Meaning	Category
ضوابط	Controls	Technology
قوانين / ضوابط	Regulations	Political
ضوابط الانبعاث	emission controls	UN
ضوابط الأثمان	credit controls	Financial
ضوابط الإنتاج	Production controls	Legal
ضوابط الأمان	safety controls	UN
ضوابط الخطية	linearity controls	Computer
ضوابط الشاشة	screen controls	Technology
ضوابط الصرف	Rules of exchange	Financial
ضوابط الطابعة	Printer controllers	Technology
ضوابط العمل	Work regulation	Economical
الضوابط المالية	financial restrictions	Administrative
الضوابط المحاسبية	accounting checks	Computer
ضوابط حدودية	Border controls	Social
ضوابط دستورية	Constitutional checks	Political
ضوابط مادية	Physical controls	Financial
ضوابط هيكلية	Structural parameters	Legal
الضوابط والموازين	checks and balances	Media

Figure 4.2 Example of search results page of Almaany (www.almaany.com/home.php?language=english&word=%D8%B6%D988%%D8%A7%D8%A8%D8%B7&lang_name=Arabic&type_word=2&dspl=0)

Online automatic translation

The earliest experiments in the field of Machine Translation (MT) took place in the 1950s, the most famous being the 'Georgetown experiment' (1954), which involved the fully automatic translation of over sixty Russian sentences into English. Despite the claim by researchers that the problem could be solved in a few years, reality proved to be more resistant. In the early 1960s, the late Yehoshua Bar Hillel formulated the radical idea that 'fully automatic high-quality machine translation' (FAHQMT) was both theoretically and practically impossible as machines must be able to process meaning. In order to prove his point, he used the now famous example: 'Little John was looking for his toybox. Finally he found it. The box was in the pen. John was very happy.' He argued that a machine would be unable to correctly determine the meaning of 'pen' in this sentence.

Since then, MT has come a long way, with a major impetus being given in the late 1980s when computing power not only increased exponentially but also became more affordable. In spite of this, the Holy Grail of FAHQMT that can rival human performance is still not within reach, even if the current state of the art suggests that FAHMQT is, at least, theoretically possible. The conundrum will only be solved in the future through the development of so-called 'intelligent computers', which can acquire and learn knowledge very much like the human brain.

One of the oldest and, until recently, one of the most powerful online machine translation engines was Babel Fish (www.babelfish.com/) initially produced by the search engine Altavista, using technology developed by SYSTRAN (www.systranet.com/translate), which has been involved in MT research since the very beginning. The SYSTRAN online translation engine does offer Arabic, in which field it has since been joined by a handful of others:

Bubbles: www.bubblestranslation.com/english/translator.html
Google Translate: http://translate.google.com/#
Microsoft Translator: www.microsofttranslator.com/
WorldLingo: www.worldlingo.com/products_services/worldlingo_translator.html

Of the four, the most versatile at the moment is Google Translate, which even offers an audio facility (albeit only for English) of the translations, whereas it is without doubt the fastest of all the online MT tools. It is the only one of the programs that is 'interactive' insofar as users are invited to contribute better translations of the automatically generated ones.

In addition to individual words or texts, Bubbles, SYSTRAN, Google and WorldLingo also offer translations of websites.

Once again, however, a word of caution is advisable; while these engines are a useful rough-and-ready tool in order to have a quick gist translation, they cannot be used for proper translation. As Table 4.1 shows, the results include the bizarre and downright incomprehensible, alongside perfectly correct translations. Indeed, what is striking above all is not the fact that source sentences are badly translated, but that the systems return ungrammatical, unnatural and/or incomprehensible translations, which violate the very rules upon which they have been built.

Table 4.1 Sample translations by online programs

English > Arabic

ST	*Bubbles*	*SYSTRAN*	*Microsoft*	*Google*	*WorldLingo*
'I don't have a book yet.'	ليس لدي كتاب حتى الآن	لم يحصل أنا يتلقّى كتاب بعد	لا يتلقى كتاب بعد	ليس لديّ كتاب حتّى الآن	أنا لا أتلقّى كتاب بعد
'Preparations are underway for work on a new swimming pool.'	تحضيرات جار لعمل على [سويمينغ بوول] جديد	تحضيرات جار لعمل على [سويمّينغ بوول] جديد	يجري التحضير للعمل في بركة السباحة جديد	يجري حاليا الإعداد للعمل على حمام سباحة جديد	تحضيرات جار لعمل على [سويمّينغ بوول] جديدة
'The horse raced past the barn fell.'	تسابق الحصان الماضي الحظيرة سقطت	[فلّ] الحصان حجر السّامة يتسابق بعد الهري	سقط الحصان تسابق في الماضي الحظيرة	تسابق الحصان الماضي الحظيرة سقطت	[فلّ] الحصان حجر السّامة يتسابق بعد الهري

Arabic > English

Bubbles	*SYSTRAN*	*Microsoft*	*Google*	*WorldLingo*	*ST*
'My sister bought a new car last week.'	'Sisters car of the new week last bought.'	'I bought my new car last week.'	'My sister bought a new car last week.'	'Sisters car of the new week last bought.'	اشترت أختي سيارة جديدة الأسبوع الماضي
'Egyptian officials are in contact with Somali leaders in Mogadishu.'	'Egyptian heads occur Somalian communications with commanders in Mogadishu.'	'Egyptian officials are contacts with leaders of Somalis in the Mogadishu.'	'Egyptian officials are in contact with Somali leaders in Mogadishu.'	'Egyptian heads occur Somalian communications with commanders in Mogadishu.'	يجري مسئولون مصريون اتصالات مع قادة صوماليين في مقديشيو
'Acknowledges that the lessor has the right and full authority to hire two-bedroom apartment.'	'The landlord avows that for him followed and the authority [aalkaamlh] [fY] renting apartment of rooms and hall.'	'Approves the lessor right and full authority in renting an apartment 2 rooms and lounge.'	'Acknowledges that the lessor has the right and full authority to hire two-bedroom apartment.'	'The landlord avows that for him followed and the complete authority in renting of apartment is rooms and hall.'	يقر المؤجر بأن له الحق والسلطة الكاملة في تأجير شقة غرفتين وصالة

When one takes a closer look at the test sentences and their target segments, it becomes clear that even though some providers had difficulty with terminology – surprisingly even in cases such as 'fell', 'swimming pool' and السلطة <الكاملة> – it is syntactic complexity that constitutes the principal stumbling block for all the programs. A case in point is the very simple – but syntactically ambiguous – sentence 'The horse raced past the barn fell', which defied every attempt at translation. The same feature also accounts for the mistranslation by all engines of the legal sentence.

Corpora and concordancers

The term 'corpus' (ذَخِيرة لُغَوِية) refers to a collection of texts or speech in one (*monolingual*) or several (*multilingual*) languages that is electronically (or digitally) stored for processing. The first computer corpus ever created was the *Brown University Standard Corpus of Present-Day American English Corpus*, which is known, simply, as the 'Brown Corpus'. It was developed in the 1960s and contained one million words of edited written American English.

Corpora are the main resource for specialists working in the field of corpus linguistics, which focuses on the use of languages as found in collections (*corpora*) of 'authentic' text, i.e. as it occurs in the real world.

The biggest corpora today are for English. The *British National Corpus* (BNC) contains a 200-million word collection of samples of written and spoken language from a wide range of sources, and thus reflects a wide cross-section of current British English, both spoken and written (www.natcorp.ox.ac.uk/). The *North American News Text Corpus* is composed of approximately 310 million words of formatted news text (https://catalog.ldc.upenn.edu/LDC95T21).

Present-day corpora come in a number of guises. The Brown Corpus, the BNC and the NAWTC are all 'balanced' inasmuch as they contain balanced samples of different types (or genres) of written – and, ideally, spoken – English, i.e. fiction and non-fiction literature, media, technical writing, etc.

These corpora are particularly useful for lexicographers, i.e. dictionary-makers, as they provide insight into word frequency, synonymy, polysemy, register, dialect, and so on.

The approach to corpora can be twofold insofar as it can be 'driven' by them, or 'based' on them. Within a corpus-driven approach, the data are the only guiding principle; in other words, if it is not in the corpus, it does not exist! For obvious reasons, most lexicographical works are therefore corpus-based in that they rely on 'authentic' meanings of words in contemporary usage. This is the case, for instance, of contemporary major English dictionaries (Oxford, Longman). Modern grammars of English, too, rely on corpora: e.g. Greenbaum's *Oxford English Grammar* (1996) was based almost entirely on information extracted from the British Component of the *International Corpus of English*, whereas the Collins *COBUILD* project has resulted in a series of reference grammars for learners of English reliant on examples culled from the *Bank of English* Corpus.

Though this approach has been used for other languages since then, its application in Arabic is long overdue and the only bilingual English–Arabic dictionary that is based on a corpus is Hinds and Badawi's *Dictionary of Egyptian Arabic* (1986). This was also a glaring lacuna in Arabic–Arabic lexicography, until the release of the monumental مُعْجَم اللغة العَرَبِيَّة المُعاصِرة 2008 , which is based on a 100-million-word corpus. Among the few Arabic grammar books reliant on a corpora for examples we find E. Badawi, A. Gully and M. Carter's *Modern Written Arabic Grammar* (2004) and R. Buckley's *Modern Literary Arabic: A Reference Grammar* (2004).[145]

The second type of corpus is a so-called *Treebank*, in which all sentences have been annotated to provide syntactic (i.e. relational) information. This process is known as 'parsing', and the information is represented in a tree structure, hence the name Treebank. The most famous of these *parsed corpora* is the *Penn Treebank* (www.cis.upenn.edu/~treebank/),[146] named after Pennsylvania University, where it was created. It is important to add that Treebanks are not balanced.

The differences in approach are linked to the aims of each type of corpus; the target audience of a balanced corpus includes people who are primarily interested in linguistic description and analysis, whereas Treebanks are typically aimed at corpus linguists who are interested in having a large collection of texts in computer-readable language that is available for tagging (grammatical annotation) and parsing with a view to conducting research in Natural (i.e. human) Language Processing (NLP).[147]

Over the years, many more corpora have been compiled for a large number of languages, including Arabic, which has received a huge boost as the initial problems of dealing with bidirectional scripts have been overcome.

While some corpora concentrate on Arabic only, several are *bilingual*, which are, of course, of invaluable use to the translator since they essentially constitute a database, which can, in turn, be used in Translation Memory management processing (see above).

Unfortunately, many Arabic corpora are not available for public use, and those that are tend to be extremely expensive.[148] Our discussion will be limited to the freely accessible corpora.

Translators are always advised to construct their own *parallel corpora*, i.e. bodies of text in parallel translation, as these provide a unique resource for future practice, as well as for further processing in, for instance, CAT tools.

The Arabic corpora fall into one of two broad types: news corpora and conversational corpora. As the latter involve corpora of telephone conversations,[149] spontaneous speech and broadcast news for use in speech recognition software, they fall outside the scope of this chapter. Instead, we shall discuss the news corpora, which may be divided into three groups:

1 Written press

In this group, we find, for instance: *Arabic Gigaword* (approx. 2 million words); the 80-million-word *Arabic Newswire Corpus* (*Agence France Presse, Assabah, Al-Ḥayāt, An Nahar, Ummah Press, Xinhua News Agency*); *An-Nahar Newspaper Text Corpus* (24 million words) from the Lebanese *An-Nahar* newspaper; the *Al-Ḥayāt Corpus* (18.5 million words); *Penn Arabic Treebank* (https://catalog.ldc.upenn.edu/LDC2004T02), a written Modern Standard Arabic corpus from *Agence France Presse* (AFP) newswire archives.

2 Audio(visual) media

This type of corpus is much rarer, and the main representative is the *Louvain Receptive Arabic Language Learning* (RALL) corpus, which comprises 320,000 words, broken down as follows: 80,000 from Algeria, Saudi Arabia and Egypt each, added with a control corpus of 80,000 words. It is important to note, however, that the storage of the corpus is still in writing.

3 Mixed

This category includes corpora that rely on both audiovisual and written media resources. The biggest are: *Corpus Linguae Arabicae* (CLARA), approximately 37 million words, a balanced and annotated corpus drawn from various geographical areas and comprising literature, press and other written materials; the *Corpus of Contemporary Arabic* (CCA),[150] 1 million words from a heterogeneous pool of both spoken and written materials.

The above corpora vary considerably in size, the type of resources from which data has been collected, geographical spread, representativeness ('balanced' vs 'unbalanced') and, most of all, accessibility and cost.

We shall now discuss corpus searching through three free corpora, arabiCorpus (www.arabicorpus.byu.edu), the *International Corpus of Arabic* (www.bibalex.org/ica/en/default.aspx) and the *Leeds Arabic Corpora* (http://corpus.leeds.ac.uk/query-ar.html).

At the time of writing, **arabiCorpus**[151] contains about 69 million words, culled from a number of subcorpora, including newspapers from a variety of Arab countries (*al-Ahrām*, *al-Ḥayāt*, *al-Tajdīd*, *al-Waṭan*), in addition to the Qur'an, classical and modern literature, 'chat' data from the internet, as well as the Penn Treebank news data. Most of the corpora are only available in combined groups, but the individual newspapers can be searched separately. Figure 4.3 shows the default search screen.

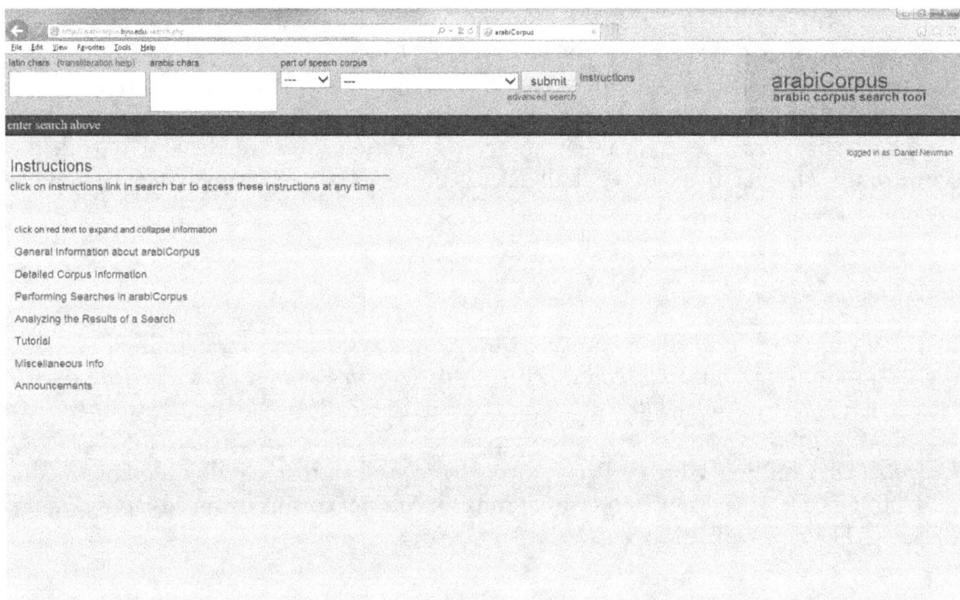

Figure 4.3 Search page of arabiCorpus (http://arabicorpus.byu.edu/search.php)

Search entries can be made either in Arabic script or in transliteration, whereas the word category (adjective, noun, verb string) can be specified, as can the subcorpus one wishes to search (a full corpus query slows down the search time considerably).

In addition to the statistics (number of occurrences, percentages) and the actual results in context ('citations'), it is possible to access a summary of the word forms, i.e. with article, adjectival forms, etc., to filter out subsections of the resources (e.g. results per newspaper, novel), as well as specifying the number of words one wishes to look at before and after the target word. Conveniently, the 'word before/after' tab takes the user to a list of occurrences of words next to the target, which, of course, is extremely helpful in determining common collocations, as well as filtering out irrelevant neighbouring words and repeated occurrences.

The **International Corpus of Arabic** (ICA) is hosted by the Bibliotheca Alexandrina in Egypt and will, once completed, contain 100 million words. At the time of writing, the corpus comprises approximately 70 million words. The corpus is unique in that it is fully representative of modern language use across the entire Arab world with data from publications from every country of the region, as well as beyond. The ICA covers a wide variety of sources (online and print) as well as genres and subjects (literature, science, technology). The interface toggles between English and Arabic, but search terms can only be entered in the Arabic script. Figure 4.4 shows the default search screen.

Figure 4.4 Search page of the International Corpus of Arabic (www.bibalex.org/ica/ar/default.aspx)

Searches can be filtered according to the number of words before and after the search term/string; word class; stem pattern; number; gender; definiteness; and country. The results provide information about the genre, source and country of origin, whereas both the sentence and wider context can also be accessed.

The **Leeds Arabic Corpora** comprises newspaper data (*al-Ḥayāt*), public Wiki data, the Corpus of Contemporary Arabic (CCA), Arabic legal data and a computer science corpus. What it lacks in size – at less than 2 million words it is quite small in comparison with the giants that are populating cyberspace – it makes up for by including technical subcorpora.

The Leeds corpora are also quite user-friendly: the corpus is divided into five subcorpora (see Figure 4.5), which can be queried individually. Unfortunately, unlike in arabiCorpus, it is not possible to search the entire corpus in one go, which is rather a limitation in view of the often small size of the subcorpora. The 'collocations' and 'concordance' facility (see below), however, is a major plus as a number of different variables can be set.

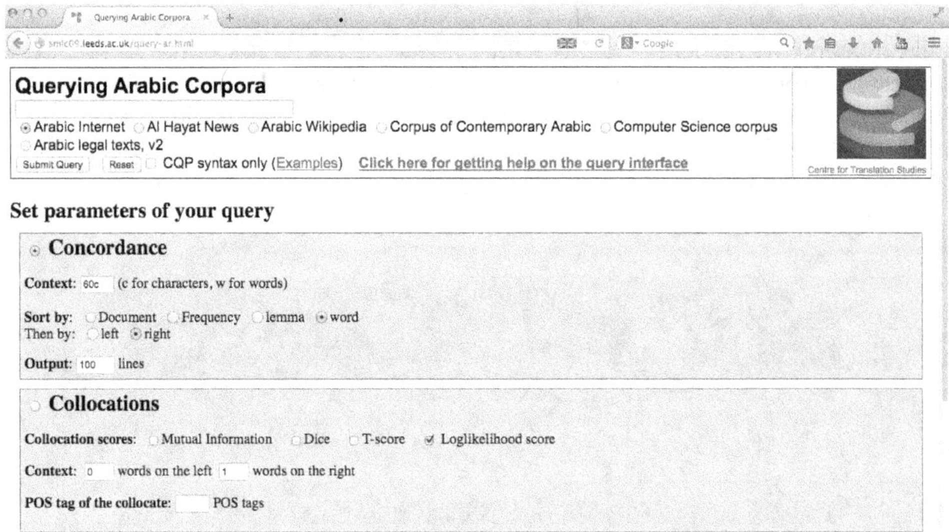

Figure 4.5 Search page of Leeds Arabic Corpora (http://corpus.leeds.ac.uk/query-ar.html)

Corpora and the translator

Corpora provide a number of significant benefits to the translator. First and foremost, they can serve as a pool from which to mine vocabulary and terminology. Secondly, they can be used to build bilingual databases of translations.

In order to make maximum use of corpora, they have to be processed in some form as raw data cannot be effectively managed. For instance, the world's biggest corpus for any language is Google search, but as this presents merely raw data, unprocessed, uncontrolled, it only becomes useful when it is 'screened' in one way or another. Probably the most important corpus-based tool with numerous applications in language-teaching and translation is *concordance*, which essentially shows a particular word in the context in which it appears; this is what corpus linguists call KWIC ('Keyword In Context').

Concordancer software 'chews' the data so that they appear in a user-friendly and useful format. A relatively big free concordancer for English is Corpus Concordance English (http://lextutor.ca/conc/eng/), which allows searches in a number of areas (all of them culled from the BNC): written language (1 million words), spoken language (1 million words), legal language (2.2 million words), medical corpus (1.4 million words) and the Brown corpus (see Figures 4.6 and 4.7).

Home > Concordancers > Corpus search input (Eng)

Corpus Concordance English (v.6.5)

With precast link extractor/exporter

French German Spanish English

Speed is 1 second per million words of corpus

Keyword(s): equals In corpus: Choose a Corpus Corpus descriptions

CONTROLS

Sort By 1 word(s) to Left of keyword | Line Width 120 Number of Lines 10,000 Gapped? No

On STARTS or FAMILY searches, "sort by keyword" gives distribution of forms

OPTION: With associated word within 4 words to Left side.

+ Scan for any recurring word (potential colloc.) within 5 words presenting <= 4 times

DEMOS: Demo 1 Demo 2 Demo 3 <<3+4 have new sort info >> Demo 4 Demo 5

Reset Get concordance

Link Extractor As discussed here and deployed here

Extractor is now replaced by fully explicit output URL + copiable link that contains this same information

Figure 4.6 Search page of Corpus Concordance (http://lextutor.ca/conc/eng/)

Figure 4.7 Results for 'resistance' in Corpus Concordance (www.lextutor.ca/concordancers/concord_e.html)

All corpora discussed above, arabiCorpus, the International Corpus of Arabic and the Leeds Arabic Corpora offer concordance searches, which are, as we have seen, very useful for collocations. Figures 4.8–10 contain screenshots of the result screens of each corpus.

Figure 4.8 Example of search results in arabiCorpus for كمبيوتر

Figure 4.9 Example of search results in the International Corpus of Arabic for كمبيوتر (http://arabicorpus.byu.edu/search.php?page=citations&sort=r BeforeW&start=1)

Figure 4.10 Example of search results in Leeds Arabic Corpora for كمبيوتر (http://corpus.leeds.ac.uk/cgi-bin/cqp.pl?searchstring=%D983%%D985%%D8%A8%D98%A%D9%88%D8%AA%D8%B1&corpuslist=i-ar-lemma&searchtype=conc&contextsize=60c&sort1=word&sort2=right&terminate=100&llstat=on&cleft=0&cright=1&cfilter=)

It is also possible to do the same thing for corpora or databases that you have collected yourself. The only thing that is needed is concordance software, which will do the text 'crunching' for you. There are a number of programs around, but most of them are quite expensive. A free and easy-to-use one (even if it is somewhat outdated now) is aConCorde, of which a sample screenshot can be seen in Figure 4.11.

Figure 4.11 Sample screen of aConCorde (http://www.andy-roberts.net/coding/aconcorde)

Glossary

Action verb A verb which denotes activity: e.g. *walk*, *read*, *look*. (>< **stative verb**).

Adjunct A type of **adverbial** which provides additional information, and is thus optional: e.g. *always*, *carefully*.

Adverb A word which modifies **a sentence, a verb, another adverb**, or **an adjective**: e.g. *sometimes*, *extremely*, *then*.

Adverbial phrase A group of words which play the grammatical role of an adverb: e.g. *with a knife*, *tomorrow morning*. The term **adverbial** nowadays denotes both single-word **adverbs** and **adverbial phrases**.

Agent In a passive sentence, who or what caused something to happen to someone or something else: e.g. in *The dinner was prepared by John*, John is the agent.

Affective meaning Related to the personal feelings or attitudes of the speaker (affection, disparagement, ...). Alternatively, it is also sometimes used to refer to the effect an utterance has on the addressee.

Alliteration Repetition of the same sound beginning several words in sequence: e.g. *parroting parading parasite*.

Allusive meaning Involves the meaning conjured up by a linguistic unit and often has an element of intertextuality: e.g. المُخضرَمون.

Anaphora For reasons of stylistic effect, the repetition of a reference to a word or phrase at the beginning of successive phrases, clauses or lines. This device is often referred to as **rhetorical anaphora**, in which case it is contrasted with **grammatical anaphora,** which involves the use of pronouns to refer to previously mentioned lexical units.

Antithesis Opposition, or contrast of ideas or words in a balanced or parallel construction.

Antonym A word that means the opposite of another: e.g. *night* vs *day*.

Apposition A construction in which a noun phrase is placed after another to modify its meaning: e.g. 'This jacket, *a hand-me-down*, is still in good condition.' ('A hand-me-down' is not connected to the subject by a preposition or conjunction.)

Archaism The use of an older or obsolete form.

Article A determiner of a noun phrase that does not have a meaning of its own. In English, there are **definite** (*the*) and **indefinite** (*a*, *an*) articles.

Associative meaning Refers to expectations associated with the referent: e.g. *That nurse is a woman*.

Assonance Repetition of the same sounds in words close to each other: e.g. *Thy kingdom come, thy will be done*.

Asyndeton Lack of conjunctions between coordinate phrases, clauses, or words.

Attitudinal meaning Attitude to the referent: choice of word indicates speaker's attitude to referent (derogatory terms).

Attributive When an adjective (or adjectival phrase) is used to modify a noun and is placed *before* that noun, it is used attributively: e.g. 'old' in 'an *old* woman'.

Borrowing A foreign word is borrowed with only minor, if any, changes (usually only phonologically): e.g. *mobile*, موبيل.

Calque (**loan translation**) The verbatim translation of a ST item into the TT, which involves the retention of the same structure: e.g. *skyscraper*, ناطحة السحاب.

Causative verb A type of transitive verb which expresses causative meaning: e.g. *raise*, *persuade*.

Clause A part of a complex sentence which contains a subject, a finite verb and a predicate. The structure of a clause is identical to that of a simple sentence.

- **Co-ordinate:** one of two clauses which are equal components of a sentence. In addition, a co-ordinate clause does not serve as a subject, complement, object or adverbial in another clause. The two clauses are linked by **conjunctions**.
- **Subordinate:** (= dependent clause) a clause which depends on the other (= **main clause**) clause of the sentence. A subordinate clause is usually introduced by a **subordinating conjunction** (*when*, *that*) or by **a relative pronoun** (*that*, *which*, *who*, *whose*, *whom*).

Code-switching The alternating use of two or more languages within the same stretch of discourse. This may involve the use of words, phrases or sentences within the same text.

Coherence The thematic consistence and development within a text that make it a structured whole, rather than a series of non sequiturs.

Cohesion The linking of parts of a text through various devices such as conjunctions (e.g. *and*).

Collocate (n.) A word that tends to co-occur with another one. See **collocation.**

Collocation A set of words that tend to go together: e.g. *a hoarse voice*, صَوْت أجَش.

Collocative meaning Meaning relating to words that regularly appear together (within certain contexts).

Colloquial Relating to the everyday (= informal) use of a language.

Communicative translation A type of translation, which is close to **free** translation and **cultural transposition,** in which ST expressions are rendered with their situationally appropriate cultural equivalents in the TT.

Compensation Information, or a stylistic effect from the ST that cannot be reproduced in the same place in the TT is introduced elsewhere in the TT: e.g, كتبتم الرسالة يا شيخ, translated as 'you wrote the letter O shaykh', with the vocative particle in English compensating for the absence of a second person pronoun equivalent to the Arabic clitic (the object pronoun تم). Compensation can be either **in kind** (as in the above example) or **in place** (with the shift of an effect occurring at different places in the ST and TT).

Complement A noun phrase which *completes*, i.e. gives additional information about the subject.

Complex preposition A preposition consisting of more than one word: e.g. *in front of*.

Compound (complex) sentence A sentence which contains two or more clauses.

Concord (= *agreement*) Refers to the relation between the number (= singular or plural) of the subject and the form of the verb.

Conjunct A word which links sentences: e.g. *besides, however, therefore.*

Conjunction A word which links co-ordinating clauses: e.g. *and, or, but, besides, alternatively.*

Connotative meaning (connotation) The thoughts provoked by a term when in reference to certain entities. Though these meanings may not be strictly implied by relevant definitions, they show up in common or preferred usage.

Copula Verbs like *appear, be, become, feel, look, prove, remain, seem, smell, sound, taste, turn,* which serve to link the subject with the complement of the sentence, and do not take an adverb: e.g. *This appears/is/ ... nice* (not *nicely). The *nice* in the example is known as a **predicative adjective.**

Cultural transposition (adaptation) The replacement of SL culture-specific items by TL culture-specific items: e.g. أثلج قلوبنا, 'our hearts have been warmed'; 'Romeo and Juliet', قيس وليلى.

Determiner A word – e.g. an *article, some, all* – which determines the referent(s) (= object or idea) of a noun phrase.

Denotative meaning (also **propositional meaning, literal meaning, dictionary meaning**) The conventional meaning of a word, utterance, etc. This is often contrasted with the **connotative meaning** (q.v.). For instance, the denotative meaning of 'winter' is that it is one of the seasons in the northern hemisphere and runs approximately from December to February. The connotative meanings of 'winter' are 'cold', 'snow', … .

Dialect A language variety which differs from another one – usually called the normative or standard variety – in grammar, syntax and lexis and that is limited to a particular geographical area.

Diglossia A situation, in a given speech community, in which there are two closely related languages, one of high prestige – which is typically used in formal contexts – and one of low prestige, which is the colloquial variety. In Arabic, the high form in Arabic is فصحى, the low form عامية (or دارجة).

Direct object A noun phrase referring to a person or thing affected by the action of the verb: e.g. 'She threw *me* (= direct object) out of the house.'

Ellipsis The process through which the subject of two or more co-ordinated clauses is mentioned only in the first and not in the others: e.g. 'He bought the ice-cream and (*he*) gave it to us.'

Euphemism Substitution of an agreeable or at least non-offensive expression for one that may be unpleasant or harsh to the listener or reader: e.g. The translation of *Piss off!* as إمشي ('Go!').

Exegetic translation A type of translation which includes information not contained in the ST with a view to explaining certain concepts to the target audience.

Explicitation The fact of introducing information from the ST that is implicit from the context or the situation: e.g. مريضه/ مريضته. The opposite is **implicitation,** which entails indicating information that is explicit in the ST: e.g. أخرج, *go out* or *come out.*

Free translation A type of translation in which there is a significant distance between ST and TT, with a correspondence at the level of the ideas found in the ST, rather than the words or sentences.

Generalization The translation of a term for a more general one: e.g. the translation of *chair, seat* as كرسي. The opposite is **particularization.**

Genre See **text type.**

Gerund A noun, derived from an *-ing* form: e.g. *The singing is nice.*

Gisting Producing a rough or outline translation of a text to provide an insight into the subject and overall content of the source text. Being less expensive and less time-consuming than a 'proper' (or 'custom') translation, gisting can be used, for example, to determine whether a text contains useful information before a custom translation is commissioned.

Head The noun in a noun phrase: e.g. 'the *children*'.

Homonym Words that are spelled the same but have different meanings. This should not be confused with **polysemy** as in the case of homonyms the meanings are unrelated: e.g. *bank* ('place to withdraw money' and 'slope next to a river').

Hyperbole Exaggeration for emphasis or for rhetorical effect.

Hyperonym A linguistic unit whose meaning is subsumed into, and thus more specific, than that of another one: e.g. *robin* is a hyperonym of *bird*. Cf. **superordinate.**

Idiolect The language variety or style used by a particular individual: e.g. the use of certain constructions, lexical units.

Idiom A fixed expression, whose meaning can often not be derived from its constituent components: e.g. *a red herring.*

Indirect object This refers to the person who receives the **direct object**: e.g. 'He gave *me* (= indirect object) the book.' OR: 'He gave the book *to me* (= indirect object).'

Interlinear translation Almost a morpheme-for-morpheme rendering of the ST – irrespective of conventional grammatical ordering – with both ST and TT appearing together. If added with grammatical information, the translation is also known as a **gloss.**

Interlingual translation The translation between two different languages or language varieties.

Intersemiotic translation Translation between semiotic (i.e. signs) systems: e.g. the meaning of a red light being 'translated', i.e. meaning that one has to stop.

Intertextuality Refers to the fact that texts are often linked to other texts, whether by allusion, imitation or the fact of belonging to the same genre.

Intralingual translation Translation within the same language; in many cases this involves paraphrase.

Intransitive verb A verb which cannot take a direct object: e.g. *to rise.*

Inversion To move a word or a phrase to another place in a sentence or a paragraph (usually for reasons of TT style).

Jargon A language variety usually associated with a given profession and which diverges from the normative variety in lexis only through the use of specialized terminology.

Lexical verb A verb which is not an auxiliary.

Lexicalized metaphor A metaphor whose meaning is stable and definable and thus appears in dictionaries: e.g. *the grim reaper.*

Literal translation A type of translation usually viewed as being at the opposite end of the spectrum from **free translation** inasmuch as it involves a word-for-word translation of the ST.

Litotes Understatement, for intensification, by denying the contrary of the thing being affirmed: e.g. 'She's not the cleverest person I ever met.'

Mass noun = uncountable noun.

Metaphor Implied comparison achieved through a figurative use of words; the word is used not in its literal sense, but in one analogous to it.

Metonymy Substitution of one word for another which it suggests: e.g. *a man of the cloth* (= 'a priest'); أَهْل البَيْت ('people of the house', to refer to the family of the Prophet Muhammad).

Modal A verb which expresses possibility, uncertainty etc.: e.g. *will*, *would*, *must*, *shall*, *should*, *ought*, *can*, *could*, *may*, *might*.

Mode (= mood) A category of the verb. English has three moods: **indicative** (denoting statements), **imperative** (commands), **subjunctive** (doubt, supposition).

Modifier A word or group of words which **modify** (= say something about) the **head** of a noun phrase: e.g. '*the boy's* school', '*the* seats *of the bus*'.

Modulation Within contrastive stylistics, a type of translation strategy that involves a shift in viewpoint between ST and TT (concrete/abstract, means/result, metaphor/non-metaphor, different parts of the same process): e.g. *he was blown away*, ذهب أدراج الرياح.

Non-finite verb A verb form which does not change with person and number, i.e. **present and past participles, imperative, infinitive.**

Onomatopeia Use of words to imitate natural sounds; accommodation of sound to sense.

Oxymoron Apparent paradox achieved by the juxtaposition of words which seem to contradict one another: e.g. *the honest thief*.

Pattern repetition Repetition of root patterns: الطبيل والتزمير. See also **root repetition.**

Phrase A group of words which form part of a clause.

- **Noun phrase:** refers to: 1) noun; 2) nominal group (e.g. *Duncan's book*); 3) pronoun (*he*); 4) pronominal group (*everyone*, *we all*).
- **Verb phrase:** part of a clause that contains an auxiliary and a main verb: e.g. *have seen*.
- **Adjective phrase:** part of a clause containing an adjective (and an adverb): e.g. (*quite*) *tall*.
- **Adverb phrase:** part of a clause containing one or more adverbs: e.g. *an* ***extremely beautifully*** *performed sonata*.

Pleonasm Use of superfluous or redundant words.

Polysemy The fact that one lexical item has several related meanings. This is usually contrasted with **homonymy** (q.v.), where the meanings are unrelated.

Pluperfect = the past perfect tense.

Predicate The part of the sentence which contains what is said about the subject.

Preterite = the simple past.

Reflected meaning When one sense of a particular word affects the understanding and usage of all the other senses of the word (**polysemy**).

Register A variety or style of language determined by a particular set of values of the context; it is determined by what the speaker is doing socially. Another way of looking at it is to perceive it as a functional variety. The concept of register is closely related to that of **diglossia** (q.v.).

Reinforcement A process whereby an item in the ST is reinforced by another item in the TT: e.g. *among the group*, من ضمن الفرقة. The opposite is **condensation:** e.g. *Do you know*…, لو سمحت هل تعرف….

Rheme A part of a clause that contains what the speaker says about the **theme.** Rheme is often used interchangeably with **comment.**

Root repetition A stylistic rhetorical device that is often used in Arabic and involves the repetition, in close proximity, of words whose root share the same letters: تخليص الإبريز فى تلخيص باريز.

Semantic repetition A stylistic rhetorical device that involves the use of (near-) synonyms: e.g. المحل، والمجاعة، والمسغبة. In English, this tends to be avoided as it is said to reflect paucity in style, and occurs most frequently in fixed expressions: e.g. *with might and main*, *last will and testament*.

Simile An explicit comparison between two things by means of *like* or *as*.

Simple sentence A one-clause sentence.

Slang A language variety that differs from the normative variety in grammar, syntax and lexis and that is confined to a particular segment of the speech community.

Social meaning Words are used to establish relationships between people and to delineate social roles. For example, the use of second personal plural pronouns in Arabic as a mark of respect.

Sociolect A language variety in which members of the same social group share a number of phonetic, grammatical and lexical features: e.g. the Queen's English.

Source language (SL) The language in which the text to be translated is written.

Source text (ST) The text to be translated.

Stative verb A verb that denotes a state: e.g. *know*, *remain*. (>< **action verb**).

Superordinate (hyperonym) A linguistic unit whose field of meaning is broader, and thus includes that of another unit: e.g. *flower* is the superordinate of *rose*. Cf. **hyperonym.**

Target language (TL) The language into which a text is to be translated.

Target readership The group of people for which a text is translated, for example subject experts, novices, prospective customers. It is important to specify the target readership when commissioning a translation so that the translator can choose an appropriate style and vocabulary.

Target text (TT) The translation, i.e. the result of the translation process.

Tautology Repetition of an idea in a different word, phrase, or sentence.

Text function The function served by a text, e.g. to sell a product, to provide instruction on the use of a product, to convey information about an event. It is important to specify the text function when commissioning a translation so that the translator can choose an appropriate style and vocabulary.

Text type Class of text (e.g. abstract, news report, light fiction, commentary) with specific characteristics of style, sentence formation, terminology, etc.

Theme That part of a clause which tells the addressee what it is about. This is usually contrasted with **rheme. Themes** are usually found in initial positions (**thematic fronting**). **Theme** is often used interchangeably with **topic.**

Thematic meaning Refers to how the order of words spoken affects the meaning that is entailed.

Transitive verb A verb that can take a direct object: e.g. 'I *saw* him' (= direct object). (<> **intransitive verb**).

Translation by addition A translation method by which the TT includes elements that are not contained in the ST. This process is sometimes referred to as **dissolution** or **amplification.**

Translation by omission A translation method by which elements included in the ST are left out of the TT. This is sometimes also referred to as **concentration** or **economy.**

Translation loss Strictly speaking, any omission in the rendering of the ST. This does not always involve grammatical losses, as the losses may be situated at the semantic, cultural or intertextual levels.

Transliteration, transcription Transforming text from one script to another, usually based on phonetic equivalences. One may distinguish between two main types of transliteration, a *broad* one and a *narrow one,* with the latter relying on a very precise grapheme-for-grapheme rendition which often involves the use of diacritical marks: e.g. *Imam* (broad) vs *imām* (narrow).

Transposition In contrastive stylistics, a translation strategy in which there is a shift in grammatical category between ST and TT: *to become penniless*, أفلس (noun to verb); *to cross*, وَضَع عَلامة الصَّليب.

Voice A category of the verb that expresses the relation between the subject and the verb. In English there are two voices: **passive** and **active**.

Notes

1 El-Gemei, 'Collocations', in Versteegh 2006–9.
2 Baker 1992: 14.
3 Beekman & Callow 1974: 164.
4 Palmer 1933: 1.
5 Palmer 1938: iv.
6 e.g. Aisenstadt 1979; Cowie et al. 1983; Emery 1988, 1991.
7 e.g. Santillán Grimm 2009; Hoogland 1993.
8 e.g. Abu-Ssaydeh 2008; Hoogland 1993.
9 e.g. Baker 1992; Abu-Ssaydeh 2001, 2004.
10 Benson 1985.
11 The division is loosely inspired by Emery 1991, who relies on Aisenstadt 1979 and Cowie et al. 1983 (as did El-Gemei, op. cit.) for a division into open, restricted and bound collocations. However, the interpretations do not necessarily coincide with ours, while the taxonomy presented here differs significantly in a number of respects.
12 Cf. Cowie et al. 1983: xiii.
13 See Chapter 4.
14 Mel'čuk 1996: 211.
15 Ibid.
16 Cf. Cowie et al. 1983: xii.
17 The examples given by Emery (1991) 'to curry favour' and 'to foot the bill' do not really illustrate the case inasmuch as they do have other collocants: *to curry* + *sauce/dish* (and *to seek/gain/find* + *favour*) and *foot* + *the expense/a meal/a room/the fare*.
18 Benson et al. 1997: 254.
19 Also known as جناس or تَجْنِيس, this common stylistic device in Arabic rhetoric relies on formal similarity rather than on any other considerations of collocation, and there are often no semantic links between the words.
20 For a more detailed discussion of this phenomenon, see Koch 1983, 1991.
21 For a discussion of this phenomenon, see, for instance, Nevins and Vaux 2003.
22 Gabrys-Biskup 1990.
23 Gorgis and Al-Tamimi 2005.
24 Benson et al. 1997: 8.
25 McArthur 1975: 9.
26 Palmer 1968: 185.
27 McArthur & Atkins 1974: 6–7.
28 For a discussion, see Ryding Lentzner 1977; Helliel 1994.
29 Aisenstadt 1979; Cowie et al. 1983; Hoogland 1993; Abu-Ssaydeh 1989, 1995, 2008; Al-Rawi 2001; Hafiz 2002; Muʿtasim 2003.
30 Heliel 1989, 1994; Shakir & Farghal 1992; Ghazala 1993a/b; Shakir & Shdeifat 1996; Abu-Ssaydeh 2001; Bahumaid 2006; al-Brashi 2005.
31 For an extensive treatment of these, see Benson 1986.
32 L'Homme & Bertrand 2000.
33 Jackson 1988: 106.
34 Cf. Qur'an: 3:67, 3:67, 4:125, 6:161, 10:105, 16:120, 22:31, 30:30.

35 For a detailed discussion, see Al-Wahy 2009: 101–123.
36 See Ali 2006.
37 Maalej 2002.
38 Ryding 2005: 205. This is also the view of Emery 1988.
39 Cf. al-Kharabsheh 2005.
40 Brook 1972: 14.
41 This is originally a Greek word, meaning 'common', which is used to refer to the link language resulting from an admixture of several dialects, with the dominant variety (the so-called Attic) constituting the principal component. However, in this context, it is more useful to draw a parallel with the Homeric (Ionian-based) poetic *koiné*, which came to be the language of epic poetry but, like Standard Arabic, never had any mother-tongue speakers.
42 Ferguson 1959b. For a full discussion of the various schools of thought, see Versteegh 1997; Holes 1995/2004.
43 It literally means 'bilingual' in Greek, which semantic ambiguity also exists in Arabic in which *izdiwājiyyat al-lugha* and *thunā'iyyat al-lugha* are sometimes variously used to denote both 'diglossia' and 'bilingualism'.
44 This situation, of course, no longer applies to Greece, where *demotiki* has been the language of education and administration since 1976, while *katharevousa* is only very sporadically encountered these days.
45 Marçais 1930: 401.
46 Ibid.
47 Ferguson 1959a: 325.
48 Ibid.: 336.
49 Ibid.: 329.
50 For an overview, see Davies, 'Dialect Literature', in Versteegh 2006–9.
51 Ferguson 1959a: 328.
52 Badawi 1973: 89–91.
53 Ibid.: 104.
54 Hinds & Badawi 1986: X.
55 Ibid.: 525.
56 Bishai 1960: 320.
57 Badawi 1973: 67–8.
58 Harrell 1960: 3–77.
59 Salib 1979: 7.
60 Badawi, himself, would later on also use this terminology equivalent; see, for instance, Badawi 1985.
61 Salib 1979: 5.
62 See El-Hassan 1978a; Mitchell 1978, 1980, 1982, 1986; Mitchell & El-Hassan 1994; Nofal 1980; Abu-Melhim 1992; Dichy 1994; Hary 1996; Boussofara-Omar, 'Diglossia', in Versteegh 2006–9.
63 Ryding, 'Educated Arabic', in Versteegh 2006–9.
64 Boussofara-Omar, 'Diglossia', in Versteegh 2006–9.
65 See Heath 1989; Bentahila 1983; Atawneh 1992; Belazi 1992; Morsly 1986.
66 The term 'code-switching' was originally used in studies on bilingualism and later extended to cover what is essentially 'register switching'. Unfortunately, in Arabic studies the term is used in both its original and more recent sense.
67 See Eid 1982, 1988, 2002; Schmidt 1975; Schulz 1981; Mejdell 2006; Bassiouney 2006.
68 Al-Tunayr 1987.
69 See Zack 2012.
70 Boussofara-Omar, 'Diglossia', in Versteegh 2006–9.
71 See Catarino 1974; Parkinson 1981, 1991.
72 Kaye 1972.
73 El-Hassan 1978b: 32.
74 Ibrahim 1997: 8–9.
75 Ibid.: 3.
76 Cairo: Dār al-Rā'id li 'l-Ṭibāʿa, 1966 (Beirut: Dār al-Andalus, 1983), 2nd ed., *al-ʿArabiyya, tārīkh wa taṭawwur*, Beirut: Maktabat al-Maʿārif, 1993.
77 See Newman 2013.

78 Ibrahim 1997; Parkinson & Ibrahim 1998; Wilmsen & Youssef 2009.
79 For a discussion of the role of the media, see, for instance, Ibrahim 1997: 46ff.; Holes 2004: 314ff.
80 The Moroccan term is especially avoided in Egypt, where in the vernacular it refers to 'feeling up' women (Ibrahim 1997).
81 In addition, there are the religious calendars that are in use in various countries, starting, of course, with the Muslim Hijra calendar, whereas in Egypt, the names of Coptic months are also sometimes added to calendar references.
82 For a more extensive list, see Ibrahim 1997.
83 The English translation is also rather unusual since it does not ordinarily denote a region and is only used to refer to the Tunisian context.
84 Ibrahim 1997: 83ff.
85 Ibid.: 86.
86 Parkinson 2003.
87 Parkinson 2008.
88 Ibrahim 1997.
89 It is important to stress that we are not dismissing a colloquial or foreign influence on MSA, which has been amply documented (e.g. Stetkevych 1970). The discussion here is whether these influences are distinguishing features between MSAs.
90 Omar 1976: 28.
91 Ibrahim 1997: 100ff.
92 Interestingly enough, this variation mirrors that in English, where the UK spelling is 'cheque' vs US 'check'.
93 Both Van Mol (2003) and Parkinson (2008) included a North African and Gulf variety in their corpora (Algeria/Morocco and Saudi Arabia/Kuwait, respectively). Wilmsen (2010) added a Syrian newspaper (*al-Thawra*) to his corpus, which allowed for a broader 'Levantine' sample.
94 It is worth pointing out that these are by no means as substantial as is commonly believed, as witnessed by the examples later on in this chapter.
95 See Newman 2013; Wilmsen 2010.
96 Ibrahim 1997.
97 Ibrahim 1997: 111; Wehr 1976: 522.
98 For a more extensive list, see, for instance, Benson 1986, 1997.
99 See, for instance, Mazraani 1997 (for Saddam Hussein's speeches); Holes 1993 (for Nasser's speeches).
100 Lefevere 1992: 64. Also see Fischer 1958.
101 For Arabic, see Sawaie 1987: 3–22.
102 Twain 1992: lvii.
103 Ḥusayn 1957: III, 200–1; quoted in Abdel-Malek 1972.
104 For this issue, see Diem 1974; Somekh 1993; Rosenbaum 1995; Zughoul & El-Badarien 2004; Abdel-Malek 1971, 1972.
105 Lewis 1993: 71.
106 Burton 1885: 15.
107 Ibid.: xi.
108 Zughoul & El-Badarien 2004 and al-Sarrani 2011 are among the few studies that have devoted attention to this topic.
109 Berthele 2000.
110 Ibid.: 589.
111 Ibid.: 589–90.
112 Also see Holes 2004: 354–55.
113 Al-Sarrani 2011: 107–8.
114 See Parkinson 1981.
115 Twain 1992: 175.
116 Al Ashmawi-Abouzeid 1994.
117 Al-Sarrani 2011: 107–8.
118 Ibid.: 114, 115.
119 Muhaidat 2005.
120 See Newman & Husni 2008.

121 *Qiṣṣat madīnatayn*, trans. M. al-Baʿalbakkī, Beirut: Dār al-ʿIlm li 'l-Malāyīn, 1959, p. 208.
122 'The End of Legalese: The Game is Over', *New York University Review of Law and Social Change*, 13, 1984–1985, p. 531 (quoted in Gopen 1987: 334).
123 Harvey 2002: 182.
124 Ibid.: 181.
125 Šarčević 1997: 11.
126 Cf. Danet 1980.
127 Cao 2007: 9ff.
128 In Šarčević 1997: 9.
129 Ibid.
130 Maley 1994: 13.
131 Tiersma 2000: 135ff.
132 Šarčević 1997: 70–71.
133 See also Kocbek 2008.
134 David & Brierley 1985; Zweigert & Kötz 1992.
135 David & Brierley 1985: 19.
136 Šarčević 1997: 70.
137 Cao 2007: 60ff.
138 Ibid.: 29ff.
139 Cf. Tiersma 2000: 139ff.; Farghal & Shunnaq 1992.
140 Cf. *Oxford English Dictionary*: 'The action of making or giving laws; the enactment of laws, lawgiving.'
141 Cf. Melinkoff 1963; Tiersma 2000; Alcaraz & Hughes 2002.
142 This is P. Tiersma's term: 2000: 61ff.
143 Šarčević 1997: 203.
144 Cf. *The English Style Guide: A Handbook for Authors and Translators in the European Commission* (2006): http://ec.europa.eu/translation/english/guidelines/documents/styleguide_english_dgt_en.pdf.
145 The former is based on an unidentified corpus of media and literary texts, whereas the latter draws its examples from a number of modern Arabic novels.
146 Penn Treebank output is distributed through the Linguistic Data Consortium (www.ldc.upenn.edu/).
147 An example of a parsed corpus for Arabic is the Quran Corpus (http://corpus.quran.com/).
148 For an overview, see: www.comp.leeds.ac.uk/eric/latifa/index.htm.
149 Cf. European Language Resources Association (ELRA): http://catalog.elra.info/index.php?osCsid=18de3c2c09e5d98c25575bdbffd8666e
150 Designed by Latifa Al-Sulaiti and Eric Atwell; see www.comp.leeds.ac.uk/eric/latifa/research.htm.
151 The corpus was created by Dilworth Parkinson of Brigham Young University, which is also the host of the corpus.

Bibliography

Abdel-Malek, Zaki N. (1971): Al-Ṣirā[c] bayna al-fuṣḥā wa 'l-[c]āmiyya: aw 'athr al-izdiwāj al-lughawī fī uslūb Yūsuf al-Sibā[c]ī', *al-Lisān al-[c]Arabī*, 8:1, pp. 175–180.

—— (1972): 'The Influence of Diglossia on the Novels of Yūsif al- Sibā[c]i', *Journal of Arabic Literature*, 3, pp. 132–141.

Abd-el-Jawad, Hassan (1986): 'The Emergence of an Urban Dialect in the Jordanian Urban Centers', *International Journal of the Sociology of Language*, 61, pp. 53–63.

—— (1987): 'Cross-dialectal Variation in Arabic: Competing Prestigious Forms', *Language in Society*, 16, pp. 359–368.

Abdulaziz, M. H. (1986): 'Factors in the Development of Modern Arabic Usage', *International Journal of the Sociology of Language*, 62, pp. 11–24.

Abdul-Hassan, R. S. (1988): 'Variation in the Educated Spoken Arabic of Iraq: A Sociolinguistic Study', unpubl. PhD diss., Leeds: University of Leeds.

Abirached, S. (1962): 'Sur le bilinguisme libanais', *Travaux et Jours*, Oct.–Dec., pp. 119–133.

Abou, Selim (1972): 'Le problème de la diglossie', *Cahiers d'Histoire Mondiale*, 14, pp. 33–43.

Abou-Seida, Abdelrahman (1971): 'Diglossia in Egyptian Arabic: Prolegomena to a Pan-Arabic Sociolinguistic Study', unpubl. PhD diss., Austin, TX: University of Texas.

Abu-Haidar, Farida (1972): 'Shifting Boundaries: The Effect of Modern Standard Arabic on Dialect Convergence in Bagdad', in E. Broselow et al. (eds), *Perspectives on Arabic Linguistics IV. Papers from the Fourth Annual Symposium on Arabic Linguistics*, Amsterdam/Philadelphia: John Benjamins, pp. 91–105.

Abu-Melhim, Abdel-Rahman (1972): 'Code Switching and Linguistic Accommodation in Arabic', in B. Comrie & M. Eid (eds), *Perspectives on Arabic Linguistics III. Papers from the Third Annual Symposium on Arabic Linguistics*, Amsterdam/Philadelphia: John Benjamins, pp. 231–250.

—— (1992): 'Communication across Arabic Dialects: Code-switching and Linguistic Accommodation in Informal Conversational Interactions', unpubl. PhD diss., Texas A & M University.

Abu-Rabia, Salim (2000): 'Effects of Exposure to Literary Arabic on Reading Comprehension in a Diglossic Situation', *Reading and Writing*, 13, pp. 147–157.

Abu-Ssaydeh, A. (1989): 'Towards a Collocational Dictionary', *al-Lisān al-[c]Arabī*, 32:5, pp. 5–15.

—— (1995): 'An Arabic–English Collocation Dictionary: Issues in Theory and Methodology', *Babel*, 41:1, pp. 12–23.

—— (2001): 'Synonymy, Collocation and the Translator', *Turjumān* 10:2, pp. 53–71.

—— (2004): 'Translation of English Idioms into Arabic: A Case Study', *Babel*, 50:2, pp. 114–131.

—— (2008): 'Collocation and the Arabic–English Dictionary: Ideas for Better Dictionaries', *Zeitschrift fur Arabische Linguistik*, 48, pp. 10–34.

Aisenstadt, E. (ed.) (1979): *Collocability Restrictions in Dictionaries*, Exeter: University of Exeter.

Al Ashmawi-Abouzeid, Fawzia (1994): 'Linguistic Problems of Translation of Spoken Arabic in Literary Texts', *Turjumān*, pp. 7–12.

Al-Batal, M. (1994): 'Connectives in Arabic Diglossia: The Case of Lebanese Arabic', in M. Eid, V. Catarino & K. Walters (eds), *Perspectives on Arabic Linguistics VI: Papers from the Sixth Annual Symposium on Arabic Linguistics*, Amsterdam: John Benjamins.

Al-Brashi, A. S. (2005): 'Arabic Collocations: Implications for Translation', unpubl. PhD diss., Sydney: University of Western Sydney.

Alcaraz, E. & B. Hughes (2002): *Legal Translation Explained*, Manchester: St Jerome.

Ali, Abdul Sahib Mehdi (1987): *A Linguistic Study of the Development of Scientific Vocabulary in Standard Arabic*, London: Kegan Paul.

—— (2006): 'Compounds', in Kees Versteegh (ed.), *Encyclopedia of Arabic Language and Linguistics*, I, Leiden: Brill, pp. 451–455.

Al-Kharabsheh, Aladdin (2005): 'The Interpretation of Terminological Constructions: The Case of Technico-scientific Nominal Compounds', *Journal of Language and Linguistics*, 4:2, pp. 161–182.

Al-Qurashi, Khedier (1982): 'The Feasibility of the Arabic Language as a Medium of Instruction in Sciences', unpubl. PhD diss., Bloomington, IN: University of Indiana.

Al-Rawi, S. (2001): 'Rendering Arabic Collocations in English', *al-Lisān al-ᶜArabī*, 52, pp. 23–27.

Al-Sarrani, Abeer Abdulaziz (2011): 'Challenges of Cross-cultural Translation of American Literary Works into Arabic: Harriet Beecher Stowe's *Uncle Tom's Cabin* as a Case Study', unpubl. PhD diss., Philadelphia: University of Pennsylvania.

Altoma, Salih Jawad (1957): 'The Teaching of Classical Arabic to Speakers of the Colloquial in Iraq: A Study of the Problem of Linguistic Duality and its Impact on Language Education', unpubl. PhD diss., Cambridge, MA: Harvard University.

Al-Tunayr, Muḥammad (1987): *Alfāẓ ᶜāmmiyya faṣīḥa*, Cairo: Dār al-Shurūq.

Al-Wahy, A. S. (2009): 'Idiomatic False Friends in English and Modern Standard Arabic', *Babel*, 55:2, pp. 101–123.

Atawneh, Ahmad (1992): 'Code-mixing in Arabic–English Bilinguals', in Ellen Broselow, Mushira Eid, John McCarthy (eds), *Perspectives on Arabic Linguistics IV: Papers from the Fourth Annual Symposium on Arabic Linguistics*, Amsterdam: John Benjamins, pp. 219–241.

Badawi, El-Said Muhammad (1973): *Mustwayāt al-ᶜArabiyya al-muᶜāṣira fī Miṣr*, Cairo: Dār al-Maᶜārif.

—— (1985): 'Educated Spoken Arabic: A Problem in Teaching Arabic as a Foreign Language', in Kurt R. Jankowsky (ed.), *Scientific and Humanistic Dimensions of Language*, Washington, DC: Georgetown University Press, pp. 15–22.

Bahumaid, Sh. (2006): 'Collocation in English–Arabic Translation', *Babel*, 52:2, pp. 133–152.

Baker, M. (1992): *In Other Words: A Coursebook on Translation*, London: Routledge.

Bassiouney, Reem (2006): *Functions of Code-switching in Egypt*, Leiden: Brill.

Beekman, John and John Callow (1974): *Translating the Word of God*, Grand Rapids, MI: Zondervan.

Belazi, H. M. (1992): 'Multilingualism in Tunisia and French/Arabic Code Switching among Educated Tunisian Bilinguals', unpubl. PhD diss., Ithaca, NY: Cornell University.

Benson, Morton (1985): 'Collocations and Idioms', in R. Ilson (ed.), *Dictionaries, Lexicography and Language Learning*, London: Pergamon Press, pp. 61–68.

—— (1986): *Lexicographic Description of English*, Amsterdam: John Benjamins.

Benson, M., E. Benson & R. F. Ilson (1997): *The BBI Combinatory Dictionary of English: A Guide to Word Combinations*, 2nd rev. edition, Amsterdam/Philadelphia, PA: John Benjamins.

Bentahila, A. (1983): 'Motivations for Code-switching among Arabic–French Bilinguals in Morocco', *Language and Communication*, 3, pp. 233–243.

Berthele, Raphael (2000): 'Translating African-American Vernacular English into German: The Problem of "Jim" in Mark Twain's *Huckleberry Finn*', *Journal of Sociolinguistics*, 4:4, pp. 588–613.

Bishai, Wilson B (1960): 'Notes on the Coptic Substratum in Egyptian Arabic', *Journal of the American Oriental Society*, 80:3, pp. 225–229.

—— (1966): 'Modern Inter-Arabic', *Journal of the American Oriental Society*, 86, pp. 319–323.

Blanc, H. (1960): 'Style Variations in Arabic: A Sample Interdialectal Conversation', in C. Ferguson (ed.), *Contributions to Arabic Linguistics*, Cambridge, MA: Harvard University Press, pp. 81–156.

Blau, J. (1973): 'Remarks on some Syntactic Trends in Modern Standard Arabic', *Israel Oriental Studies*, III, pp. 173–231.

—— (1976): 'Some Additional Observations on Syntactic Trends in Modern Standard Arabic', *Israel Oriental Studies*, VI, pp. 158–190.

—— (1977): *The Beginnings of the Arabic Diglossia: A Study of the Origins of Neoarabic*, Malibu: Undena Publications.

Bonaffini, Luigi (1997): 'Translating Dialect Literature', *World Literature Today*, 71:2.

Boucherit, Aziza (1996): 'Arabe classique-arabe dialectal. Produit d'une rencontre', *The Arabist*, 17, pp. 15–17.

Bowers, Frederick (1989): *Linguistic Aspects of Legislative Expression*, Vancouver: University of British Columbia Press.

Brook, G. L. (1972): *English Dialects*, London: Deutsch.

Burton, Richard (1885): *A Plain and Literal Translation of the Arabian Nights' Entertainment, Now Entituled The Book of a Thousand Nights and one Night*, Benares: The Kamashastra Society.

Byrne, Jody (2006): *Technical Translation: Usability Strategies for Translating Technical Documentation*, Dordrecht: Springer.

Cao, Deborah (2007): *Translating Law*, Bristol: Multilingual Matters.

Catarino, Vicente (1974): *Syntax of Modern Arabic Prose*, 2 vols, Bloomington, IN: Indiana University Press.

Chroma, M. (2005): *Legal Translation and the Dictionary*, Tübingen: Max Niemeyer Verlag.

Cohen, David (1962): 'Koinè, langues communes et dialectes arabes', *Arabica*, 11, pp. 119–124.

Cowie, A. P., R. Mackin & I. R. McCaig (1983): *Oxford Dictionary of Current Idiomatic English. Vol. 2: Phrase, Clause and Sentence Idioms*, Oxford: Oxford University Press.

Cunningham, Clark (1992): 'The Lawyer as Translator', *Cornell Law Review*, 77:6, pp. 1298–1387.

Cruse, D. (1986): *Lexical Semantics*, Cambridge: Cambridge University Press.

Danet, B. (1980): 'Language in the Legal Process', *Law and Society*, 14:3, pp. 447–563.

David, R. & J. Brierley (1985): *Major Legal Systems in the World Today*, London: Stevens.

De Cruz, P. (1999): *Comparative Law in a Changing World*, London: Cavendish Publishing.

Dichy, Joseph (1994): 'La pluriglossie de l'Arabe', *Bulletin d'Etudes Orientales*, XLVI, pp. 19–42.

Dickins, J., S. Hervey & I. Higgins (2002): *Thinking Arabic Translation: A Course in Translation Method: Arabic to English*, London/New York: Routledge.

Diem, Werner (1974): *Hochsprache und Dialekt im Arabischen. Untersuchungen zur heutigen arabischen Zweisprachigkeit*, Wiesbaden: Franz Steiner Verlag.

Eid, Mushira (1982): 'The Non-randomness of Diglossic Variation in Arabic', *Glossa* 16:1, pp. 54–84.

—— (1988): 'Principles for Code-switching between Standard and Egyptian Arabic', *al-ʿArabiyya*, 21, pp. 51–79.

—— (2002): 'Language is a Choice: Variation in Egyptian Women's Written Discourse', in A. Rouchdy (ed.), *Language Contact and Language Conflict in Arabic: Variations of a*

Sociolinguistic Theme, London: Routledge, pp. 203–332.

El-Hassan, S.A. (1978a): 'Educated Spoken Arabic in Egypt and the Levant: A Critical Review of Diglossia and Related Concepts', *Archivum Linguisticum*, 8, pp. 112–132.

—— (1978b): 'Variation in the Demonstrative System in Educated Spoken Arabic', *Archivum Linguisticum*, 9, pp. 32–57.

—— (1987): 'Aspectual Distinctions in English and Written Arabic', *International Review of Applied Linguistics in Language Teaching*, 25, pp. 131–138.

—— (1992): 'Semi-imperfectives and Imperfectives: A Case Study of Aspect and Tense in Arabic Participial Clauses', *Lingua*, 86, pp. 301–330.

Elshakry, Marwa S. (2008): 'Knowledge in Motion: The Cultural Politics of Modern Science Translations in Arabic', *Isis*, 99, pp. 701–730.

Emerson, Frances B. (1987): *Technical Writing*, Boston, MA: Houghton Mifflin Company.

Emery, Peter G. (1988): 'Compound Words in Modern Standard Arabic', *Zeitschrift für Arabische Linguistik*, 19, pp. 32–43.

—— (1991): 'Collocation in Modern Standard Arabic', *Zeitschrift für Arabische Linguistik*, 23, pp. 56–65.

—— (1993): 'Legal Arabic Texts: Implications for Translation', *Babel*, 35:1, pp. 1–11.

Ennaji, Moha (2002): 'De la diglossie à la quadriglossie', *Langues et Linguistique*, 8, pp. 49–64.

Ethnologue: Languages of the World: https://www.ethnologue.com/.

Farghal, M. & A. T. Shunnaq (1992): 'Major Problems in Students' Translations of English Legal Texts into Arabic', *Babel*, 34:4, pp. 203–210.

Ferguson, Charles (1959a): 'Diglossia', *Word*, 15: pp. 325–340.

—— (1959b): 'The Arabic Koine', *Language*, 35, pp. 616–630.

—— (1996): 'Epilogue: Diglossia Revisited', in Alaa Elgibali (ed.), *Understanding Arabic*, Cairo: The American University in Cairo Press, pp. 49–69.

Fischer, John L. (1958): 'Social Influences on the Choice of a Linguistic Variant', *Word*, 14, pp. 47–56.

Franco Aixelá, J. (2004): 'The Study of Technical and Scientific Translation: An Examination of its Historical Development', *Journal of Specialised Translation*, 1, pp. 29–49.

Gabrys-Biskup, Danuta (1990): 'Some Remarks on Combinability: Lexical Collocations', in J. Arabski (ed.), *Foreign Language Acquisition Papers*, Katowice: Universytet Slaski, pp. 31–44.

Ghazāla, Ḥ (1993a): 'Tarjamat al-mutalāzimāt al-lafẓiyya: Inklīzī–ᶜArabī', *Turjumān*, 2:1, pp. 7–44.

—— (1993b): 'Tarjamat al-mutalāzimāt al-lafẓiyya: ᶜArabī-Inklīzī', *Turjumān*, 2:2, pp. 1–33.

Gibbons, J. (ed.) (1994): *Language and the Law*, London/New York: Longman.

Gómez González-Jover, Adelina (2005): 'Specialized Bilingual Dictionaries for Translators (Some Considerations for a User-oriented Approach)', *Revista Alicantina de Estudios Ingleses*, 18, pp. 71–78.

Gopen, G. (1987): 'The State of Legal Writing: Res Ipsa Loquitur', *Michigan Law Review*, 86:2, pp. 333–380.

Gorgis, Dinha & Yasser Abdullah Tamimi (2005): 'Binomials in Iraqi and Jordanian Arabic', *Journal of Language and Linguistics*, 4:2, pp. 135–150.

Hafiz, T. (2002): 'Arabic Collocations: The Need for an Arabic Combinatory Dictionary', *International Journal of Arabic–English Studies*, 3, pp. 95–104.

Hamad, A. H. (1986): 'Diglossia in the Phonology of Second Language', unpubl. PhD diss., Lincoln, NE: University of Nebraska-Lincoln.

Hamzaoui, M. Rachad (1965): *L'Académie arabe de Damas et le problème de la modernisation de la langue arabe*, Leiden: Brill.

—— (1975): *L'Académie de Langue arabe du Caire*, Tunis: Université de Tunis.

Hannaoui, A. (1987): 'Diglossia, Medical Arabic and Language Policy in Morocco', unpubl. PhD diss., Stony Brook, NY: State University of New York.

Harrell, Richard (1960): 'A Linguistic Analysis of Egyptian Radio Arabic', in C. Ferguson (ed.), *Contributions to Arabic Linguistics*, Cambridge, MA: Harvard University Press, pp. 3–77.

Harvey, M. (2002): 'What's So Special about Legal Translation?', *Meta*, XLVV:2, pp. 177–185.

Hary, Benjamin (1996): 'The Importance of the Language Continuum in Arabic Multiglossia', in Alaa Elgibali (ed.) *Understanding Arabic*, Cairo: The American University in Cairo Press, pp. 69–90.

Hass, W. (ed.) (1982): *Standard Languages: Spoken and Written*, Manchester: Manchester University Press.

Hatim, Basil & Ian Mason (1990): *Discourse and the Translator*, Essex: Longman.

Heath, Jeffrey (1989): *From Code-switching to Borrowing: Foreign and Diglossic Mixing in Moroccan Arabic*, London: Kegan Paul International.

Heliel, M. M. H. (1989): 'Al-Mutalaāzimaāt al-lafẓāiyya wa-l-tarjama', *FIT Newsletter*, 11:3, pp. 31–44.

—— (1994): 'Verb-Particle Combinations in English and Arabic: Problems for Arab Lexicographers and Translators', in R. de Beaugrande, A. Shunnaq & M. Heliel (eds), *Language, Discourse and Translation in the West and Middle East*, Amsterdam and Philadelphia, PA: John Benjamins Publishing Company, pp. 141–151.

Hinds, Martin & El Said Badawi (1986): *A Dictionary of Egyptian Arabic: Arabic–English*, Beirut: Librairie du Liban.

Holes, C. (1993): 'The Uses of Variation: A Study of the Political Speeches of Gamal Abd al-Nasir', in Mushira Eid & Clives Holes (eds), *Perspectives on Arabic Linguistics V: Papers from the Fifth Annual Symposium on Arabic Linguistics*, Amsterdam: John Benjamins, pp. 13–45.

—— (1995): *Modern Arabic: Structures, Functions and Varieties*, London: Longman (2nd rev. edition, Washington, DC: Georgetown University Press, 2004).

Hoogland, Jan (1993): 'Collocation in Arabic (MSA) and the Treatment of Collocations in Arabic Dictionaries', in K. Dévényi et al. (eds), *Proceedings of the Colloquium on Arabic Lexicology and Lexicography*, Budapest: Eötvös Loránd University & Csoma de Körös Society, pp. 75–93.

Hussein, Taha (1957): *Ḥadīth al-Arbaᶜa*, Cairo: Dār al-Maᶜārif.

Ibrahim, M. (1986): 'Standard and Prestige Language: A Problem in Arabic Socio-Linguistics', *Anthropological Linguistics*, 28:1, pp. 115–126.

Ibrahim, Zeinab (1997): 'Egyptian and Lebanese Written Modern Standard Arabic: Are they One and the Same?', unpubl. Ph.D. diss., Washington, DC: Georgetown University.

Jackson, Howard (1988): *Words and their Meanings*, London/New York: Longman.

Kaye, A. S. (1972): 'Remarks on Diglossia in Arabic, Well-defined vs. Ill-defined', *Linguistics*, 81, pp. 32–48.

—— (1994): 'Formal vs. Informal in Arabic: Diglossia, Triglossia, Tetraglossia, etc.: Polyglossia-multiglossia Viewed as a Continuum', *Journal of Arabic Linguistics*, 27, pp. 47–66.

—— (2001): 'Diglossia: The State of the Art', *International Journal of the Sociology of Language*, 152.

Killean, Carolyn (1980): 'Demonstrative Variation in Oral Media Arabic in Egypt', *Studies in the Linguistic Sciences*, 10:2, pp. 165–78.

Klinge, Alex (1994): *Legal Discourse and Modality: An Investigation of Semantic and Pragmatic Aspects of Modality in Insurance Policies*, Copenhagen: Handelhojskolens erhvervssproglie Fakultet.

Kloss, Heinz (1993): '*Abstand* Languages and *Ausbau* Languages', *Anthropological Linguistics*, 35, pp. 158–167.

Koch, B. (1983): 'Arabic Lexical Couplets and the Evolution of Synonymy', *General Linguistics*, 23:1, pp. 51–61.

—— (1991): *Repetition in Arabic Discourse: Paradigms, Syntagms, and the Ecology of Language*, Amsterdam/Philadelphia, PA: John Benjamins.

Labov, William (1994): *Principles of Linguistic Change*, Oxford: Blackwell Publishers.

Lefevere, Andre (1992): *Translating Literature: Practice and Theory in a Comparative Literature Context*, New York: Modern Language Association.

Lewis, B. (1993): *Islam and the West*, New York: Oxford University Press.

L'Homme, Marie-Claude & Claudine Bertrand (2000): 'Specialized Lexical Combinations: Should they be Described as Collocations or in Terms of Selectional Restrictions?', in S. Evert, U. Heid, E. Lehman & C. Rohrer (eds), *Proceedings of the Ninth EURALEX International Congress*, Stuttgart: Universitat Stuttgart, pp. 497–506.

Kocbek, Alenka (2008): 'The Cultural Embeddedness of Legal Texts', *Journal of Language and Translation*, 9:2, pp. 49–70.

Maalej, Zouhair (2002): 'English–Arabic Translation Guidelines for Nominal Compounds': http://simsim.rug.ac.be/Zmaalej/syncom.html.

Maley, Y. (1994): 'The Language of the Law', in J. Gibbons (ed.), *Language and the Law*, New York: Longman, pp. 11–50.

Marçais, William (1930): 'La diglossie arabe', *L'Enseignement public*, 97, pp. 401–409.

Mazraani, Nathalie (1997): *Aspects of Language Variation in Arabic Political Speech-making*, London: Curzon Press.

Meiseles, Gustav (1980): 'Educated Spoken Arabic and the Language Continuum', *Archivum Linguisticum*, 11:2, pp. 118–148.

McArthur, Tom (1975): *Dictionary of English Phrasal Verbs and their Idioms*, London: Macmillan.

McArthur, Tom & Beryl Atkins (1974): *Dictionary of English Phrasal Verbs and their Idioms*, London/Glasgow: Collins.

Mejdell, G. (2006): *Mixed Styles in Spoken Arabic in Egypt*, Leiden: E. J. Brill.

Mel'čuk, Igor (1996): *Cours de morphologie générale*, vol. 3, *Moyens morphologiques. Syntactiques morphologiques*, Montreal: Les Presses de l'Université de Montréal/Paris: CNRS Éditions.

Melinkoff, D. (1963): *The Language of the Law*, Boston, MA: Little, Brown & Co.

Mikkelson, Holly (2000): 'Introduction to Court Interpreting', in *Translation Practices Explained*, vol. 1, Manchester: St Jerome Publishing.

Minnick, Lisa Cohen (2004): *Dialect and Dichotomy: Literary Representations of African American Speech*, Tuscaloosa, AL: University of Alabama Press.

Mitchell, T. F. (1978): 'Educated Spoken Arabic in Egypt and the Levant, with Special Reference to Participle and Tense', *Journal of Linguistics*, 14:2, pp. 227–258.

—— (1980): 'Dimensions of Style in a Grammar of Educated Spoken Arabic', *Archivum Linguisticum*, 11:2, pp. 89–107.

—— (1982): 'More than a Matter of "Writing with the Learned, Pronouncing with the Vulgar": Some Preliminary Observations on the Arabic Koine', in *Standard Languages: Spoken and Written*, Manchester: Manchester University Press, pp. 123–155.

—— (1985): 'Sociolinguistic and Stylistic Dimensions of the Educated Spoken Arabic of Egypt and the Levant', in *Language Standards and their Codification: Process and Application*, Exeter: University of Exeter, pp. 42–57.

—— (1986): 'What is Educated Spoken Arabic?', *International Journal of the Sociology of Language*, 61, pp. 7–32.

Mitchell, T. F. & Shahir El-Hassan (1994): *Modality, Mood and Aspect in Spoken Arabic. With Special Reference to Egypt and the Levant*, London: Kegan Paul International.

Morris, Marshall (ed.) (1995): *Translation and the Law*, Amsterdam/Philadelphia, PA: John Benjamins Publishing Company.

Morsly, Dalila (1986): 'Multilingualism in Algeria', in Joshua A. Fishman, Andree Tabouret-Keller, Michael Clyne, Bh. Krishnamurti & Mohamed Abdulaziz (eds), *The Fergusonian Impact: In honor of Charles A. Ferguson on the Occasion of his 65th Birthday*, Berlin: Mouton de Gruyter, pp. 163–174.

Muhaidat, Fatima Muhammad (2005): '*A Tale of Two Cities* in Arabic Translation', unpubl. PhD diss., Binghamton, NY: State University of New York.

Muʿtaṣim, M. (2003): 'Fī sabīl muʿjam ʿarabī li-mutalāzimāt al-ism wa-l-ṣifa', *Proceedings of the International Congress on Al-Maʿājim al-ʿArabiyya*: al-*Wāqiʿ wa 'l-Āfāq. Hasan II University in ʿAyn al-Šaqq*, Casablanca.

Nevins, A. and B. Vaux (2003): 'Metalinguistic, Shmetalinguistic: The Phonology of Shm-reduplication', *Proceedings from the Annual Meeting of the Chicago Linguistic Society*, 39:1, pp. 702–721.

Newman, D. (2013): 'The Arabic Literary Language: The Nahda (and Beyond)', in Jonathan Owens (ed.), *Oxford Handbook of Arabic Linguistics*, Oxford University Press, pp. 472–494.

Newman, Daniel & Ronak Husni (2008): *Bilingual Modern Arabic Short Story Reader*, London: Saqi Books.

—— (2013): *An A to Z of Arabic–English Translation*, London: Saqi Books.

Nofal, Loutfy M. (1980): 'Language Function Analysis in Modern Standard Arabic, with Pedagogical Implications for the Teaching of Arabic', unpubl. PhD diss., Erlangen-Nürnberg University.

Olsen, F., R. Alexander Lorz & Dieter Stein (2009): *Translation Issues in Language and Law*, London: Palgrave Macmillan.

Omar, Margaret (1976): *Levantine and Egyptian Arabic*, Washington, DC: Foreign Service Institute.

Palmer, F. (1968): *Selected Papers of J. R. Firth 1952–59*, Bloomington, IN/London: Indiana University Press.

Palmer, H. E. (1933): *Second Interim Report on English Collocations*, Tokyo: Kaitakusha.

—— (1938): *A Grammar of English Words*, London: Longman.

Parkinson, Dilworth (1981): 'VSO to SVO in Modern Standard Arabic: A Study in Diglossia Syntax', *al-'Arabiyya*, 14, pp. 24–37.

—— (1985): *Constructing the Social Context of Communication: Terms of Address in Egyptian Arabic*, New York: Mouton De Gruyter.

—— (1991): 'Searching for Modern Fusha: Real Life Formal Arabic', *Al-Arabiyya*, 24, pp. 31–64.

—— (2003): 'Future Variability: A Corpus Study of Arabic Future Particles', in D. Parkinson & S. Farwaneh, *Perspectives on Arabic Linguistics XV*, Amsterdam: John Benjamins, pp. 191–211.

—— (2008): 'Sentence Subject Agreement Variation in Arabic', in Z. Ibrahim and S. Makhlouf (eds), *Linguistics in an Age of Globalization: Perspectives on Arabic Language and Teaching*, Cairo: The American University in Cairo Press, pp. 67–90.

Parkinson, D. & Zeinab Ibrahim (1998): 'Testing Lexical Differences in Regional Standard Arabics', in Elabbas Benmamoun (ed.), *Perspectives on Arabic Linguistics XII*, Amsterdam/Philadelphia, PA: Johns Benjamins, pp. 183–202.

Pinchuck, Isadore (1955): *Scientific and Technical Translation*, London: André Deutsch.

Plag, I. (2003): *Word-formation in English*, Cambridge: Cambridge University Press.

Quirk R., S. Greenbaum, G. Leech & J. Svartvik (1985): *A Comprehensive Grammar of the English Language*, London: Longman.

Robinson, Ludmilla (1994): *Handbook for Legal Interpreters*, Sydney: The Law Book Company.

Rosenbaum, Gabriel M. (1995): '*Fusha* within Dramatic Dialogue written in the Colloquial', *Israel Oriental Studies*, 15, pp. 143–176.

Rotman, Edgardo (1996): *The Inherent Problems of Legal Translation: Theoretical Aspects*, Bloomington, IN: Indiana University School of Law.

Ryding, K. (2005): *A Reference Grammar of Modern Standard Arabic*, Cambridge: Cambridge University Press.

Ryding Lentzner, Karin (1977): 'Semantic and Syntactic Aspects of Arabic Prepositions', unpubl. PhD diss., Washington, DC: Georgetown University.

Salib, Maurice Boulos (1979): 'Spoken Literary Arabic: Oral Approximation of Literary Arabic in Egyptian Formal Discourse', unpubl. PhD diss., Berkeley, CA: University of California.

Sallam, A. M. (1979): 'Concordial Relations within the Noun Phrase in Educated Spoken Arabic (ESA)', *Archivum Linguisticum*, 10, pp. 20–56.

Santillán Grimm, P. (2009): 'Collocation in Modern Standard Arabic Revisited', *Zeitschrift für Arabische Linguistik*, 51, pp. 22–41.

Šarčević, Susan (1985): 'Translation of Culture-bound Terms in Laws', in J. C. Sager (ed.), *Multilingua: Journal of Inter-Language Communication*, Amsterdam: Mouton Publishers, pp. 127–133.

—— (1988): 'Translation of Legislation with Special Emphasis on Languages of Limited Diffusion', in P. Nekeman (ed.), *Translation, our Future: Proceedings of the XIth World Congress of FIT*, Maastricht: Euroterm, pp. 455–562.

—— (1989): 'Lexicography and Translation across Cultures', in M. Snell-Hornby et al. (eds), *Translation and Lexicography. Papers read at the Euralex Colloquium held at Innsbruck 2–5 July 1987*, Amsterdam: John Benjamins Publishing, pp. 211–221.

—— (1991): 'Bilingual and Multilingual Legal Dictionaries: New Standards for the Future', *Meta*, 36:4, pp. 615–626.

—— (1994): 'Translation and the Law: An Interdisciplinary Approach', in M. Snell-Hornby, Kaindl, Pochhacker (eds), *Translation Studies: An Interdiscipline*, Amsterdam: John Benjamins Publishing Company, pp. 301–307.

—— (1997): *New Approach to Legal Translation*, The Hague: Kluwer Law International.

—— (1997): 'Creativity in Legal Translation: How Much is Too Much?', in A. Chesterman et al. (eds), *Translation in Context*, Amsterdam: John Benjamins Publishing Company, pp. 281–292.

Sawaie, M. (1987): 'Speakers' Attitudes toward Linguistic Variation: A Case Study of Some Arabic Variation', *Linguistische Berichte*, 107, pp. 3–22.

Schmidt, Richard Wilbur (1975): 'Sociolinguistic Variation in Spoken Egyptian Arabic: A Re-examination of the Concept of Diglossia', PhD diss., Providence, Rhode Island: Brown University.

Schulz, David Eugene (1981): 'Diglossia and Variation in Formal Spoken Arabic in Egypt', unpubl. PhD diss., Madison, WI: University of Wisconsin-Madison.

Shakir, A. & M. Farghal (1992): 'Collocations as an Index of L2 Competence in Arabic–English Simultaneous Interpreting and Translation', *FIT Newsletter*, 11:3, pp. 227–245.

Shakir, A., & O. Shdeifat (1996): 'The Translation of Collocations as an Indicator of Development of FL Competence', *Al-Manarah*, 1:3, pp. 9–27.

Somekh, Sasson (1993): 'Colloquialized *fusha* in Modern Arabic Prose Fiction', *Jerusalem Studies in Arabic and Islam*, 16, pp. 176–194.

Sotiropoulos, Dimitri (1977): 'Diglossia and the National Language Question in Greece', *Linguistics*, 197, pp. 5–31.

Stetkevych, Jaroslav (1970): *The Modern Arabic Literary Language: Lexical and Stylistic Developments*, Chicago, IL: The University of Chicago Press.

Tiersma, Pieter (2000): *Legal Language*, Chicago, IL: The University of Chicago Press.

Tomaszczyk, J. (ed.) (1999): *Aspects of Language and Legal Translation*, Łódź: Łódź University Press.

Turkī, A. (1965): 'Qaḍiyat al-fuṣḥā wa al-lahjāt fī naẓr baʿḍ al-udabā' al-muʿāṣirīn', *Hawliyyāt al-Jāmiʿa al-Tūnisiyya*, 2, pp. 57–73.

Twain, Mark (1992): *Tom Sawyer and Huckleberry Finn*, Ware: Wordsworth Editions.

Van Mol, Mark (2003): *Variation in Modern Standard Arabic in Radio News Broadcasts: A Synchronic Descriptive Investigation into the Use of Complementary Particles*, Leuven: Peeters.

Versteegh, Kees (1997): *The Arabic Language*, Edinburgh: Edinburgh University Press.

Versteegh, Kees et al. (eds) (2006–9): *Encyclopedia of Arabic Language and Linguistics*, Leiden: Brill.

Wardhaugh, Ronald (2002): *An Introduction to Sociolinguistics*, Oxford: Blackwell.

Wehr, Hans (1976): *A Dictionary of Modern Written Arabic*, ed. J. Milton Cowan, 3rd ed., Ithaca, NY: Spoken Language Services.

Wilmsen, D. (2010): 'Dialects of Written Arabic: Syntactic Differences in the Treatment of Object Pronouns in Egyptian and Levantine Newspapers', *Arabica*, 57, pp. 99–128.

Wilmsen, David & Riham Osama Youssef (2009): 'Regional Standards and Local Routes in Adoption Techniques for Specialised Terminologies in the Dialects of Written Arabic', *The Journal of Specialised Translation*, 11, pp. 192–210.

Wright, Sue Ellen & Leland D. Wright, Jr. (eds) (1993): *Scientific and Technical Translation, American Translators' Association Scholarly Monograph Series*, Vol. VI, Amsterdam/Philadelphia, PA: John Benjamins.

Zaccaria, Giuseppe (2001): *Translation in Law, Yearbook of Legal Hermeneutics*, 5, Berlin: Lit Verlag.

Zack, Liesbeth (2009): *Egyptian Arabic in the Seventeenth Century: A Study of Yūsuf al-Maghribī's* Dafᶜ al-ᶜiṣr ᶜan kalām ahl Miṣr, Utrecht: LOT.

—— (2012): 'Quenching the Thirst for Knowledge: An Analysis of the Colloquial Material in al-Xafāǧī's *Šifā' al-ġalīl fīmā fī kalām al-'arab min al-daxīl*', in M. Meouak, P. Sánchez & Á. Vicente (eds), *De los manuscritos árabes medievales a internet: la presencia del árabe vernáculo en las fuentes escritas,* vol. 6, *Estudios de dialectología árabe*, Zaragoza: Universidad de Zaragoza, Área de Estudios Árabes e Islámicos, pp. 193–220.

Zweigert, K. & H. Kötz (1992): *An Introduction to Comparative Law*, trans. T. Weir, Oxford: Clarendon Press.

Zughoul, M. R. & Mohammed El-Badarien (2004): 'Diglossia in Literary Translation: Accommodation into Translation Theory', *Meta*, 49:2, pp. 69–93.

Index

For Product Safety Concerns and Information please contact our EU
representative GPSR@taylorandfrancis.com
Taylor & Francis Verlag GmbH, Kaufingerstraße 24, 80331 München, Germany

www.ingramcontent.com/pod-product-compliance
Lightning Source LLC
Chambersburg PA
CBHW081921130726
47908CB00018B/2697
9780415478854